# Namma

## A Tibetan Love Story

### KATE KARKO

D0003417

SCEPTRE

Copyright © 2001 by Kate Karko
First published in 2001 by Hodder and Stoughton
A division of Hodder Headline
A Sceptre Paperback

The right of Kate Karko to be identified as the Author of
the Work has been asserted by her in accordance with the
Copyright, Designs and Patents Act 1988.

10 9 8 7 6 5 4 3 2 1

A CIP catalogue record for this title is available from the British Library

ISBN 0340 767405

Typeset by Palimpsest Book Production Limited,
Polmont, Stirlingshire
Printed and bound in Great Britain by
Mackays of Chatham PLC, Chatham, Kent

Hodder and Stoughton
A division of Hodder Headline
338 Euston Road
London NW1 3BH

For Tsedup
who is my inspiration.
That he may be understood.

And for the people of Machu
who gave me so much.
This book is my way of giving back to them.

# CONTENTS

# LIST OF ILLUSTRATIONS

Tsedup's eldest brother, Rhanjer and younger brother, Gondo

Gondo's son, Dorlo

Tsering Samdup outside the tiger's lair at Lhamo

Rhanjer's son, Samlo

Tsedup in winter *tsokwa*

Gondo's wife, Tseten, Gondo, Tamba and friend

Tsedup's sister, Dombie

Dombie's son Yeshe; her daughter Dawa with Dickir Che;

girls in *tsokwas* – *in front*, Rhanjer's girls, Lhamo Tsering and Rinchenchet with eldest daughter, Gurra, *centre back*; Tselo in the grassland

Dickier Che and Rinchenchet knitting

Sirmo's son, Tsering Dhondup

Kate wearing the rings that Annay gave her

Our son, Gonbochab

*All photographs from the author's collection. Chapter illustrations by the author.*

# FAMILY TREE

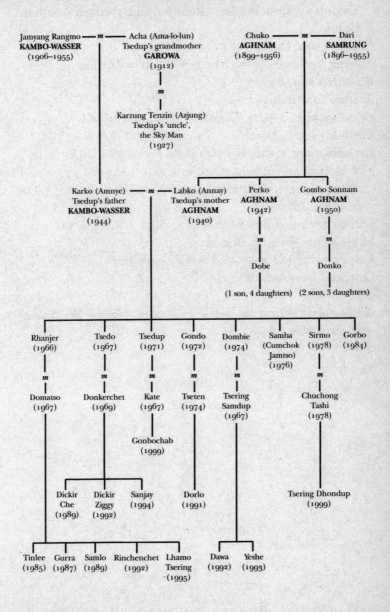

Jamyang Rangmo — *m* — Acha (Ama-lo-lun)
**KAMBO-WASSER**   Tsedup's grandmother
(1906–1955)   **GAROWA**
   (1912)

Chuko — *m* — Dari
**AGHNAM**   **SAMRUNG**
(1899–1956)   (1896–1955)

*m*

Karzung Tenzin (Azjung)
Tsedup's 'uncle',
the Sky Man
(1927)

Karko (Amnye) — *m* — Labko (Annay)   Perko   Gombo Sonnam
Tsedup's father   Tsedup's mother   **AGHNAM**   **AGHNAM**
**KAMBO-WASSER**   **AGHNAM**   (1942)   (1950)
(1944)   (1940)

*m*   *m*

Dobe   Donko

(1 son, 4 daughters)   (2 sons, 3 daughters)

Rhanjer   Tsedo   Tsedup   Gondo   Dombie   Samba   Sirmo   Gorbo
(1966)   (1967)   (1971)   (1972)   (1974)   (Cumchok   (1978)   (1984)
   Jamtso)
   (1976)

*m*   *m*   *m*   *m*   *m*   *m*

Domatso   Donkerchet   Kate   Tseten   Tsering   Chuchong
(1967)   (1969)   (1967)   (1974)   Samdup   Tashi
   (1967)   (1978)

Gonbochab
(1999)

Dickir   Dickir   Sanjay   Dorlo   Tsering Dhondup
Che   Ziggy   (1994)   (1991)   (1999)
(1989)   (1992)

Tinlee   Gurra   Samlo   Rinchenchet   Lhamo   Dawa   Yeshe
(1985)   (1987)   (1989)   (1992)   Tsering   (1992)   (1993)
   (1995)

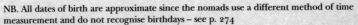

NB. All dates of birth are approximate since the nomads use a different method of time measurement and do not recognise birthdays – see p. 274

# ACKNOWLEDGEMENTS

With thanks to those who understand. To all of our friends, especially Jemima and Lamakyab who know more than anyone what this book means. To Ells, Chloë and Kats who were part of the adventure. To Tsedup's family for giving me a home. To my family for their love: especially to Dad for his unfaltering support, to Mum for her help with editing and for believing in me, and to Phil.

But mostly to Tsedup, without whom there would be no book. There would be no Gonbochab. And without whom I would be lost.

For the background on Shamanism and Buddhism, I am grateful to Alexandra David-Neel, *With Mystics and Magicians in Tibet*, Penguin, London, 1931; and Keith Dowman, *The Sacred Life of Tibet*, Thorsons, London, 1997.

# *Prologue*

We met in the shadow of the Himalayas. In a place where monkeys ran on tin roofs and flying squirrels leapt like bats from pine to shivering pine. Where the roar of monks' horns from the monastery blasted the summer sky, and glaciers shone like cut diamonds.

It is so difficult to talk about love, how it all started, but the drama of ours changed my life.

It was in McLeod Ganj, an Indian hill station, at a roof-top party, full of Tibetans and drunk Punjabis, that I saw a man dance, his eyes closed, long hair swirling in a dervish-spin. Around him the chaos reeled, and he must have seen me looking at him, for he came and sat with me and we looked out at the black night. Then he began to tell me, very carefully, about the great, golden eagles in the mountains of his homeland. He spoke of nature with such integrity, as if he was part of the earth, not just on it.

I had no idea how he felt about me so I tailed him. He used to sit on the dusty street opposite the Dalai Lama's monastery, strumming a guitar and selling bread he'd made. I diverted my walks so that I would pass him each day, or I would see him stroll down the bustling street from my balcony. Once he brought me an eagle feather.

Then one morning, in a voice so serious, he told me he'd dreamt of me. Later, in his tiny house, our life began. We took a room in a valley of corncobs, with a cow downstairs who mooed at night. We spent days walking in the forest and swam naked in a pool of melt-water. When we stopped on a rock at night he sang to me. 'From now on there is no yours and mine,' he told me. We would share everything.

Right from the beginning we were inseparable. We spent hours holed up in our small house talking. He already had a good grasp of English as he had been studying at a school before we met and had quite a few English friends. Despite our different cultures, we discovered we were uncannily compatible. He coaxed out all that had lain dormant in me: he encouraged me to paint, to play music, to speak from the heart. I knew that he had an energy I did not possess and his unbounded enthusiasm for life became the inspiration for mine. I listened as Tsedup spoke of the relatives he had left behind in Tibet, the tribe, the yaks, the mountains. He missed it all.

He was born by the first bend of the Yellow river, a Tibetan nomad in a yak-hair tent in a nomads' land. At four he rode bareback and shot his father's rifle. At twelve he told his family he wanted to go to school. In the town he watched Kung Fu films and wished he had been born Chinese. At eighteen he escaped to India on foot over the mountains, with some money taken from a box in the tent. He didn't tell his family first – they would never have let him go.

I was born in the London suburbs, and had a happy middle-class childhood in a free country. I meandered along the well-worn track from school, to university, to art college. Then, one summer holiday, I went travelling: I felt the need for adventure.

Now here we were in India, across the border from Tsedup's country and four thousand miles from mine. A step down from the Tibetan plateau and a step away from any notion of home. We were in the middle, geographically, spiritually, culturally. Tsedup was in exile; I was just visiting; India was our half-way house.

Meeting him was unexpected, but I had never been so sure of anything in my life. That summer, I came home, dumped college and worked to save money to go back. In the winter we were together again, my parents worrying for my sanity. Tsedup had only planned a short trip to India, a couple of years to learn some English, and then it would be back to the tribe. He hadn't banked on meeting me and he never made it back over the mountains.

The year after we met, we were married in India, in a small registry office with plastic plants and a fat notary who muttered, 'Visa marriage,' under his breath as he stamped our certificate. It resembled a sheet of school loo paper (the kind you use for tracing maps in Geography). It had all the romance of an auction. Afterwards we sat and ate noodles quietly. I hadn't told my parents. Even when they came out to see us for a week, we didn't whisper a word. We didn't feel married, not properly. We just wanted to be together and, besides, I wanted them to get to know Tsedup before I broke it to them that he was their son-in-law. A nomad in a family tree is something to get your head around.

It was hard enough for them to cope with our living conditions. I had spent the whole day cleaning before they arrived, but still my father recoiled when he saw our house. It was beyond him to imagine living in a room that resembled his garage. From the relative comfort of their three-star hotel on the lip of a cliff overlooking the valley, he helped save us from that 'shocking existence' by writing a letter to the British High Commission in Delhi. In a month we would be interviewed for Tsedup's British visa, which would enable him to live in England with me. My father was happy to use his status at the bank to offer his support, and I was touched. As well as everything else Tsedup brought to my life, he taught me that there was no limit to my parents' love for me.

After waiting for three months we were summoned to Delhi. We had no idea what to expect. As an exile, Tsedup had had no papers and we had bribed an official to get him an Indian passport. The next morning we dressed in new clothes. At the crowded High Commission, Tsedup was called in first. I passed him afterwards in the corridor, sitting in an armchair smiling encouragingly at me. When I pushed open the door I was pleased to see the Englishwoman sitting behind the desk. At least we could relate to each other.

She introduced herself. 'Right,' she said, eyeing me coldly through mascara fronds, 'I see eight couples a day, every day. All of them say they're in love. Most of them are lying. If you lie to me once, it will be the last thing you do in this office.' Then she proceeded to interrogate me, rifling through our love letters and photographs, making me recite his family tree, all seven of his brothers' and sisters' names, in order. At the end, I was ashamed of my country. I understood that she had a job to do, but she did it with such cruel calculation that I could have slapped her. I had been living with a man for whom trust and honesty were sacred: nomads don't lie. But she wasn't to know that.

'I'm going to give him the visa. I believe him,' she said finally, 'but if he ever turns out *not* to be the nice man he appears to be, you will inform us, won't you? We would be very interested to know.'

I found Tsedup sitting on the grass outside.

'We've got it,' I cried, but he was too distraught to care.

In him she had provoked the desired response, but at a cost. 'You come from nothing. Your family have nothing. You're just using this English girl to get to the West,' she'd said to him. She had no idea how he had suffered, missing his family all these years, or the depth of his feeling for his homeland.

He had leapt from his chair and, with both fists on her desk, had shouted in her face, 'How dare you insult my family and my country? I am proud of them and I love my wife.' It was his first encounter with a British authority figure and I was sorry that he had seen the ugly side of my culture so soon.

It was a struggle for a nomad in London, an education for us both, and life had not prepared me for living with the pain of an exile. But I was quick to learn, and so was he. I saw through his eyes. Things that were commonplace became exceptional: an escalator ride; using a knife and fork;

sitting on a loo. He was sick in cars, claustrophobic on the tube. He slept a lot: this new land was too alien to face each morning. I had to leave him while I went to work, so it was a lonely time for him. He spent his days in a cloud of nostalgia, preparing Tibetan food, patiently re-creating the smells of his homeland in our small kitchen, with chilli and chives, meat *momos*.

We lived in my parents' rented flat in North London, on the top floor on a hill bustling with traffic. The house vibrated when the buses passed. My mother would come up from Winchester on Mondays and Tuesdays to do her psychotherapy course. In the evenings Tsedup and I sat in the bedroom quietly, while her clients cried through the wall. 'Don't they have any friends?' he asked. He would sit and look at the Heath from the back window, desperate for a vista: there were no mountains, nothing to look up at. The streets were closed in. Tsedup felt the world hurrying past him; there were more people in this city than in his whole country. He had dreams about flying, and his father hunting on the Heath, and woke in a sweat, afraid that the police would get him.

'You are my family here,' he said. 'You're all I've got.' I loved him enough to want to be everything to him, but I was not. Beyond our existence lay another world and a part of him I had yet to discover. Until I saw him in his homeland I would never truly know and understand him.

He spoke to his parents. It was the first time they had had contact in four years. (No mail had got through between India and Tibet.) Nomads cannot conceive of a life without family, and they had been desperate for news of their son. They rode six miles to the only international telephone in town and waited at a prearranged time for it to ring. The whole family crowded round the receiver. His mother had never used a phone before.

She cried into the mouthpiece, 'When are you coming home?' But they told him not to come back until he had papers: it wasn't safe. They could not visit him in England. They would need Chinese passports for that and the likelihood of acquiring them was almost impossible. We waited for his British passport, and my father wrote to Tsedup's father, reassuring him that we were taking care of his son. He received a reply on fragile paper in the most exquisite hand, a silk prayer scarf enclosed. Tsedup translated:

It is almost inconceivable that two families, so very far away from one another, should be joined, as we have been, in the coming together of Tsedup and Kate.

That was how we felt. I wanted to write to his mother. She was illiterate, but I knew that Tsedup's father would read my letter to her. 'I miss you and I don't even know you,' I wrote. 'But we are both living under the same moon. When I look up at it I will think of you.' Later she told Tsedup that when he brought me home she would love me as one of her own daughters. She had two; now I had become the third. I had not even met them and yet I was part of them, as Tsedup had become part of us.

In England he watched TV for the first time, and it became a window through which he could look and learn about all sorts of things – 'From the leader of the country to how to make pasta,' he said. He spent hours watching nature programmes, learning about animals he had never known existed and observing the microscopic lives of insects. The images blew him away: he had always been close to nature, but never that close. Soon we were watching him on the screen: he became a model and actor. They booked him as an Eskimo, a Cherokee, a Mongolian warlord, but never a Tibetan – most people didn't know what that was. They liked his look, they said, exotic. So he played along: the cultural chameleon. He had the English friends he'd known in India and soon they became my great friends too. He even made some Tibetan friends, although there were only a few in the UK. Most spoke the Lhasa dialect of the capital, which was different from the eastern region of Amdo, where Tsedup was from. But he was lucky enough to find a couple of Amdo friends and they became his lifeline, sharing his memories. He was always elated after he'd seen them.

I found work as a magazine designer and we became more comfortable. One day I broke it to my parents that we were married. 'We have a son-in-law,' my mother cried. We decided to celebrate with those who had helped us through hard times and had an intimate blessing service in a small Hampshire church. It was a joyful day, but we felt the absence of his family. We showed slides of them through the service, to try to make them a part of it, for Tsedup's sake. He saw a picture of his parents smiling inside the tent as he took his vows. The vicar even allowed our Tibetan friends to read a Buddhist prayer. I had never been so moved.

Gradually he assimilated, but never conformed. That would have meant losing a part of himself. He missed his people and resolved not to live like an Englishman. If there was such a thing as a modern nomad that was what he'd become, he said. He wanted to go home, to live his life between two worlds. Somehow we endured the waiting, the bureaucracy and the indifference. The Home Office would not issue a British passport until he had been in the country four years. We had enormous reserves of hope when the waiting got too much. And we had each other. One day, eating chips in a pub on the Euston Road I handed him the visas. After nine years of waiting he was going home.

Tsedup had crossed the widest cultural gap I could ever have imagined and survived. Now it was my turn: I was leaving a glossy, society magazine to go to the Roof of the World. For six months I would live with his tribe as a nomad bride in the Machu grasslands of Amdo. As far as I knew, I was the first western woman ever to have done it. I was making history. My parents wanted to come with us for the first week, to be with him in case there was a threat to his safety and to be part of the reunion. He telephoned his parents to tell them we were coming. His father had ridden back from a three-day hunting expedition. That was all he had wanted to hear, he said.

# ONE

## *The Reunion*

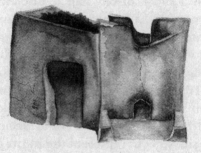

H e wanted the window-seat. From there he could see
the carpet of cloud beneath him and the amber sun
falling over the edge of the world. He sat quietly, tracing the
ice crystals on the glass outside with his fingertip. It was only
a few minutes until landing.

To reach his remote home we had flown east from London
to Beijing and were now on the internal flight westwards to
Lanzhou, capital of Gansu province. From there we would
travel ten hours by road up to the Tibetan plateau and the
grasslands of Amdo. Although Tsedup's family had told us
we would be met at the airport, I wasn't sure that they would

make it. The Tibetan lunar calendar is different from ours and I wondered if they'd got the right week. My heart hammered like a machine-gun and I struggled to suppress the butterflies in my belly. I glanced at Tsedup, who looked composed, but when I squeezed his hand I felt him shaking.

As the plane touched down, the lockers sprang open and Chinese businessmen grappled frantically with their briefcases. It was hot in the terminal and the baggage inspector was a pedantic soul. As we struggled to locate the tickets among our belongings, he stared at us suspiciously from beneath a shock of oily hair. I cast my eyes around the modest entrance hall, which was empty. As Dad pushed the last tag into the man's fist, another man approached us, grinning furiously. 'I am your driver. Come this way, ple—'

Suddenly the swing doors in front of us burst open and a crowd of Tibetan nomads, children and monks surged towards us in traditional costume. They solemnly placed *kadaks* around our necks. It was the Tibetans' custom to offer a white silk stole to represent the purity of their heart. I was shocked: there were so many of them and they looked so incongruous in this place, so wild with their long hair, dark skin and jewellery, the monks serene in their vivid pink robes.

I stood still for a moment as my new relations moved around me in a blur of unfamiliar syllables and smiles. Then, slowly, I began to recognise Tsedup's brothers, Rhanjer, Tsedo, Gondo, Cumchok. Tsedup stood in the middle of the throng, stunned and grinning, until they led us to a car beside which a tiny, nomad woman stood weeping. It was Tsedup's cousin, Dolma. Tsedup took her in his arms and spoke softly to her in their dialect: there was no need to cry, he was too happy for that. I knew that he must have been feeling a tumult of emotion, but he was brought back to earth with a bump.

My father stood before him covered in *kadaks*. He was panicking. 'Tsedup! Where is our luggage?' he asked, and pointed to the pavement. 'I just left it here and it's gone!' Tsedup calmed him. It is the Tibetan custom to operate smoothly and hospitably at all times, and he assured Dad that the bags were already in the cars. In Tibet Dad was going to have to learn to relax. In fact we all learnt that here, though things might sometimes seem out of control, they were always sorted out perfectly in the end.

We set off in convoy to the city. Tsedup and I took Sando's car. He was Dolma's husband and had a job as a driver in their town. Unlike his wife, who wore traditional costume, he was dressed in a shirt and slacks. Dolma had recovered her composure and sat next to him in the front chattering excitedly, with her small son on her lap. Gondo sat with us in the back, smoking and rarely talking. He was Tsedup's closest brother, only a year younger, but taller. They had been like twins when they were growing up. The last time Tsedup had seen him he had been a boy. Today, instead of tickling each other as they used to, they sat awkwardly side by side, trying to be normal after nine years of silence. Tsedup did most of the talking, jabbering questions, and occasionally Gondo would flash a smile and laugh. For most of the journey he was reserved, his tousled black hair and sheepskin *tsarer* a direct contrast to Tsedup's freshly chopped locks and western shirt and trousers.

We arrived at the Legend Hotel in the centre of the city after a two-hour drive through industrial wasteland. My parents had booked it through an agent in the UK and predictably, it was plush. We went to the desk to check in, followed gingerly by Tsedup's brothers and their children, who loitered uncomfortably under the enormous glass chandelier. This was not their territory.

'Are they country people?' asked the Chinese manager, as he cast his eye over their attire.

They stood fingering their massive coral necklaces, their sheepskin *tsarers*, which resembled large wrap-around coats with brightly patterned trim and huge red sashes tied around their hips. They provided a colourful contrast to the cream and chrome of their surroundings.

'They are our family,' I replied.

Rhanjer, Tsedup's oldest brother, a short, portly young man with mischievous eyes and a wide smile, accompanied us to our room to help us deposit our bags. Then we left Mum and Dad to sleep off the excitement of the day and went for some food. The boys took us to a small restaurant in a back-street, where an old Chinese woman sat on the pavement stirring a cauldron of broth. They laid out trestle tables and we sat down. I was in the middle opposite Tsedup. Their conversation, which I didn't understand, appeared stilted. They were either overwhelmed to see him, embarrassed at my presence or both. Either way, they didn't talk much, but the beer flowed as the overhead strip-lights sang in our ears and soon there was sporadic laughter and enthusiastic slurping of noodles. I didn't realise then, but this was the nomads' way. Their silence and composure disguised emotions deeper than I could have imagined.

That night in our bed Tsedup told me he felt as if he had been asleep for nine years. Seeing his brothers had made him feel as if he had jumped from boy to man in one day. As his mind had flooded with memories, he had also realised how much he had changed. We talked long into the night and I held him. This was only the start. Although I shared his euphoria, I suddenly became aware of the gap in our experience, for here Tsedup had a whole history of reference to draw on. I had only what he had told me in England, along with snippets of what I had read and some old photos. This was all new for me. Yet he was grasping at the threads of his old life and beginning to reconstruct a picture. I had noticed a change in him: he was now confident, taking control, guiding my parents and me, organising, explaining, translating. This was *his* territory and I could already feel our roles reversing. I was elated to see him so self-assured.

The next morning the family collected us from our hotel and, after we had distributed a packet of travel-sickness tablets between us, we set off for Machu, his home. Many of the nomads had been sick on the way to Lanzhou: they were not used to long car journeys or pollution. It was stiflingly hot and the sky above the city and surrounding industrial landscape was tinged a curious shade of orange. We were glad to escape.

The convoy of cars blazed a trail through Gansu province. It was an ugly place of occasional belching factories and isolated no-stop towns, occupied by Chinese Muslims who cycled suicidally down the middle of the road. We drove through markets with row upon row of suspended cattle carcasses and colourful fruit, the strains of Chinese music wailing from shabby shop doorways to compete with the Tibetan tape in the car. It was raining and through the drizzle I watched the landscape change. The further we got from Lanzhou, the greener it became. Melon fields spanned the valley, bordered by rocky hills peppered with scrub into which small caves had been excavated by the farmers. Avenues of poplar trees lined the road and, beyond, fields of barley rolled in the wind.

Soon the sheer scarp of mountain ranges were ahead. It was such a dramatic change in the landscape that we knew the Tibetan plateau was not far away. We began to climb through precipitous mountain valleys, dodging barren chasms and clefts of jagged rock. Then, high up between two peaks standing sentry at either side of the road, we stopped. It was the old border between China and Tibet.

As we crossed the high pass we were ecstatic. A *chorten*, a white and gold monument draped in prayer flags, marked the border of the area known as Hortsung by the Tibetans. There, I saw the first Tibetan man walking along the road in his *tsarer*, and Tibetan writing on a whitewashed wall. At the side of the road, a woman with long, plaited hair sat spinning yak wool on a finger-sized spindle. We had arrived. Before us lay the great plains of central Asia, land of the nomads, a vast panorama of flat grassland and green hills, soft and undulating, receding into the horizon. Sometimes we saw rocky crags rearing in the distance. Tsedup breathed in and told me he could smell home. I felt as if I had passed into an unknown world of solitude and mystery.

Suddenly the featureless landscape of our earlier journey was marked by curious totem-pole structures. On top of each tall mountain we passed was a collection of wooden stakes and prayer flags, spiking up into the sky. I asked Tsedup what it meant. He told me that they were holy mountains, *laptse*, and that these structures marked the Tibetans' offering sites to the mountain spirits. At the foot of a hill we passed a small monastery and a monk collecting water from the stream, his fuchsia robes bright in the dull afternoon.

At eleven thousand feet my ears popped. Tsedup's friend

Gondi took the wheel – Sando had been driving for seven hours and needed a nap. He soon fell asleep on the back seat and began to snore gently. I was beginning to feel conspicu-ously underdressed in my thin, linen skirt and T-shirt beside Dolma, resplendent in full traditional costume. With her tiny frame, delicate features, leopardskin *tsarer* and strings of coral and turquoise, she was, without doubt, the prettiest woman I had ever seen. She smiled at me as Sando let out a loud grunt and the two of us giggled. It was strange not being able to talk: so much was left to instinct, gesticulation and facial muscles. But we played with Gonbochab, her little boy, who at first clung to his mother to escape the weird white woman next to him, then relaxed enough to let me play with the little doll that he insisted on banging on Gondi's head as he drove.

Soon we turned off the main road and continued the last part of the journey on a winding dirt track through the mountains. We stopped to wait for the rest of the convoy beside a huge lake surrounded by snow-capped mountains. Tsedup told me this was a bird sanctuary. The cold wind ruffled the water towards me as I peed in a ditch. Then I slipped and ruined my skirt. My sandals were now full of muddy water as well and I sighed. Not only did I feel underdressed for meeting my in-laws, I was now cold and wet. What I had been thinking of when I chose to wear my office clothes to come to such a wilderness, I shall never know. I don't think I had grasped the concept of where I was going.

As we moved on, nomad encampments of black yak-hair tents became visible in the valleys; yaks and sheep were grazing on the slopes. In the steady drizzle of the early evening the tents seemed to offer little in the way of shelter for their inhabitants and I began to wonder if our new home would be the same. These were pitched close to the road on blackened scrub and looked considerably less attractive than I had imagined. In contrast to the breathtaking vista I had witnessed when we first arrived at the Tibetan plateau, this land was more closed in and claustrophobic. I saw a nomad woman in a sodden sheepskin *tsarer* shovelling yak dung into a basket and children staring at the cars as we passed. I looked forward to seeing the true splendour of the Machu landscape, as Tsedup had described it: although I had been excited at the prospect of living in a tent, I had also hoped that the beauty of the surroundings might compensate me for the loss of home comforts. This area was bleak and I couldn't conceive that somewhere like this would feel like home. I felt anxious.

After two hours of winding through the mud-sludge and mountain fog, we rounded a sharp bend at the top of a pass. The convoy stopped and Tsedup fumbled with the door handle.

'This is the Wild Yak range!' he exclaimed. 'This is Machu soil!' Then he jumped out and ran to the cliff edge of the road. We followed and everyone stood in the pattering rain to survey their beloved homeland.

Far below, the first bend of the Yellow river meandered through the mist that shrouded the grassland. The Amnye Kula mountain range, deep green and dense with peaks and valleys, rolled into the distance. Herds of black yaks grazed on the shallow escarpments and a flock of sheep scrambled beneath us on the shale and rocks. The horizon was blurred by rainclouds, but it was an exhilarating sight and I was stunned by the power and drama of the landscape before me. It was just as Tsedup had described it.

The men climbed up to a stony ridge high above the track, where prayer flags flapped wildly from wooden stakes. Tsedup gave a wild, triumphant cry and flung his arms in the air. At last he was home, and as his voice ricocheted around the mountains, the other men began whooping and shouting, called repeatedly upon the mountain gods, giving thanks for his safe return, tossing fistfuls of *long hda*, 'wind horses' – small paper squares with pictures of horses – into the wind. The thin slivers of paper fluttered down into the valley and out of sight.

We descended from the high pass to the small town of Machu, which lay in the flat river basin. The car accelerated down a long, straight track of dust and stones, crunching over the gravel and spitting out shingle from the tyre grips. The last pale shades of thin light still illuminated the sky, but dusk would be swift tonight as the sun had already been snuffed out by the creeping fog. It was a race to get there before dark, and Tsedup explained that we still had another six miles to drive through increasingly rough terrain. I hoped the Santana was up to it, and wondered how my parents were faring in the car behind. Ten hours of breakneck roads and precipitous valleys had probably finished them off.

As we sped through the deserted streets, I realised that the town was not quite as I'd expected. I had often asked Tsedup what it was like and, in his search for a suitable parallel, he had told me it resembled a town in the Wild West. I had imagined sandy streets, wooden buildings, tumbleweeds and saloon brawls, but apart from the horses standing outside restaurants, it seemed like just another concrete rural town with rows of squat buildings lining the road. Everyone had shut up shop and it had the air of a ghost town. I glimpsed two streets that day, and Tsedup told me that there were only three altogether. It certainly was a small town and, as this was to be my only haven of civilisation for the next six months, I hoped I would be able to unearth its charms before too long.

At the end of the main street we turned westward and saw a small group of nomads brandishing prayer scarves, an old woman with some children. 'Drive on,' said Tsedup. We were behaving like spoilt royalty, but time was running out and Tsedup's parents were waiting. Later he discovered that the old woman had been his grandmother.

We left the town, then negotiated the ditches of the next rutted track through the grasslands. We seemed to be driving into nowhere, an infinite horizon of vast green plains and mountains that spread for ever in the dim half-light. This was the end of the earth. Tsedup was quiet: it seemed that he wanted to savour the sight of his home for, despite the rain, he had wound the window right open and was leaning out. I watched him and wished I could share his thoughts right then.

As we approached the site of Tsedup's tribe the light was almost gone. We turned off the track on to the grass, and I could just make out the silhouette of black tents huddled in a valley between two ridges. This was the Valley of the Rocks. Suddenly the convoy stopped. Everyone opened the car doors and got out. As we stood peering into the dark, I could see figures moving slowly towards us. Then one broke free and ran faster. An old woman in a dark *tsarer*, grey hair streaming, necklace thumping on her chest, arms outstretched. It was Tsedup's mother. She flung herself around him, weeping. I watched her clinging and sobbing and stammering with joy. I was already crying when she pulled me to her and held me tight. I could smell the outdoors in her hair.

'Namma, *shata go*! *Shata go!* Bride, thank you! Thank you!'
She wept.

I didn't know what she was thanking me for, but the
pain and relief in her voice touched me. Then his father
came, followed by his sisters, brothers, uncles, aunts, their
children and dogs, and I saw him standing before Tsedup:
he wore his *tsarer* and a smart waistcoat beneath the tufts of
tangled sheepskin. He was a real nomad, a proud man with
a fine, lined face. He stood still for some time, staring into
Tsedup's eyes.

We were guided back to the tent. His mother held my
hand and I felt the warmth of her rough fingers as she led me
through the wet grass, carefully sidestepping the yak dung.
Tsedup was the first to enter. We waited behind him as he
paused at the doorway and wept into his hands. The sight
of the tent was too much: he wept with recognition of all
he had missed, for the lost years, the waiting, for his aged
parents, for love of Tibet.

The tent was empty. At its heart the clay fire danced orange
and red, casting shadows over the yak-wool roof. They had
laid out their best woven rugs and a table of bread and meat.
The smell of juniper and dung smoke filled the air. It was all
so perfect, just as he had remembered, and in a moment
Tsedup was a child again. We all sat down in the warm glow
and they served us tea. Then Tsedup turned his head to me
and smiled as I have never seen him smile, before or since.

'I am home,' he said.

# TWO

## *In the Tribe*

'She sells sea-shells on the seashore.' The next day Rhanjer was in full swing. Having mastered the basics of the English language he was feeling rather pleased with himself. The tent was full. The rest of the tribe had allowed us time last night for the joyful reunion but now they flocked impatiently to see Amnye Karko's son. Everyone seemed to be a relative. There were hordes of dreadlocked children clustered in the entrance to the tent staring at the strangers. We sat inside breathing the thick, fragrant dung smoke, as the nomads talked together and the rain fell on the yak hair outside. It seemed that we had achieved minor celebrity status and I began to feel slightly self-conscious.

Last night had been a riot of excitement and talk before eventually we had retired to our white tent with Gondo and Rhanjer, who drank beer with their brother into the small hours. I had had an interesting time tackling an army of ants that had built a nest directly under my sleeping mat. This morning my parents were nursing pounding heads from a sleepless night of fear: the altitude, and the Tibetan mastiffs who had sniffed round their tent and barked all night, had sent them into pulmonary palpitations. Today we were all a little deflated.

But it was wonderful to see the landscape revealed now that the darkness had lifted. The grassland was lush and covered with summer flowers. Herds of yaks and sheep wandered the hillsides above the tents and as I looked down the valley I saw the Yellow river and the cobalt mountains of the Silver Horn range. There was an overwhelming sense of space. Machu had exceeded my expectations.

We ate breakfast in the main tent, then Tsedup and I were presented with our own *tsarers*, which my new sister-in-law, Shermo Donker, had sewn. Shermo was the title by which she referred to me and I her from now on. I had only been here a day and had already acquired two new names: Shermo and Namma. I was part of the tribe. My *tsarer* was made from thick black fabric in the shape of a long coat, trimmed with snow-leopardskin, silk and gold piping with a colourful woven hem called *tugh*. She had obviously spent hours making it for me. She helped me to dress, carefully readjusting the length until she was satisfied, then tied the long red sash, the *kirok*, tightly round my waist. I could barely breathe. But I felt the part.

As I sat quietly watching Tsedup, a thousand eyes seemed

to bore into me, but there were smiles of encouragement from his mother Annay. She knelt by the fire, fingering her prayer beads in a steady rhythm between thumb and forefinger, mumbling the Tibetan prayer, '*Om mani. Om mani. Om mani. Om mani,*' a twist of religious tokens around her plump neck.

Behind her Shermo Donker, small and jumpy, giggled into her cupped hands and Sirmo, Tsedup's youngest sister, hid shyly in the back of the tent behind the crowd. She was tall and exquisite with full Cupid's-bow lips, a pale skin and soft, dreamy eyes that flashed when she smiled. She wore full traditional costume: her *tsarer* of emerald-green velvet, with six strings of coral beads around her neck. Across the top of her head and over her sleek black plaits, a string supported two enormous silver and coral earrings that dangled as low as her shoulders. I couldn't help but stare at her. She seemed so graceful among the bustling throng.

Soon the conversation turned to song as Choegetar, Tsedup's second cousin, took a banjo and began to pluck the strings. He sang an Amdo song of reunion, his voice rising in a clear vibrato, his eyelids flickering with concentration. It was dark in the tent, except for the slit of pale light and thin rain drifting through the gap in the roof. Everyone was dressed in traditional costume with about a kilo of coral necklaces apiece. Tsedup's father, Amnye, sat by the fire. He was a fine-looking man with dark skin and broad cheekbones, tight curly hair, a twinkle in his eye and a goatee beard. A wooden cosh protruded from inside his sheepskin *tsarer* and a cigarette from his mouth. He never smoked a whole one, kept half for later. Gorbo, Tsedup's sixteen-year-old brother, crouched by the dung pile, an enormous silver and coral earring dangling from his left earlobe. He sniggered as Tsedup strummed a western song, embarrassed by his brother's peculiar taste in music.

We had brought gifts for the family and handed them out one by one: a portable tent for his father to take hunting and the same for Gorbo; cloth for his mother; silver jewellery, perfumes and soaps for Shermo Donker and Sirmo; watches for Rhanjer and Gondo; boots for Tsedo and a kite for the children. They clucked admiringly. Amnye and Rhanjer turned each object over and over in their hands, studying them. As soon as the rain had abated we set up the tent for the children and they squealed around inside. 'Let's go and fly the bird!' they said. On the mountain it soared and arced in the sky as the sun beat down. They had never seen a kite before.

That evening, as the sunset spilled over the mountain, I watched Gorbo herding the yaks home. He guided them in on his father's white stallion, down through the valley from the higher slopes where they had spent the day grazing. My sister-in-law tied them up while the children chased the errant calves. I was introduced to my yak, Karee Ma, White Face, for the first time. Tsedup had asked his parents if I could have one of the herd as a birthday present a few years before. I approached her uneasily. She was the ugliest one of all, with a huge, white head and albino, pink-rimmed eyes. She resisted my wary touch. Still, we would bond in time.

Each day we were invited to a different tent and I was beginning to learn exactly what it was to be a guest of the nomads. Pride of place was always closest to the fire on the top right-hand side and this was where we always sat. Plates were piled high with *momos*, the traditional steamed parcels of meat, like miniature Cornish pasties, along with deep-fried bread, hunks of boiled meat and yak intestines stuffed with mince and black pudding. *Djomdi*, a mixture of small brown beans dug from the earth, rice, sugar and melted butter, was always on offer, a particular delicacy, along with a bowl of *tuckpa*, a soup of rice noodles and meat. All this was washed down with a bowl of strong tea. They watched us intently, constantly urging us to eat more with the command, '*Sou! Sou!*' They didn't mind if we abstained, but in Tibet it is customary to offer hospitality to a guest. Annay said, via Tsedup, 'We cannot talk to one another, we do not understand each other's language, but I can talk to you by offering food. It is the only way that I can communicate with you.' Communication was not a problem. In the tenth home, I tried to remember the Tibetan for 'I'm full', as I chewed tentatively on another morsel of fat. I had never been a great fat fan. I was going to have to get used to it. I was going to have to get used to a lot.

I could already sense the tribe's acceptance of me, and was amazed at their spirit of generosity. Most had probably never seen a western person before and suddenly I was their relative. I remembered Tsedup telling me about when he had first seen western people as a child: a fat man with a ginger beard and a thin woman with sunken cheeks, two ghosts eating noodles in a restaurant. He had run away. He had never seen such ugly people in his life. Today no one ran, they just stared – at our long noses. They were proud: I was their Amdo *namma* and they called me that often, laughing.

I didn't look like your average nomad bride, after all. I was a curiosity. Mostly I think they were just happy to be accepted by us. Years of repression and reproach from their Chinese neighbours had led them to believe that other people saw them as a barbarian race, a backward people. As a child, Tsedup remembered the whole family travelling on a pilgrimage to Lhasa. They stopped on the way in Lanzhou. None of the hotels would have them so they pitched tent in a field in the city. He and his father and brothers went to buy food and when they returned the tent was surrounded by hundreds of Chinese and piles of bicycles. They all covered their noses with their hands. In the middle of the staring, pointing throng sat Tsedup's mother, nursing her baby and crying. Gorbo was two months old. It was then that Tsedup began to question his identity.

Amnye, Tsedup's father, told us that just before our arrival a man from a neighbouring tribe had returned home with his fifteen-year-old daughter. He was a nomad but had settled in the city with his Chinese wife. His daughter had never seen his home but when he brought her to the tent she would not go in. She recoiled in disgust and sat in the jeep crying. Today, the sense of relief was almost tangible.

My parents were shown particular honour and respect. They had wanted to witness the reunion, to see their son-in-law back with the tribe, and despite the hardships, they had made it. I was proud. Initially, my mother had found it difficult to cope: she couldn't sleep at night because of the dogs, her pulse was accelerated and she had dizzy spells. We feared it might be acute mountain sickness, in which case she would have had to be moved to a lower altitude. She felt like a neurotic westerner, but she recovered with the aid of Annay, who brought her *samker*, a mixture of barley, salt, milk and water, and prayed over her as Mum lay in her tent. Mum wanted to tell her that she knew how much Annay had longed for her son's return – she had her own son and understood her pain. She had wanted Annay to know how long she had waited to meet her and how glad she and Dad were to have her son in their family, but she couldn't. Instead she gave her a picture of Tsedup and me on our blessing day, laughing.

At every home the families thanked my parents for looking after Tsedup in England. They were fascinated by my father's gadgetry and much was made of the camera, binoculars, penknife and compass he had brought for the trip. The father of each family, and Tsedup's eldest brother, Rhanjer, would ask him endless questions about the West and he, with Tsedup as interpreter, responded enthusiastically to their thirst for knowledge of the outside world. They stroked his arm. Body hair seemed a mystery as they had virtually none of their own. They admired his portly appearance and hearty laugh, and they thought my parents were beautiful, especially my father's huge green eyes. Compared to Tsedup's parents they looked so young. In fact, Tsedup was shocked at how frail and aged his parents had grown over the years.

My mother's sketching skills were a revelation, and Annay and Amnye sat patiently for her as she immortalised them. The tribe never once seemed curious about her hands. As a child she had fallen into the fire and they were disfigured; a constant source of anguish for her. She often hid them when meeting people for the first time: she didn't want to shock them or have to explain. Unlike their western counterparts, even the children did not stare or point.

The tribe's encampment formed a large circle of twenty black yak-hair tents in the middle of the grassland, in the shape of a turtle. In Tibetan culture, the turtle is the symbol of water and earthly spirits, so a family's home is believed to be protected if they settle on land with either water or earthly spirits. All the tents faced due south. As the sun moved from east to west in the sky, the beam of sunlight that penetrated the slit in the tent roof moved from west to east inside, telling the family what time it was. It was very precise. At eleven o'clock when the sun began to bake the cool ashes at the side of the clay stove, Annay would call Gorbo to herd in the yaks for milking. Our tent had survived four or more generations. During the Chinese Cultural Revolution it had been purloined and used for yaks and sheep to sleep on, but half of it had survived. It was later given back and patched up by the tribeswomen.

Every tent looked the same inside. At its heart was the fire. Women sat on one side, men the other. Most had an altar in the top corner. A small cupboard contained pictures of Tibetan lamas, small, brass cups, *thib*, for filling with water as an offering and butter lamps burning fragrantly. An enormous vat of yoghurt, cooking pots, wooden pails, water barrels and the milk churner occupied the women's side. Then there was a mountain of dried dung, its size a direct reflection of the women's industriousness. (The bigger the better, it seemed.) To the rear, under a sheet of plastic, were skin-clad boxes of butter, sacks of barley, rice, flour, cheese, clothes and rush baskets of tea. An injured tape-recorder sat on the battery box. The nomads have discovered solar power and every family had a panel, which was placed on the roof of the tent each morning to catch the sun's rays. Everything had its place, and although the tent became dishevelled at times, with the children running around, people eating, mud on the mats, every effort was made to treat it with respect and it was frequently swept with a small brush made from twigs. (This produced an amazing amount of dust.) Before Amnye returned the tent was always tidied and the mats positioned neatly for him to sit on.

Our tent was inhabited by Tsedup's father, Amnye Karko, his mother, Annay Labko, Tsedup's elder brother Tsedo, his wife, Shermo Donker, and their three small children; also Sirmo, Tsedup's youngest sister, and Gorbo, his youngest brother. Our arrival had made it slightly more cosy than before. The remainder of his family had married away, which was a blessing, as there were eight of them and it would have been a trifle too cramped if they had stayed. Rhanjer, Tsedup's oldest brother, had his own family tent in the tribe. Thankfully, we had our own white tent to sleep in, as did Tsedo and his wife, which allowed for a modicum of privacy.

In the evening the tent was the best place to be. After the yaks had been tied up everyone sat around the fire and we talked and laughed, played cards and ate our supper, usually *tuckpa* or *momos*, which we made together. The children collapsed after a day of hard playing. There was a conscientious search for nits in their clothes, then they were put to bed in a row in a sheepskin, three heads poking out of the top. They lay listening to the soporific lull of family chatter in the firelight, the distant howl of a lone wolf, the dogs barking, their father sucking on his pipe.

The last few days with my parents were spent picnicking. On the first day, the whole family set up tent by the Yellow river – the Tibetans call it Ma Chu. We piled the children, food and tent into Rhanjer's truck, then bounced the half-mile or so through the grassland to the river on the back of the boys' bikes. Annay rode the stallion in a Stetson, one of the dogs running alongside. The flat plain was covered in flowers, and birds trilled. (Skylarks, my father said.) Butterflies flitted from daisy to daisy, and the misty mountains rolled on into the infinite haze of the summer-blue horizon. We made *momos* together as the sun shone and the children made flower garlands for our heads. Then they ran naked and shrieking into the water as Tsedup's grandmother cried out warnings from the hillside. The current was fast. The Yellow river had been given its name for a reason: it churned up silt into an opaque, ochre flow. Froths of bubble-mush collected along the banks. Tsedup showed off his swimming skills, while his brothers sploshed crudely. It wasn't appropriate for a woman to expose her flesh, so I watched jealously from the bank. Then we played volleyball until dusk.

On the second picnic, we made a trip deeper into the Valley of the Rocks to see Tsedup's uncle. His home was at the foot of a mountain. He had erected a tent for us on a grassy knoll and we sat inside and ate as the yaks grazed in the drizzle outside. Then we climbed to a cave high up on the side of one of the valley slopes. Outside it were the rubbled remnants of an abandoned *chorten*. It had been the site of worship for an old monk, a lama who lived in the cave three hundred years ago in complete isolation. He spent his entire life in contemplation of the holy mountain peak visible through the crack of light at the opening to the cave. When he died a rainbow took his soul, so the story goes. We looked down through the valley from our rocky outcrop. He had not been the only one to die here: on one particular day during Mao's Great Leap Forward, fifty women from the tribe had been widowed. When the fighting was over, they came down from the mountain to perform the traditional sky burial. It was usually the task of men. They had to scalp each father, son, husband, brother. Then they chopped up their bodies and left them as carrion for the vultures on a mountain peak.

As we said goodbye, Tsedup's uncle gave my father a book wrapped in soot-stained, burgundy cloth. It was a long, rectangular Tibetan manuscript, which had been in the family for generations and had survived burial during the purges by the Chinese. It was dedicated to the second rein- carnation of the founder of Labrang Monastery, Genchen Jigme Rhongwo. It was three hundred years old.

The night my parents left Machu we all stayed in the town- house near the monastery. Tsedup's parents had invited them for a last supper. Annay walked the six-mile journey, since she couldn't face riding in the jeep my parents had hired – it made her sick. Amnye arrived from the town on his brakeless bicycle. The house stood in a field of tall grass surrounded by a stone wall. It was ramshackle with odd windows and two steps up to the wooden door. Inside were two cobbled rooms, a clay stove in the first. On the wall there was a collage of faded posters: a wooded lake glistening in the morning light; two fat cherubs holding a hundred-yuan note; galloping horses, snorting dragons, fierce tigers. There was a picture of Tsedup at school with cropped hair and flares, a skinny boy, smiling. Behind a woven cloth sacks of barley husks, stored for twenty years, nudged boxes of butter covered in skin. By the door was a collection of musty canvas bags, the brush made from a yak's tail, the dung tray, some old boots. In the second room there was a sleeping platform of straw and wood, a metal stove and an old Victorian sewing-machine, with 'Flying Angel' painted in scrolled gold lettering on its side. Next to it, the altar cupboard stood in the corner. A rotating light illuminated the lamas' images and brass cups, like a small, silent siren. On the wall were photographs of Tsedup and me and my parents, in a frame. It was strange to see them here. We had sent them so long ago. It was like a shrine to their missing boy.

That night we talked, a sensitive task for Tsedup, since he did all the translating and most of it was about him. Annay and Amnye told my parents how grateful they were to them for having taken care of him in England and bringing him home. My parents said that they had been happy to help their son and to have him for a son-in-law. By knowing him their lives had changed. The tears flowed freely down Annay's cheeks. She left the room to fetch a stained cloth, then sat dabbing at her eyes, thanking them over and over. My parents said it was a wonderful thing for them to be there with his family.

Until that point, Ama-lo-lun, Tsedup's tiny octogenarian grandmother, had sat silently reciting her mantra and turning her *korlo*, prayer wheel. Suddenly she looked up at my parents. 'Please look after him. He is my heart,' she said, clasping her bony hands to her breast. Amnye got up from his seat and pretended to fuss with the butter lamps on the altar. Then he walked out of the door. It was not the thing to do, to stay and cry.

I had just one thing to say. I said it to Amnye when he came back in. He readjusted his wooden cosh in his *tsarer* and sat on the platform cross-legged, then removed the white Tilley hat that Dad had brought him.

I said, 'How do you feel that your son has married a western girl?' I knew that I wasn't quite what he had expected for his son.

He lit a cigarette, drew in a lungful of smoke. 'All my sons are free to do what they wish with their lives,' he stated simply. That was it. He smiled at the very corner of his mouth, giving nothing away. Did he like me? Was I a

*Top*, the family tent; *left*, Tsedup's mother, Annay Labko; *right*, Tsedup's father, Amnye Karko.

View of Machu from the Wild Yak range.

*Top*, Ama-lo-lun, Azjung (the Sky Man) and Rhanjer's son, Tinlee; *bottom*, Tsedup's brother, Cumchok Jamtso seated centre at the ceremony to worship the holy mountain.

A *chorten* at Labrang monastery.

This page *top*, Tsedup's youngest brother, Gorbo; *above left*, Mum; *above right*, Dad and boys from the tribe. Opposite page *top*, view of Jerko's tent; *bottom*, Nawang, Tsedup and Tsedo's children – Sanjay, Dickir Che, Ziggy and me inside the white tent.

Above and below photographs by Cloë Lederman

Me, Sirmo and Shermo Donker pose for a picture before our trip to town.

social embarrassment? He was an important man in the tribe and in the town. I guessed that Tibetan fathers-in-law were not used to such impertinence in the average *namma*.

Maybe I should have kept quiet, but I said, 'I know how much Tsedup loves Tibet. I love it too. I don't want to take him away from his home. I want to be part of it.'

Annay wept again. I had meant it. I wanted to be a part. Surely it couldn't be that hard.

# THREE

# *Palace of the Lamas*

As day dawned, the mist hung in delicate trails over the town in the valley below the house. We clattered out of the yard in the jeep, loaned by the mayor, as Annay waved at the gate and Ama-lo-lun called after us, in a tiny voice, 'I will look for your return.' Tsedup and I were taking my parents to Labrang, the site of the biggest monastery in Amdo, where we would say goodbye to them. Amnye had set off before dawn on the local bus. He was a local councillor who represented the nomad tribes. There was a meeting in Gannan or Hezou, as the Chinese called it, the county's seat, which was only two hours away, so he said he would join us in Labrang later that day. That was the plan, anyway.

My father had never been a good back-seat passenger; he had also never been in the metal box of a Beijing jeep. As we bounced on the rusty springs, trying not to hit the roof, negotiating precipitous, blind bends high up on the passes, he muttered expletives under his breath. I had to laugh. But it was no laughing matter when we stopped at one of the small towns on the way.

It was just another dusty Chinese settlement, low-rise concrete, ugly, cattle and people wandering vaguely in the midday heat. We parked on a street corner and sat in the jeep as Tsedup bought some water from a stall on the other side of the road. Predictably, a crowd began to form around the vehicle, pressing their noses up to the glass and pointing. The prospect of opening the windows and relieving ourselves of heat-stroke was not an option. We endured, until Tsedup returned with the water and we drove off, leaving the bemused voyeurs in a cloud of black exhaust fumes. We had not gone fifty yards down the street, when a Chinese police officer stepped out into our path and ordered our driver into the police compound. News had travelled fast.

We drove through the gate into the gravel yard and parked in the shade of a tree. At a table in the sunlit courtyard sat a group of about eight uniformed policemen, playing cards and eating noodles. They had their feet on the table and their jackets hung from the back of their chairs, exposing the holstered pistols slung from their hips. Their Ray-Bans glinted fake golden as they drew languidly on their cigarettes. They didn't look up and I found their nonchalance the most threatening thing about them. We sat in the jeep, awaiting our fate, as a fat officer, obviously the superior of the pack, finished his last mouthful and rose wearily. His deputy, who stood at his side with a cigarette dangling from his mouth, motioned to our driver to get out of the jeep. He gingerly stepped down to join them.

We watched anxiously as they spoke. It was worse not knowing what they were saying. Our driver was Tibetan, and whatever it was they wanted, he was not in a position to negotiate. He came back to the jeep and, in a trembling voice, summoned Tsedup. My mouth went dry as I tried to block out my parents' hysteria and concentrate on the figure of my husband in front of the policeman. They exchanged a few words, then Tsedup came back and asked us for our passports, including his own. The documents were passed lazily around the group, who scrutinised them upside down, methodically turning the pages. One of the officers came up to the jeep and peered at us dispassionately for a few moments. Then there appeared to be a small commotion; they were all pointing at something and getting excited. Tsedup seemed to be making some progress. Suddenly they handed him back our passports and appeared to be waving us on. We couldn't believe our luck, but sat quietly as our driver, visibly shaking, chain-smoked his way out of town.

When we were far enough away to feel safe, Tsedup revealed the details of his experience to us. He had got out of the jeep and the fat sergeant had asked him, 'Where are you from?' He'd told him Machu. The policemen had then deduced that he was a local and the deputy had asked him for his identity card, which all nationals are obliged to carry. He'd told them he didn't have one. The fat man had groaned while his deputy had exclaimed incredulously, 'You haven't got one?' They had been mentally limbering up. It might mean prison, a fine, anything.

'What are *they* doing here?' the fat man had demanded, pointing out the westerners, huddled in the back of the jeep.

'They are my family,' Tsedup had said. 'There is my wife in the middle and her mother and father.'

They had had no idea what he was talking about.

'Go and get those people's passports,' the fat one had bellowed.

Tsedup had brought them back the passports and the sergeant had examined them slowly, one after the other. One of the young policemen with his feet on the table had suddenly grabbed one of the passports out of the sergeant's thick hands to have a look for himself. He had nearly fallen off his chair when he saw the picture inside. Immediately he had passed the document to his superior. 'Look! Look!' he had cried out in shock. The fat officer had not deigned to look at Tsedup until that point.

Suddenly he had turned to him. 'Where did you get this?' he had demanded.

'London,' Tsedup had replied.

'What? In England? London?' he'd exclaimed.

'Yes,' Tsedup had said. 'I am a British citizen.'

The shift in mood was almost tangible: the policeman had slipped from barking orders to an ingratiating tone. 'Well, you be very careful,' he had said. 'We don't want to make any trouble. We will get the blame if any harm comes to you, so please look after yourselves. Normally when we catch foreigners driving in a private vehicle we impose a massive fine, but I'll let you off.' Then he had offered, 'You can extend your visas in Labrang if you need to.'

Labrang, or Xiahe as it has been renamed by the Chinese, stands at about 8,400 feet (2,820 metres) above sea level and is near the Hexi Corridor, part of the old Silk Road, which was once the main thoroughfare for military, economic and cultural exchanges between Asia and Europe. It is home to one of the six major lamaseries of the Gelugpa, or Yellow Hat, sect of Tibetan Buddhism founded by Tsong Khapa around AD 1400. Labrang literally means 'Palace of the Lamas'. For Tibetans, it carries a unique religious and cultural heritage. It was established in 1709, according to the guidebook, and at one time housed up to four thousand monks. Now there are about 1,300. The lamasery, or 'The Grand Golden House' as the Tibetans call it, was cradled between the mountains, the golden rooftops of its temples winking in the sun. Each building was terracotta red, the colour of warm earth, and had white and black detailing under the gilded roofs and around the windows. Each window was of traditional Tibetan style, with the bottom slightly wider than the top of the frame, like a blunt triangle.

On the main street of the town, fuchsia-robed monks jostled with nomad pilgrims and western tourists. In the profusion of trinket stalls and shops that lined the road to the monastery, Chinese traders sold Tibetan carpets, prayer beads, cymbals, jewellery and *thankas* – religious paintings. In customary style the Chinese modern architecture of the town was concrete and unimaginative. What had once been temples was now a mass of breeze-block hotels and glass-fronted shops.

We arrived late in the afternoon. The hotel that my mother had chosen was the former Summer Palace of the lama Jamyang Jhapa, the reincarnation of the founder of Labrang Monastery. It sat among the flutter of birch leaves and the gurgle of water in the rocky riverbed. It was quiet and out of reach of the throb of the main town. The receptionist wore the traditional Tibetan dress of the Lhasa region, which was coincidentally what I was wearing that day. It consisted of a full-length, sleeveless, silk pinafore dress tied at the back, with a woven apron of thin, horizontal coloured stripes and a long-sleeved silk blouse underneath. She stood in front of a huge mural of the grassland, which covered the entire reception wall. Yaks and sheep grazed behind her head and a nomad woman fetched water from a blue river to take back to the tent in the background. A real Tibetan hotel. Tsedup smiled and greeted her in Tibetan. But she did not speak Tibetan.

In curt Chinese she stopped him short. 'Speak Chinese!' she commanded. His tone changed to indignation and he switched language. It appeared that the dress and the painting were nothing more than a sham for the next bus of tourists.

We were led to our rooms through a circular garden with flower-beds radiating out from its centre. Around the edge of the circle, positioned just like a tribe, were Tibetan tents, not the black yak-hair variety that we had just come from but white festival marquees with blue swirling patterns on them.

'Wow, real tents! This is great,' exclaimed Tsedup, prepared to forgo his displeasure. I could tell that he was beginning to worry about whether my mother would be happy staying in a tent again. But his fears were allayed when he reached the entrance to ours. As he touched the white surface, his face fell. It was concrete. The inside was fitted with all the usual hotel amenities, TV with thirty channels, plastic shower slippers, hot water twice a day. It was surreal.

Tsedup and I took a rickshaw into town to meet Amnye.

A collection of lethargic drivers lazed around the gate of the hotel and we took our pick, haggled, and were ripped off. It was a motorbike with a metal cart attached and it buzzed with great ferocity along the road, past terracotta mud huts and over layers of barley straw. The local farmers required the assistance of passing vehicles to crush their barley husks and release the seed. We crossed the bridge over the river, passing rain-washed prayer flags and hundreds of red and gold prayer wheels lining the wall of a monastery. Nomads and monks were circumambulating the lamasery in the early evening light, performing their *kora*, turning each wheel as they passed it. They would be reciting the Buddhist mantra *Om mani padme hum*, as they moved clockwise round the temple, although I couldn't hear them for the rickshaw's whine.

We alighted at the White Conch Hotel in the centre of town where we were due to meet Tsedup's father. Inside, the Amdo receptionist said that he had not been there and that there was no note. We decided to check out the Tibetan hotels and come back later. Perhaps the bus had been delayed. We walked slowly in the gutter as cycle rickshaws clanked past, churning up the dust on the tarmac road. On either side of the street we passed shops crammed with hats, shoes, cauldrons, kettles, steamers and piles of plastic buckets. This was where the nomads came to stock up on provisions. The prices in Labrang were often much lower than in their own nearby towns, so it was not uncommon for a pilgrimage to be combined with an annual shopping spree. They bartered loudly with the Chinese owners, often in their own language, so both parties were left shouting over the other in total incomprehension. Most of the nomad men could speak basic Chinese, and for women, most transactions were covered by a knowledge of numbers and the word for noodle soup. But some of the older generation were none the wiser. Pointing and shouting seemed to work best.

Eating-houses with names such as Snowlands Restaurant and Yak Restaurant cluttered the balconies above the street. Inside, monks stared unblinking at sunburnt backpackers chomping nostalgically on fried omelettes and honey pancakes, while a group of Muslim boys, in white caps, chopped and steamed and stoked in the grimy back kitchens. On the pavement stood a wooden stall hung with yak and sheep carcasses. The fat had yellowed in the heat and had seduced a cloud of flies into frenzied activity. A bored and bearded Muslim man in a blue worker's uniform swatted them lamely with a dead yak's tail. Next to him, under a small striped parasol, sat an equally bored-looking Chinese girl in red nylon trousers and a frilly flowered blouse. She was selling ices from her refrigerated cart and her face was covered in white makeup that stopped at her jawline, revealing a tawny neck. This painted mask was completed by a perfect circle of neon pink rouge on each cheek. She looked like an Aunt Sally. It appeared that, unlike their western counterparts, these Chinese women loved to be white. Instead of topping up on bronzer they bought ivory sticks of foundation to smear it all over their faces.

We reached the side-street just before the monastery. A row of ramshackle hotels stretched the length of the earthy track opposite stalls of Tibetans selling trinkets. Beyond, a green field of barley waved to the wooded hills. At each doorway Tsedup asked if anyone called Karko was staying there. He knew that his father's favourite hotel, the Dolma, was in this street so he left a message there that we were at the hotel by the river. Then we caught another rickshaw up to the monastery. Tsedup was taking me to meet the monks from his tribe who lived there.

We pulled up alongside a huge wall stained with clay water. The red-brown expanse was divided by a narrow passageway leading to a golden-roofed temple. We dismounted the sputtering vehicle and Tsedup had a short dispute with the driver over the fare, then we entered the shadow of the alley. About twenty yards down and set in the right-hand wall was a wooden door. Tsedup pushed it open and a brass bell tinkled above our heads as we stepped over the threshold.

We had entered a courtyard bordered by beautifully con-structed wooden rooms on all sides. It was like a sanctuary from the outside world. '*Arro!*' Tsedup called. Immediately a monk appeared from inside one of the rooms and made his way towards us over the wooden porch. He was dressed from head to toe in the customary fuchsia robes with a patchwork of pink silk on the bodice of his tunic. He beamed from ear to ear when he realised it was Tsedup and they embraced warmly, then Tsedup introduced me and we shook hands and smiled.

Aka Damchu led us into the cool of his room and prepared some strong tea on his iron stove. The room was simple and immaculately clean, symmetrical in shape, with a sleeping platform on either side spread with colourful Tibetan rugs. In the centre of each platform was a low wooden table painted orange with small drawers in each side. On one of the tables lay an old traditional Tibetan book, not bound, but a long, thin sheaf of thick sepia-stained paper with calligraphy on each page. After a page had been read it was lifted with great care from the top, turned over and placed down on the table above the pile. This book had been left open in such a manner and I concluded that we had disturbed his contemplation. He didn't seem to mind, though, but chatted amiably with Tsedup, catching up on the years of news with the usual animated exclamations characteristic of the nomads.

I nodded and smiled as I sipped the black tea. In the calm atmosphere of the cool room I took in the beauty of the space. Along the length of the back wall were shelves of books and a cupboard painted with peacocks and tigers. Above it sat a glass-fronted cabinet containing more books, *thib*, butter lamps and photographs of Tibetan lamas with *kadaks* draped around them. Everything inside the room and out had been painstakingly carved and painted by hand. Tsedup told me that the money for the construction of the monks' quarters had been provided entirely by his tribe.

It wasn't long before the other monks began arriving, their meditation punctuated by the guffaws coming from our room. Each one greeted Tsedup with great joy and they hugged. The Tibetans were fond of stories and soon they were all sharing memories of their past together. Aka Damchu used to chase yaks with Tsedup in the grassland when they were boys; Aka Tenzin was Tsedup's mother's cousin's son; all were either related or had shared some particular intimacy with him. They were not all named 'Aka', however: all monks are addressed by this respectful title. It was a great reunion. I had never been in the company of so many monks at once and was humbled, especially as I was a woman in their chambers. But they were not interested in formalities and made us stay and eat *tuckpa* with them. We sat slurping together as the night came down.

But the search for Amnye had not been forgotten. As we bade them goodnight, after refusing a fourth bowl of *tuckpa*, they told us to come back the next day with my parents to meet the child lama. We accepted their mysterious invitation, closed the tinkling door to the sanctuary and stepped out into the dark passage.

On the street Tsedup hailed a cycle rickshaw clanking towards us in the dusklight. He told me to get on and go back to the hotel while he wandered around to see if he could locate his father. I went off into the night air, the cyclist panting up the hill. Around me towered the monastery walls and black mountains. As we crossed the bridge and passed alongside the barley-field, I saw small fires glowing near the river. Groups of nomad pilgrims had set up camp and were cooking in their white tents. They bustled and sang, the smoke from the stoves coiling up into the moist, night air, and I thought how much I would have preferred to be staying with them there under the stellar canopy than returning to my concrete tent.

Back inside I checked on my parents, who were lying on their crisp-white-sheeted beds. The world did not seem such an alien place for them now that they had recovered a few of the trappings of civilisation. They were anxious to hear about the whereabouts of Amnye, however, and were concerned when I had nothing to report.

'Perhaps the bus was delayed,' I said. 'He'll probably come back with Tsedup soon and all will be well.'

'Let's hope so,' said my father. Then he turned to other matters. It was a rare moment for my parents to have the chance to speak to me alone. They seized it. 'Will you be all right staying here for six months, Kate?' my father began tentatively. 'If things get too much for you, you will come home, won't you? You know, you could just stay for a couple of months until your visas run out then come back.'

I had always felt the burden of my parents' anxiety. I was

proud of them for coming with us. They had done it for us, as much as to satisfy their intense curiosity. Despite my mother's various neuroses (lavatory phobia, dog phobia, insomnia phobia), and my father's seeming lack of command (he wasn't used to other people taking charge), they had made a real bond with the tribe and family that would last a lifetime. They would never forget this trip. Also they had shown me the greatest part of themselves. It had been hard for them enduring the discomfort of life in the tents, such as not washing, being debilitated by mountain sickness and eating offal, but they had conquered their fears. Yet that didn't stop them worrying about their daughter.

'Dad, I'll be fine.' I sighed. 'It'll be great, don't worry.'

We were young and carefree. What did they know? We had been desperate to be here for years and were not about to cut short our stay. However, I suppressed the desire to describe at length the horror that was provoked in me by the prospect of a thousand-mile journey to Hong Kong to renew our visas. We were just hoping that the local authorities would be able to do it when the time came. We had flexible tickets on the international flight back to London from Beijing precisely because we could never be sure how it would turn out. But I hoped it would all come right in the end. 'It'll be fine,' I repeated, distractedly chewing my nail.

Suddenly there was a knock at the door. I opened it, expecting to see Tsedup and his father and indeed it was Tsedup, but with him were two men in leather trench coats. They looked like secret agents, but not so secret: the enormous sunglasses of the moustached one were a bit of a giveaway at this time of night.

'I can't find my father,' said Tsedup. 'I've left messages all over town but he is not here.'

'Maybe the meeting went on longer and he stayed in Gannan,' Dad offered, trying not to stare at the strangers, but clearly flustered.

'Oh, these are my friends Tsorsungchab and Sortsay,' Tsedup said. At the mention of their names they broke into smiles, peering into the room over Tsedup's shoulder. 'I ran into them in town. They are from Machu.' The word Machu also triggered a nod and a wider grin from them both. Relieved, we greeted them warmly repeating 'Arro' several times, with more enthusiastic nodding.

'We're going to have a drink in our room next door,' said Tsedup. 'I'll say goodnight now.'

'Tsedup, don't worry about your father. We'll find out what has happened to him tomorrow,' my father said.

I said goodnight and left them to sleep.

Next door the men were cracking open the beers. The reason for their appearance was not that they were members of some underground operation but that they were townsfolk. The leather trench coats signalled their position in the community. Sortsay, a small, rotund, merry-faced fellow with cropped black hair and acne on his cheeks, was mayor of Tsedup's tribe. Tsorsungchab, taller, thinner and permanently wearing shades, due to a driving accident that had left his eye damaged, worked for the education department. Anyway, it was cool to wear big shades. They had come to Labrang because both of their wives were sick and were attending the outpatients' service at the hospital. Machu did not have adequate medical care at its small hospital. They were pleased to be reunited with Tsedup and took the opportunity to laugh and drink heartily with him. As the evening progressed they teased me, 'Shermo, drink your beer!' It was a bit of a novelty, a woman who drank beer.

Just then there was a knock at the door. Sortsay, who was nearest, opened it. The Chinese girl from Reception stared sourly into the room. She frowned as she said something to Tsedup, then stood obstinately by the door, waiting for his response. He turned to me with a look of disbelief on his face.

'She just asked me what I am doing here,' he said, perplexed.

I rounded on her. 'He is my husband!' I exclaimed, exasperated. It was a futile attempt to defend him since she couldn't speak English.

'I am a paying guest,' he added in Chinese, then translated my outcry. She didn't appear to have grasped the concept of interracial marriage, and the furrows in her brow deepened. She clearly presumed that he was a local, planning a free night in their luxury hotel with his friends. Tsedup told her to go away and check with the manager if she didn't believe him.

Perhaps I was wrong to expect anything else, but the frustration of seeing Tsedup submitted to this humiliation was almost unbearable. We were shocked that he had to suffer the indignities of racism in the place that he knew as home. I guessed he had forgotten: he had been away a long time. I was beginning to realise why he had left.

Right on cue there was another rap at the door. This time it was the manager. He was Tibetan and his bloodshot eyes and ruddy cheeks betrayed a fondness for the beer that he glimpsed out of the corner of his eye on our table. Once again, Tsedup was asked what he was doing there.

'I have paid for this room for me and my wife to stay in,' Tsedup replied, struggling to control his temper. Then the manager pointed to Sortsay and Tsorsungchab and asked why they were in the room. They leapt to their own defence and explained that they hadn't seen Tsedup for nine years. They were having a drink as guests and would be off to their own hotels soon. Disgruntled, the man walked away from the incomprehensible situation and returned to his bottle, as Tsedup called after him, 'Go and check your records.'

After our friends had left, Tsedup and I lay in the dark of the concrete tent and pondered the experience. I knew his pride was hurt and there was little I could do to console him. But mostly he was worried about his father's whereabouts.

The next morning when we arrived at the monastery, Aka Damchu was sitting in the sun on the wooden seat outside his room. He was spinning a prayer wheel, a small barrel of intricately moulded metal that rotated on a wooden stick. A marble-sized ball was attached by a thin chain to the barrel and swung round keeping the momentum, as he flicked his wrist in a constant rhythm. He was introduced to Dad by Tsedup and greeted him heartily. My mother had stayed behind to sketch and rest; she would join us for a tour of the monastery later, and although I understood that she had her limits, I was forced to disguise my disappointment and embarrassment. How often would she be offered the chance to have a private audience with a child lama? He was the sixth reincarnation of Ja Metoch Kamto, the tutor of Jamyang Jhapa, the founder of Labrang Monastery. The social order of the lamasery followed a strict hierarchy. Jamyang Jhapa, whose full name was Jetsun Losang Jigme Tubten Chogyi Nyima Palzang Po, was the head lama and beneath him were four sub-lamas who occupied 'golden thrones'; beneath these were seven more and so on. The boy, Jarsung, whom we were about to meet, was one of the four who occupied a golden throne; he was therefore of considerable rank.

We walked solemnly behind Aka Damchu through the wooden archway into the next courtyard holding our prayer scarves in both hands. As we passed through the gate, my father and I watched Tsedup for tips on decorum. Then we glimpsed the boy sitting waiting to receive us on his throne. He couldn't have been more than thirteen years old, but his eyes held the seriousness of a much older man. He wore wine-red robes and a length of fuchsia fabric across one shoulder. In his left hand he methodically counted the beads of his *tranger* between thumb and forefinger as he surveyed his foreign guests with curiosity. Following Tsedup's lead, we kept our heads lower than his out of respect. We approached him in our small procession, holding out our *kadaks*. He leant forward, took them from our outstretched hands and placed each one around our necks. This was all performed in total silence. He seemed so isolated, surrounded by monks much older than himself, and I wanted to ask him so many things. Had he forgotten how to be a boy? What was it like to be discovered as a reincarnate, to live your life in the image of someone else? Had he been a monk before they found him or was he living with his family? Did he realise his destiny before that time? Was he happy? But I never had the chance to display my ignorance.

We followed Aka Damchu to the other side of the court-yard, still bent in supplication, taking care not to turn our backs on the lama. Our friend led us into a shrine dedicated to Jarsung. As far as the eye could see there were books, all written by the six Jarsungs of the past, lining the walls. Butter lamps glowed fragrantly in front of an altar containing a row of pictures of the Jarsungs. Tsedup prostrated himself in front of them as I inspected their faces. The first four pictures were drawn in ink and showed old men, one in the amazing cockatoo-shaped yellow hat of the Gelugpa sect of Buddhism. The last two pictures were photographs, and one was of a tiny boy. He looked out of place next to these grand old faces. Tsedup pointed at the child. 'He has written all of these books,' he said. It seemed unlikely to me that a thirteen-year-old boy had achieved such a feat. But then I stopped. Tsedup's comment had revealed to me the true nature of the Tibetans' belief in reincarnation. As far as Tsedup was concerned, Jarsung had been the same Jarsung for hundreds of years; it was only his physical appearance that had changed throughout his various lives. He went on to explain that Jarsung had always been gifted throughout his reincarnations and, true to character, the boy we had met today was famed for being a conscientious and exceptional student.

I was moved by this strange encounter. It was a reminder of the atmosphere of mystery that surrounds Tibet: the unknown, magical and isolated Tibet. Such beliefs have a fascination for us in our logical and largely non-spiritual techno-culture, and the practice of determining the rightful successor to a lama upon his death was mystifying to me. Buddhism teaches that the energy derived from the physical and mental activities of a life will embrace a new life when dissolved by death, and has been fundamental to the Tibetan belief system for centuries. A lama's disciple will often search for years to find his reincarnated spirit, and his journey may take him many thousands of miles. When a likely candidate is located he is set a series of tests. These usually consist of the disciple placing objects that belonged to the late lama in front of the candidate, hidden among ordinary things that did not belong to him. The reincarnate will always select the lama's possessions with uncanny immediacy and a peculiar sense of familiarity. He is then recognised and ordained. It is a great honour for his family.

We took tea with Aka Damchu, who presented us with a framed picture of Lama Jarsung sitting on his golden throne. Then Tsedup, who was increasingly anxious about his father, signalled that we should leave. Dad thanked Aka Damchu for his kindness and we left for the town, but not before we had been offered a personal guided tour of Labrang Monastery that afternoon.

My father and I waited in a café while Tsedup played detective. It was a dry, hot day and the sun beat down on the dusty tarmac. He returned some time later with no news, but with a leg of mutton poking out from inside his jacket. Despite his worries for his father, he had had time to visit his uncle. That explained the mutton.

We walked into the main enclave of Labrang Monastery, past the tourists and buses and up an earthy alleyway beside one of the main temple buildings. Tsedup led us up some stone steps to a doorway. At the top, inside the cool shade of a room penetrated by shafts of sunlight, we could see a row of monks prostrating. They began in a standing position then lay full length on the wooden floor, polished smooth by hundreds of years of supplication. Tsedup pointed out his seventy-year-old uncle who, he told us, prostrated here five hundred times a day. He certainly looked fit. Tsedup gestured to him from the door and caught his eye. The old monk squinted at us then shuffled over. When he got to the door and saw Tsedup, he cried out in recognition, showing a row of broken teeth. We followed him to his small wooden house, which smelt musty inside from the soot on the ceiling. We drank tea, and Tsedup and his uncle exchanged news. My father asked if he could take a picture of him and he agreed. He seemed fascinated by the camera, which my father gave him to study, along with his mobile phone. He held them gently, feeling the smoothness of the casings. Through Tsedup, he told us he had never seen a telephone before. My father began to tell him about satellites, at which point he handed it back quickly, saying, 'Be careful with that.'

As we left, Tsedup placed the leg of mutton by his uncle's stove – he had kept it hidden in the monastery for fear of causing offence. It was disrespectful to parade part of a freshly killed animal before the eyes of the compassionate monks to whom we were all sentient beings, even the sheep. Then he stepped outside and told his uncle what he had done. A look of surprise came over the old man's face. 'Meat!' he exclaimed. 'I can't eat that.'

'Oh, yes, you can. It will do you good,' said Tsedup. 'You know you haven't really given it up, so why protest?'

The old man's eyes twinkled and he smiled. 'Thank you,' he said quietly.

That afternoon we met my mother, who told us she had chastised the manager for his treatment of Tsedup the night before. 'Do you understand? He is my *son-in-law*,' she had protested, pronouncing the words with emphasis and volume. As a child I remembered cringing many a time in the supermarket queue on one of our annual trips to France as she spoke louder and slower in English to a stunned shop assistant, who sat waiting impassively for her to go away. Yet this time she had been really angry: she was mighty when defending her brood. But her outburst had been met with silence. An apology was out of the question.

Still, a tour around the monastery would cheer her up. As the other tourists trailed around in groups we were given the undivided attention of Aka Tenzin and Aka Damchu, and were able to view the rooms quietly. Labrang Monastery was beautiful. The main temple building was vast, dark and cool inside. From the lofty ceiling hundreds of *thankas* hung like the dense foliage of a forest canopy, into which red and gold columns soared like tree-trunks. Yellow cushions were arranged in rows between the columns for the monks to sit on during prayer. Along the back wall of the room was a series of altars, with displays of unbelievable riches: a golden statue of the Buddha adorned with coral, turquoise, amber and silken *kadaks*; golden butter lamps, silk flowers, and hundreds of Tibetan books stacked on shelves from floor to ceiling, wrapped in yellow cloth with a small blue, red and gold silk marker hanging from each. Order and precision prevailed, suggesting the care and attention lavished on the monastery. The whole place was a manifestation of the nomads' enduring faith and a clear indication of their wealth, for it had been funded entirely by the donations of nomads from the four corners of Amdo. It felt ancient and precious. Dust turned in the rays of sunlight that pierced the gloom. The familiar, musty scent of Uncle's room was also prevalent here, mixed with the thick, rancid smell of butter burning in the lamps. In the next room monks were chanting their prayers, and the rhythmic resonance of their deep voices boomed through to us in the dank air.

Outside, in the blinding sunlight, we passed pilgrims prostrating at one of the temple doors in a courtyard. An offering site, made of clay and painted white, scented the air with fragrant juniper, which burned and crackled at its heart. The Tibetans love that smell and juniper is often bought and burned as an offering. According to pre-Buddhist belief, juniper is the symbol of life, a representation of the goddess of fertility.

At another temple we were shown intricate murals of the deities, painted in the style of the *thankas*. I was not used to such unabashed use of colour: I thought of our churches, which often verge on the clinical in some modern dioceses, and wondered what had happened to real craftsmanship in our society. It seemed that only the absolute devotion of a population could produce such works of beauty. Here, the monks worked for the love of the place, and practised their art as they had for centuries.

Finally we visited the museum in the grounds, which housed examples of Tibetan scripts, and other fascinating paraphernalia including a fossilised dinosaur egg. The Tibetans believed it to be the egg of a bird often depicted in religious paintings, holding a snake in its beak. In the centre of the room was a *mandala*, Wheel of Life, an elaborate, symmetrical picture made from coloured sand. The grains were painstakingly laid on the surface using a metal instrument in the shape of a thin cone with a tiny hole in the end. A monk, who had received special training in the art, would rub a stick along the serrated side of the instrument causing it to vibrate and the grains to fall from the hole. He could control the exact number of grains that would go to make up the picture with incredible precision. The 'painting' was not flat; often there were grooves dividing the patterns, delicate peaks and troughs or tiny paths of triangle-shaped relief. The *mandala* we saw had been preserved in a glass case for viewing, but usually they are made at the start of a religious festival then thrown to the elements on the last day, as a symbol of the impermanence of life. I thought of the work of street painters in the West, whose masterpieces are washed away by the rain. Generally, apart from the most modern conceptual art, the material value of a painting in our consumer society is paramount. The older it is, the more value it acquires; it is unthinkable to destroy it. Seeing the *mandala* reminded me of how we sometimes attach the wrong kind of significance to objects in the West. Sometimes we just can't admit life's impermanence.

After our splendid tour we bade farewell to Aka Damchu, and Aka Tenzin accompanied us into town. He proved a useful accomplice. Tsedup told us to buy nothing and just look around, while he made more enquiries about his father. The monk and he made off down the road while my parents and I sauntered around the shops and stalls of the hot street. Scrawny Muslim boys called to us from their trinket havens, beckoning and thrusting pipes, knives and necklaces under our noses. My mother picked out a pair of embroidered silk tapestries of birds that had caught her eye. Then, further down the parade, she chose a *thanka*, but we did not buy, just as Tsedup had instructed. Instead we waited for him in a café under the shade of a canopy, while the flies buzzed around us and a woman with a twisted body begged for change. She wore the old blue Mao uniform and a black scarf tied around her head. I paid her and watched her limp away on her crutches, muttering plaintively. Then Tsedup appeared, and I gathered from his expression that he had still not found Amnye. What if there had been a crash? Tsedup had only just got home after nine years. What a dreadful tragedy it would be if he had lost his father the week after they had been reunited. It just didn't bear thinking about. He had phoned a friend in Machu town, but apparently Amnye had not returned. He must be in Gannan, but Tsedup didn't have the number of the meeting-place. He said that Sortsay and Tsorsungchab might know it. They were also helping to sort out my parents' car to Lhanzou so Tsedup would find them later.

He asked my mother what she had found to buy. We described the items, where they were, and told him what prices we had been offered. He laughed drily. 'Wait here. We'll go and buy them for you,' he said.

The best person to shop with in Labrang is a monk. Monks know the prices and they never get ripped off. In fact, it is better that you are not there at all: send a monk.

When they returned they had bought everything my mother had asked for, at about a fifth of the tourist price. We thanked Aka Tenzin for his help, and he grinned, happy to have seen justice done. Then we drank some tea together and I accompanied my parents back to the hotel. Tsedup stayed to look for the men in leather coats.

Later that evening the three friends arrived at the hotel, all smiling. Tsedup had spoken to his father. Apparently the bus had broken down in the middle of nowhere and the passengers had waited all day for help. This had made him late for his meeting. He would not be able to come to Labrang. He had seemed unfazed by the experience, as if things like this happened all the time. What had his son been worried about? Tsedup had reprimanded him for not contacting him when he had got to Gannan, but had had to conclude that he was behaving like an Englishman. It would be a slow process to get the West out of his system. Time means little to a nomad. As long as Amnye had his pouch of *tsampa* and cheese with him, he could wait patiently for days for any delay to resolve itself.

We all went to the bar. It was dark and sober inside, with

leather seating and a row of fancy drinks in optics with tantalisingly exotic names. We opted for beer. Sortsay and Tsorsungchab had come to inform my parents that they had arranged the car and driver, which would leave the next day; it had been 'loaned' by the town mayor. My parents seemed very pleased, so we 'forgot' to give them the exact details. One thing was for sure: the mayor's chauffeur would be hotfooting it back to Labrang tomorrow afternoon before the boss found out or there would be a high price to pay for a little overtime on the side. The two plotters toasted my mother and father with great gusto and downed many drinks in their honour, as we sat laughing at each other across the lacquered table.

The next morning I woke and got up. I have never liked leaving my parents, although I have done it many times. There was still some invisible sinew that held me to them. It was true that things would be easier when we didn't have to worry about their welfare, and I wouldn't have to witness them fighting over the video camera any more, and part of me was looking forward to a break, although I knew I would miss them. However, as the car rolled up to the hotel gate and we loaded their bags, I had to put on a brave face. My father hugged Tsedup – he had not done that before, being an emotional man who rarely betrays his emotions. A very English man. Then he hugged me and I felt the warmth of his plump, safe embrace. My mother was trying not to cry. She clung to me and I held her, and tried to suppress the feeling welling up inside me. If she didn't cry then I could control it.

Then I just stood and watched the arms waving from each window, right over the bridge, through the barley-field, down past the mud huts, out of sight.

# FOUR

## *Out on a Limb*

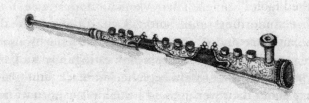

We left the concrete tents immediately and took a room in town where our two friends were staying with their families. They were returning to Machu the next day and had promised us a lift. The upstairs rooms overlooked the street, providing an interesting perspective on the scurrying life beneath the smeared window. Ours was a simple room with a linoleum floor, three single beds with cleanish sheets and pillows stuffed with what appeared to be sand. On the wall was a mirror, and underneath the window, a table. A bare lightbulb hung from the ceiling and an old-fashioned washstand, containing a tin bowl, stood sentry by the door.

In the courtyard lurked the public toilet; its putrid stench provoked convulsive retching at a distance of ten yards. It was becoming clear to me that, for all their striving for development, public sanitation was not high on the Chinese list for improvement. In fact, I had not been aware of a drainage system since leaving Lanzhou. Obviously the Tibetans had got it right: wandering off inconspicuously into a field had its merits.

We joined Sortsay, Tsorsungchab and their families in a room down the hallway. They had just got back from the Tibetan hospital across the road. It was my first time in the company of Tibetan townswomen, who were quite different from the nomad women. These women's appearance owed more to Chinese dress sense. Sortsay's wife, Dolma, sat on the bed looking pale and ill. She wore black polyester trousers, a white patterned blouse under a pink cardigan and a large gold ring. On her feet were high-heeled black shoes, and her long hair was woven into one thick plait, not two tied at the bottom, as the nomads wore it. She smiled weakly at me, then scolded her eight-year-old son, Tenzin, as he hit her knee with a small plastic gun. Meanwhile Tsorsungchab's wife, Tashintso, who needed treatment for a blood disorder, sat on a chair splitting melon seeds between her teeth and spitting the husks into a plastic bucket. She was beautiful, with a soft face and large, slightly drooping eyes, and was dressed in a similar fashion to Dolma. She had a curious indigo tattoo on her left hand: a series of dots in a circle. I wondered whether it related to some form of treatment or if it was a symbol of something. In the corner of the room sat Sortsay's mother, who was a true nomad and was dressed accordingly in her *tsarer* and jewellery. She seemed incongruous in this setting and was the only reminder that, despite these families' adoption of modern dress and all the trappings of 'civilisation', they were nomads, who had been born in tents.

It began to rain outside, the first drops heavy. The air was cooling after days of scorching heat. We sat in the crowded room and the smoke from the Chinese cigarettes hung torpidly in the fug. I was feeling a bit alienated. With Mum and Dad gone, I was beginning to grasp that Tsedup was the only person with whom I could communicate effectively. I wanted desperately to be able to talk to these women, but they seemed as embarrassed as I was to initiate a conversation, which would inevitably grind to an abrupt halt after the first sentence. We just giggled as Tsedup attempted to start things off by teasing Tashintso and trying to make her talk to me. I hoped they liked me. Perhaps they thought I was strange. I felt as if I was under a microscope.

The atmosphere lifted, however, when Tashintso's four-year-old son, Lhamochab, who had inherited the lovely brown eyes of his mother, was cajoled into performing a dance for us in the centre of the room. He was the most cherubic-looking child you could imagine, with a cheeky plump face and a quizzical smile. He strutted around, flailing his arms, in his bright yellow and black striped jumper, like a distressed bee, while singing at the top of his voice the words of the only Tibetan song he knew: '*Ah latze, ah latze, ahhh latze, ah latze, ah latze, ahh latze* . . .' Needless to say, it was somewhat repetitive, but had the whole room in uproar. Lhamochab was pleased with his new-found fame and spun round and round, until Tenzin poked him in the eye and it was curtains for the show. He sat grizzling on his mother's lap as Tenzin gloated, then ran out of the door screeching. His parents were obviously used to such behaviour for they made no attempt to discipline him. Dolma continued to smile weakly and Sortsay chuckled and smoked some more.

That evening I sampled my first karaoke. We had all dined on broth, cooked by a young Muslim man over the open fire at his street stall, under a plastic awning out of the drizzle. We slurped in unison from the clay pots that contained various ingredients, such as furry, tentacled stomach, which I ignored. Then we went back to our hotel and up the steep staircase at the other side of the courtyard to a glass-fronted room. Inside was a dimly lit bar with Formica tables and chairs and a dance-floor. A Chinese man sat at a table fiddling with the knobs on the karaoke machine, which winked synchronised neon blue lights out of the darkness, while the barmaid leant lethargically over the counter. The only customer so far was an inebriated Chinese man talking to himself by the wall. From the ceiling hung coloured lights, flashing brazenly like a school disco, and an enormous television screen that was belting out Chinese pop music. On the screen a bikini-clad girl wandered around a park, followed by a cameraman, who was wasting no time with his zoom lens. Sex on TV is censored in China, but there seemed to be an awful lot of sublimation going on. Karaoke is big in China, and even in remote parts, the locals take it seriously.

As the men fetched some drinks and we sat down at a table, the barmaid came to life. She took the microphone stand and began howling in a pseudo-operatic whine. She was loving it. Tashintso looked at me, attempting to suppress her mirth, but we burst into fits of giggles that were drowned, none the less, by the cacophony. The men joined us and we sipped our drinks and surveyed the menu of songs. I was lucky: there was nothing in English, so I would not have to humiliate myself. But I was soon invited to dance, and reluctantly joined Sortsay on the floor for a quick turn. He was remarkably gentlemanly and guided me in some kind of waltz to the strains of a love song, singing along to the words. I struggled not to stand on his feet as I wrestled with the intricacies of the steps and he smiled encouragingly. This was a world away from a club night in the West End, not that I was ever a fervent party-goer. Soon everyone took their turn at the mike, and their familiarity with Chinese popular culture became evident in that they knew every word and inflection to every song. The best songs were those about Tibet, in Chinese, of course, but sung to evocative images of nomadic life on the video screen: yaks and sheep, festivals and horse-racing, dancing and monks.

The inevitable happened later. The song list changed and I found myself with no excuse to avoid singing an English song. I stood blushing under the glitterball that rotated in the disco lights and trembled my way through the Beatles' 'Yesterday', as the drunk man shimmied around in his blue Mao suit and cap, splashing beer over the lino. When I finished the whole room cheered and clapped, and I have to say that in some strange way I found the experience quite liberating, if surreal.

When we returned to our room, bleary-eyed and a little the worse for beer, someone was in one of the beds. Aka Tenzin had found his way in and was snoring in the lamplight. I guessed he fancied a change from the monastery. I felt most uncomfortable with the idea of undressing in front of a monk, so climbed into my bed on the other side of the room fully clothed as Tsedup woke him to chat. I fell asleep to the rise and fall of their voices and the barmaid's final song.

\* \* \*

The next morning we left in another Beijing jeep, as Aka Tenzin waved from the noodle shop where we had breakfasted. I sat in the back with Tsorsungchab and Tashintso, who held Lhamochab on her knee. Tsedup sat in the front next to the driver as he was prone to travel sickness. It wasn't him that we had to worry about this time, however; we had gone only fifty yards when Lhamochab was sick over his father's legs. Many Tibetans are not used to motorised vehicles, especially the nomads who traditionally prefer the horse if they have any distance to travel, but for these townsfolk the vibration of the engine, the smell of the petrol and the sense of claustrophobia were an unfamiliar hazard. Tsorsungchab did not drive because of the car crash that had damaged his eyesight. When he took off his dark glasses to wipe his weeping eye I saw the two-inch scar that ran beneath it. He told me, quite cheerily, that beer had caused the crash and ruined his sight. Now he didn't drink.

We had been five hours on the road and the weather was inclement. An all too familiar English grey had dissolved the sky, and I searched the smudged landscape through the steamy windows for signs of home: a curve of a mountain, the sweep of the grassland that fell from the Wild Yak range. I had missed my surrogate family and the tribe. The few days of drifting in Labrang had left me feeling displaced and I craved a sense of being rooted. I had never been much of a pioneer; too much a suburban girl at heart. However, now that his role as tour guide was officially over, Tsedup was desperate to return to Machu town to be reunited with his friends. He still hadn't seen many and was as keen to make contact with them as he had been to meet his family again.

First, though, we went to Tashintso's house. It transpired that she and Tsorsungchab also had a daughter,
Tsepharchab, who must have been about eight and had
been staying with her grandmother while they were in
Labrang. She burst into tears as soon as she saw her
parents and clung to them, in her yellow dress and pink
socks, as we got out of the stuffy car. Their house was in the
heart of the town, among the sprawl of concrete dwellings
and courtyards divided by a grid of narrow alleyways and
high walls. They unlocked their metal gate and we made
our way into the courtyard, up the little path, past the tap –
a much-coveted item – and round to the back of a shambles
of outbuildings. In front of a red-brick inner courtyard was a
gaily painted house with a conservatory of fashionable blue
glass displaying potted plants. We sat at the table under the
glass roof and Tashintso brought us some beer.

They had just finished building the house. It was simple,
with a lounge area and two bedrooms all with wooden
floors. In the front room sat two armchairs, a coffee table,
wardrobe and dresser with silk flowers and a clock on it;
otherwise the room was bare. The bedrooms contained
only a bed with a neatly folded shiny pink quilt and a small
cupboard. The house looked as if they had never set foot
inside it.

The outbuilding crouching opposite in the yard was their
real home and had been for years. It consisted of a parlour,
with an electric cooker and glass-fronted cupboards, a bedroom with a small stove and television, and a back room
for eating and for the children to sleep in. Its walls were
decorated with newspaper but it was clear that Tashintso
and Tsorsungchab had all the mod cons – except a fridge;
that was the ultimate goal. If you had a fridge, you were

someone. Tashintso's brother had a fridge; one day she would have one.

As we sat and drank our beer, Tsorsungchab busied himself. Something trilled shrilly from under the table and I was astonished to see that he had a mobile phone, which he answered proudly. I could see that he was fond of gadgetry – a land-line telephone sat on a small table in the corner, covered by a handkerchief to protect it from dust. Whether the calls were work-related or not was difficult to say. He looked important anyway, as he puffed on his cigarette and grunted loudly and repeatedly into the mouthpiece, '*Ah . . . Ah . . . Ah . . .*' meaning 'what'. He seemed oblivious of anyone speaking to him, for the whats continued for some time before he settled into a rhythmic and repetitive boom of '*Oh . . . oh . . . oh . . .*' meaning 'yes'. Whoever was struggling to get a word in gave up after a short time and Tsorsungchab turned off the phone without saying goodbye. Amdowas don't say goodbye, they just say, '*Da de chi roi,*' which means, 'OK, that's it.' I laughed eventually as his monosyllabic retorts seemed to be the only thing he was uttering and he laughed heartily back. 'Shermo, drink beer!' he cried, flicking ash into the green china ashtray. I was as much a source of humour to him as he was to me.

Tashintso busied herself with the children and unpacking. Lhamochab was turning circles on his tricycle in the yard, while his sister grizzled on the flower-bed wall. She had been abandoned and was not going to let her parents forget it. Her mother cooed comfortingly as she simultaneously swept the floor, put away the clothes and chatted animatedly with Tsedup and her husband.

'Tashintso is a policewoman,' Tsedup told me. I don't know why, but for some reason I found this difficult to believe. In my limited understanding of local authority and the machinations of this alien society, it seemed inconceivable that a Tibetan man could be a policeman, let alone a Tibetan woman, but I suppose this was Communist China, and women were just as likely as men to occupy positions of authority.

Tsedup pointed to a green uniform, which hung on a peg by the door. 'Look. That is her uniform.' She was indeed a woman of the law. Paranoia kicked in. Perhaps she was watching us. We should be careful. As if he was reading my mind, Tsedup explained, 'Tashintso is going to help us. She says she will arrange for us to meet the local police sergeant soon. He will want to have an interview with me.' Perhaps it would be a good thing to have a friend in the police station after all, but the thought of an interview made me shudder.

The next day as I was brushing my teeth in a tin bowl in the sunny yard a familiar figure appeared. He wandered around the edge of the outbuilding and said, 'Hello, Kate.'

I was so shocked to hear a Tibetan speaking English that I nearly choked. He looked older, but it was unmistakably Tsempel. He had been a great friend of Tsedup's in India when we had first met, but had returned to Tibet soon after I left for England. I had not seen him for five years. His front teeth were chipped now from splitting melon seeds and around his eyes were deep lines I didn't remember. He was thin and slightly stooping, with an apologetic air, and he spoke calmly and quietly in a low, husky voice.

'*Arro*, Tsempel. *Cho demo?*' I asked, as we shook hands firmly.

He replied in English again, 'I'm happy to see you.'

Namma

I ran to the bedroom to wake Tsedup and he sprang out of bed. The two embraced warmly in a blurt of excited dialect, and it struck me, as I looked at them together, how much time had passed. It seemed now almost as if they were from two different worlds. Except, as with all the other reunions I had witnessed, there was an immediate connection between them. It didn't need to be spoken; they were like brothers. Whatever they had experienced, whichever path they had chosen, they were essentially the same. They were 'Amdo boys', and that, I had learnt, was a phenomenon unto itself.

The clarity of the concept is derived from the exiled community in India, which is split into the three regions of Tibet: Kham, Amdo and the Tibetan Autonomous Region, (TAR) with those who have been born in exile. For the most part they live harmoniously, but certain hostilities and prejudices exist. For a start they all speak different dialects. The majority, who are from the TAR or who were born in India, do not understand the regional dialects of Amdo and Kham, and it is the responsibility of the latter to learn the dialect spoken by the TAR. Meanwhile the Amdowas and the Khampas always stick together in their regional groups, like small tribes. They are from farther away and as most of them have left their families behind, the young men are freer than the others to express themselves and take advantage of their new-found freedom. When I met Tsedup, he shared a tiny cell-like room with seven other Amdo boys where they baked bread to sell on the street. They relied on each other for everything and an even greater bond existed between them than when they were in Tibet. The 'Lhasa boys' are often afraid of the Amdowas who, like their Khampa neighbours, have a reputation for brutality in fights. The

Amdowas are often made to feel coarse and crude by the older Lhasa Tibetans especially, being 'countryfolk'. But they are also revered generally for their dominance of Tibetan literature and music, of which Amdo is the heartland.

The average Amdo boy is fiercely loyal and would die for his friend. He conducts himself with something verging on medieval gallantry. He is brutally honest, so candid, in fact, that he does not understand the meaning of tact. If you are fat he will say so. If there is a dispute to be had, there is no subtle sidestepping: the cards are always on the table. The 'civilised' world would describe it as naïveté and it was the source of much miscommunication in the early days of Tsedup's and my relationship. I had not realised the levels of cunning to which we westerners aspire. A complicated combination of emotional bribery and evasive action had always worked for me. Now things were different. The Amdo boy is also proud; he does not display the arrogance of the foolish but has a genuine sense of identity and belief in self that comes from being a member of a tribe. He is often contemplative, and it is, presumably, the vastness of the grasslands that has prepared him for his lateral observation of life. But the Amdo boy is also mad, with a wild sense of humour, and is full of teasing tricks, which prevents him from appearing too dour. When the jokes are over, the Amdo boy is, above all, sincere. I had never heard anything as sincere as my husband's first words of love.

Tsedup and Tsempel stood giggling in the early heat. Tsempel wanted us to come to their friend Rabtan's house, so we thanked Tashintso for her hospitality and watched as she swung her leg over the saddle and cycled off down the alleyway in her uniform and oversized officer's cap. She called after us to stay whenever we liked; we were always welcome. Tsorsungchab was still in bed and the children were at school so we went off down the dusty track of dried mud. Rabtan was another friend from India, one of the seven who had shared the tiny house. Today he lived with his wife and baby in one of the houses close by, in the network of alleyways.

We arrived outside an orange wooden door in a wall and Tsempel pushed the bell. It rang somewhere within and an electronic voice announced our arrival in Chinese. The door opened, and another familiar face presented itself. 'Hello!' Rabtan exclaimed joyously, as he popped his cigarette back between his lips to free his hands and threw his arms around Tsedup.

Rabtan was not your average Amdo boy: with a nose for business and a finger in every pie, he had wised up to the idea that to get on you had to know Chinese, and although he didn't have a job – he had given up his shop which he found unprofitable – he was a seasoned wheeler-dealer. Judging from his house, he was doing all right. He led us into a small concrete courtyard past several outbuildings, sauntering like a hood from the Bronx. He bowled along in his tracksuit bottoms, letting his weight rest on one leg for longer than the other as if he had a limp, but it was done smoothly and consciously. An enormous holstered knife bounced threateningly on his hip; the last vestige of his nomadic costume. He touched it sporadically to remind himself it was there; one never knew when it would be needed. He was always ready either to defend himself or cut up a sausage. A beautiful young woman stood at the entrance to their blue-glass conservatory, smiling shyly. She wore dungarees and a red T-shirt, with long black hair tied in a ponytail at her neck and some gold jewellery. A tiny boy, who was a miniature replica of his father, clutched her leg and looked up at me in astonishment.

They had been expecting us, and the smell of steaming *momos* and tart chilli teased our nostrils. We were seated around a table inside the cool of their lounge on a leather-upholstered sofa. The room was flagged with tiles and had an iron stove against the wall, which sported colourful posters of galloping horses and a pop star. Beneath the pictures was a row of lacquered cupboards and a dresser with a large mirror, on which stood several black and white photographs of Rabtan, in which his moustache was more prominent and his hair was longer and hung loose over his shoulders. There was a TV and a sophisticated stereo system in a black glass cupboard. But the most startling piece of décor was a yak's skull, which hung on the wall like a hunting trophy. It stared down at us with glowing eyes, since Rabtan had placed a lightbulb in each eye socket. Chains hung about its horns. It was macabre, but Rabtan was proud of his artistry and asked me what I thought of it. 'It's nice,' I replied, noncommittally, with typical western deceit. He smiled wryly. He was used to westerners.

Rinchen, his ever-attentive wife, fussed and scurried from parlour to table, bringing dish upon dish of fried, steamed and boiled food. My offer of assistance was firmly refused, and I had to remain seated as she took orders from her husband, who occasionally barked a little too vehemently for this or that. He had tasted the world outside, but here he was a true Amdo husband. I withheld my prejudice: it was not my place to judge the roles that each member of this family played. However, a degree of mutual respect was a prerequisite of marriage, as far as I was concerned, and being barked at was something that had never worked with me. Rinchen was little more than a girl. When Rabtan had returned from India, his mother, who was old and infirm, begged him to stay as she had few children and her husband was dead. She wanted him to marry and stay with her in Machu, and she made him promise he would. Rinchen was selected as a match by their respective families, a schoolgirl at the time. Her older brothers insisted that she complete her education before the marriage so Rabtan had to wait for her. As he carefully poured our tea, his shirtsleeve lifted and a tattoo of her name in English was exposed on his arm. Rabtan showed a trace of honour.

Half-way through the copious meal the doorbell rang and the Chinese voice announced another guest's arrival. It was Nawang, a relative of Tsedup. His brother, Tsering Samdup, was married to Tsedup's sister Dombie. The Tibetan family tree is a vast and convoluted mesh of branches and sub-branches and I became more confused the more relations we met. I could pinpoint Nawang, however: this piece of genealogy was just about comprehensible and I was pleased with myself. Nawang had also been one of the magnificent seven who had shared the cell and baked bread in India. He approached us clumsily in black army boots and a bomber jacket. His long curly hair was tied back and his moustache etched out a permanent grin that sent his small eyes deeper into the crease of his brow until they were little more than two black buttons. If Tsempel was the gentle one and Rabtan was the wheeler-dealer, Nawang was the clown. He stood before us laughing as Tsedup teased him. Another friend was embraced and another round of beers were clinked together and downed. '*Shabda!*' they cried in unison, then began the long recounting of shared memories.

Many hours later I climbed alone into Rabtan and Rinchen's

bed. They wouldn't hear of Tsedup and me sleeping on the sofa and after much protestation I had accepted their generous offer and settled down beneath another pink shiny quilt.

'*Nanka a nyee hdar jig n'jowjer*,' Rinchen said, as she tucked me in. I didn't understand anything but *nanka*, meaning 'tomorrow', so she mimicked the action of riding a horse. As she turned out the light I smiled. Was I going riding with her tomorrow? I had only been on a horse once and had been completely out of control. I prayed that I would be saved from this humiliation as, in the next room, the Amdo boys slapped backs and broke into drunken song.

Thankfully my fears were allayed. As we woke and break-fasted on soft-baked bread and broth, Tsedup told me that we were going to watch the annual horse-racing. Today my equestrian skills were not required. Rinchen was dressed in her *tsarer* and coral necklace especially for the occasion and looked splendid. Tashi Thondup, their diminutive son, was sporting his baseball cap and matching jacket. He sat on his own tiny chair by the stove in his knitted split-crotch trousers, chewing a piece of bread and staring at me. He still hadn't worked out what I was.

Tsedup's younger brother Gondo arrived, in full nomad attire, on his motorbike. He gave it one last rev as he pulled up in the yard in his sheepskin *tsarer* and sunglasses, a cigarette dangling from his lips and his hair dishevelled. He had heard we were here and offered to ferry us to the grassland nearby for the races. Nawang also had a bike, so between them our lifts were secured. Bikes were the new thing and the young nomad men had converted from four legs to two wheels for getting around. I was amazed that biker chic was cross-cultural. With no access to the film *Easy Rider*, the boys had emulated the certain something that had given Dennis Hopper his ticket to Coolville. For they were cool, of that there was no doubt.

But despite the gradual 'civilisation' of the nomads, in terms of transport at least, horses were still their passion. As we rode out across the flat grassland from the town, I could see a large crowd assembling along the bank at the side of the track. Tsedup and I sat among them and waited for the others to arrive. Around us, men, women and children had settled in groups and were picnicking together. Old men cradled babies and young men huddled in their gangs smoking silver pipes. Among the mingling crowd were about fifty horses, each with a boy in the saddle, some no older than twelve. Their steeds whinnied and chewed clover, their silver-studded bridles clinking like bunches of keys. The manes of some had been clipped and stood stiff and straight, like a monk's hat. The people chatted and the air of expectancy was broken only by the occasional bout of laughter or excited cry. A flock of sheep dallying on the track were dispersed by the sharp beep of a motorbike horn, as Gondo and Nawang arrived with Rabtan, Rinchen and Tashi Thondup.

On the other side of the track, the racecourse stretched out in a flat sprint from the town boundary, and the first group of jockeys were walking their horses down to the starting point. Among them I was delighted to see Tsedup's youngest brother, Gorbo, on his father's white stallion. Apparently the rest of the family had teased him for choosing that horse to race: it was too slow, they had said. Behind the jockeys, someone in a white Tilley hat was shouting orders. It was Amnye, and he appeared to be the master of ceremonies. I felt a curious mixture of pride, affection and amusement as

I watched him officiating, pointing his wooden truncheon and yelling at any errant boys. His was a responsible role for today the boys were racing in the presence of a visiting lama, who would present the winner with a prize. The holy man and his entourage of monks had made an encampment on the hill adjacent to the racetrack and were watching the proceedings from a white tent.

Suddenly there was a commotion. The sky was filled with what sounded like an Apache war-cry as all the young men flicked their tongues and cried out in a primitive chorus. People moved closer to get a glimpse of the race, and we joined them on the lip of the bank. Tsedup stood beside me hollering at the top of his voice and I laughed. Women didn't do the war-cry thing, so I restrained myself. The horses that had assembled in the distance were now moving abreast in steady formation. Behind them, the backdrop of Machu town lay flat on the massive green plain, and the azure river meandered into the horizon. The horses were so far away that the thud of their hoofs was mute in the haze of blue, white and yellow flowers. A motorbike buzzed alongside them on the mud track, and the shouting increased as they got closer to the finishing line. I could see the small boys swinging their lassoes above their heads in great arcs and flicking the horses' hindquarters. Some were bareback. But Gorbo was in front. My heart thumped in my chest. Come on, Gorbo. You can do it! 'Yahoo!' I cried, like the embarrassing sister-in-law I so obviously was. But I didn't care. Gorbo was going to win and as he crossed the line he looked magnificent. Everyone cheered as the horses slowed, and the barefoot older boys ran to catch them in the sweat and nerves of the post-race wind-down. '*Che, che, che, che, che . . .*' they shushed, as someone threw coloured ribbons around Amnye's slow horse. Gorbo had been right.

But this was only the first heat and there would be no lama's prize for him that day. Race followed race and the white horse got tired. Gorbo had had his one taste of glory. A small boy riding bareback won the final and, to the applause of the onlookers, Amnye escorted him to the lama's tent for the prize-giving. It was amazing to have seen the young boys handling horses with ease, and as I looked at Gorbo, I found myself imagining how Tsedup would have been when he was a young nomad child. Each one of his brothers and sisters had had a horse and could ride before they could walk; it was second nature to them. He had once been wild and free, laughing and galloping in the grassland. How could my childhood compare with that? And how much of that wildness and freedom of spirit would return to him on this trip I had no idea. He was a man now, and so much had changed in his life, but I couldn't help feeling, and hoping, that there would be an awakening in him.

We said goodbye to Rabtan and his family and went with Gondo up to the lama's encampment. Several white tents were arranged in a circle on the hill and Tsedup's tribe had their own. The yaks and horses grazed lazily beneath the rocky peaks of the mountains and the clouds made shadow patterns on the golden-tipped grass. A nomad woman played with her children in the afternoon heat, and the young men and monks had set up a volleyball net and were involved in a tournament. Tsedup's father joined us at the tent, where piles of meat and offal were laid out on a plastic sheet inside, ready for feasting, should anyone fancy it. Tsedup's brothers, Tsedo and Gondo, sat in their *tsarers*, smoking an enormous pipe made from antelope horn, decorated with patterned silver from ten melted coins and encrusted with coral and turquoise. They puffed expertly and spat the last chip of hot tobacco into the fire. They had bought the pipe for Tsedup to take home to England and it was a most beautiful object. I imagined Tsedup lounging around in his slippers watching TV and puffing on it. That was an incongruous image.

It was hot in the tent so I decided to go and watch the volleyball. No sooner had I sat down among the scattering of onlookers than the young nomad children who had previously been engaged with the match found something better to stare at. I was suddenly surrounded by urchins whose eyes were glued to my every move. If I spoke to them they hid behind each other, especially the older ones, who lost the power of speech when addressed. I really was an extra-terrestrial: I was not of their earth. Then one of Tsedup's friends joined me and I recognised him as one of the boys who had collected us from the airport. He had been the one with exquisitely polished shoes. It was peculiar how that detail had remained in my mind from the chaos and emotion of that day. I welcomed the company, especially the cold beer he proffered; but should I drink it and risk appearing more bizarre than before to these kids? I decided I was trying too hard to please – they were only children after all. I sipped from the icy bottle as they giggled uncontrollably. Suddenly I was tired of being a spectacle and I felt a new sympathy for hounded Hollywood stars. In Labrang it had been different, with so many tourists around. Back in Machu, where I was the only white person, I was conspicuous. It would take a lot of getting used to. But I comforted myself with the thought that this was a small place. Soon everyone would know me and I wouldn't be such an oddity. I just had to give it time. I really did think that would be the case. I had no idea.

As the evening sun stretched our shadows over the grass-stalks, we left the lama's encampment for the tribe. After the confines of the town I was thrilled at the prospect of living in the grassland again. There, I could just be Namma and would have a home. Speeding through the undulating grassland on the back of the bike under the infinite dome of the blue sky, I felt the wind in my hair and the falling sun on my face, and the sense of space that filled me was overwhelming. I might not have had the wildness of a young nomad jockey, but right then, inspired only by the vast emptiness of this grand spectacle of nature, I felt a freedom of spirit unequalled in my life.

# FIVE

# *Earth Taming*

That week I saw my first kill. I had woken early and, after struggling to dress in my *tsarer*, which required inordinate patience for one so inexperienced, emerged from our tent into the morning mist. The scene outside was new. While we were in Labrang the tribe had moved to their summer location and I was sorry to have missed that most nomadic experience: the dismantling of the tent; the slow procession of yak and sheep herds down the valley to fresh grass. But there would be another move with the onset of winter and I would not miss that.

The tents were now spread out in a circle in the vast Yellow river valley on the flat grassland. They were bordered by the rocky mountains of their spring and winter site to the north and the green-blue mountains of Ngoo Ra, the Silver Horn range, to the south. Eastwards and westwards the valley extended to the horizon and on for ever into a horizon that was blank apart from one other encampment, visible a few miles to the west. Our new home was more exposed than it had been at the former site. Fresh winds swept the corridor from west to east on good days, and from the east, bringing chilled air and rain, on bad.

Beyond the main tent two horsemen were skulking through a sheep herd. Tsedo and Gorbo were barefoot and wrapped in *tsarers*, their breath clouding upward with the warm air from the horses' snorting nostrils. They carried lassoes casually at their sides and ambled with deceptive nonchalance among the ignorant sheep. At a glance, I knew their intent. The animals shifted lazily in a dumb crowd from left to right, then scuffled, bleating, and parted ranks as a rope arced overhead and swung wasted between them. One stood stunned for a moment, unsure which way to turn, then the two horses closed in and it bolted, isolated, as they cantered after it past our tent and towards the stream. Deranged with fear it crashed down the bank into the water, pursued by Gorbo, who lassoed it around one horn, dismounted his horse and wrestled it out of the water to open ground. I felt an overwhelming sadness as I watched the animal struggling and whispered, '*Om mani padme hum.*' They hadn't noticed me – killing was a man's domain and it was forbidden for Tibetan women to slaughter livestock. Although they helped in the preparation of the meat, they were not permitted even to watch the death. Still, I felt a morbid curiosity and wanted to witness it. I had never seen an animal killed before and somehow felt that I should. I took advantage of my sheltered position next to the white tent and spied. Tsedo was shouting at his younger brother, and it seemed as if things hadn't gone to plan. From what I could gather this was Gorbo's first catch and Tsedo was chiding him for leading the sheep to the water, causing it undue stress. He dismounted, straddled the animal's neck and dragged it nearer the family tent. There, he bound the sheep's muzzle with the rope, smothered its nostrils with his hands and held on tight as the animal bucked and writhed, gagging and retching, for what seemed an eternity, until at last it resigned itself and, with one final shiver, relaxed in his grip and fell limp. Gorbo stood over them spinning the *korlo*, and praying as Tsedo began skinning.

I slipped back inside the tent, feeling like a voyeur, but there was so much to learn and I was tired of being a hypocrite. I had only ever known pretty packaged food that bore no resemblance to the animal it had come from. Choice cuts, Cellophane wrapping, best-before dates in a clinical setting. When Tsedup first went into a supermarket in England he remarked that, once you had bypassed the fresh-bread odour pumping from the entrance vents, the food did not smell. He preferred to seek out markets, where buying food was a sensory experience. He could imagine eating it. Here, however devastating the experience, I could understand where my food had come from. I could take responsibility for eating it and give thanks for the animal's spirit, for killing is a necessity of life in Tibet. Meat forms the main component of the nomads' diet, but their Buddhist faith means that they hold a deep respect for all living things and regret their brutal task.

As I hid, Amnye appeared from the family tent and came

to a small mound on the grass not five yards from me. He knelt over it and poured on to it smouldering ashes he had collected from the hearth in the tent. He held a cloth sack containing *tsampa* and a gold cup. I watched as he simultaneously sprinkled the *tsampa* and water from the cup on to the mound, which smoked in soft grey clouds, while chanting in a rhythmic murmur. He didn't look up and I stood peering patiently through the crack in the tent until he had finished. It was his daily practice to make offerings to the deities, as did the head of each family in the tribe. They were not prayers he uttered but a constant stream of mesmeric monologue: he was addressing the family deities, asking for protection for his family, the land, his animals. I waited quietly as the smoke merged with the mist, watching Shermo Donker and Sirmo finishing milking the last row of yaks and the children scurrying back and forth from the tent with wooden pails of milk.

I was soon to discover the true value of the nomads' ancient rituals, for it was the fifteenth day of the sixth month in the lunar calendar and an auspicious day. Today the men would abandon the grassland to make their annual offering to the holy mountain, Amnye Kula. They would join the rest of the tribes in the Lhardey Nyima, Sun Valley, area of Machu, on the north side of the Yellow river. I was to stay behind with the other women.

I woke Tsedup and told him about the kill I had just witnessed and he repeated the prayer '*Om mani padme hum.*' I asked him if he had ever killed a sheep and he said no, but as a child he had helped his father skin three hundred after an epidemic that destroyed their herd. The shock of my experience waned as the realisation of the true hardships of life here reached a new clarity. Suddenly there was so much

I didn't know about the closest person to me in my life. More and more I was to realise that he had seen suffering in a way I could never before have understood. I kissed him, then went to wash in the stream.

Inside, the main tent was a bloody commotion of slicing and mashing. Tsedo and several other men from the tribe were busy butchering the freshly killed sheep for the trip. I was ushered to my usual honorary position close to the fire and picked my way carefully past the splayed carcass on the floor, taking care not to step over anyone. To do so is considered bad manners in nomad society and would be to show disrespect for the person, animal, food or book that had been straddled. I had made that mistake many years ago in India when I had been playing with Tsedup's friend's baby and had jumped over her. Tsedup had been quick to berate me and I had been hurt by his vehemence. I had not intended to offend but had been ignorant of the social code. I never did it again. It is also polite to pass behind someone, not in front, but this morning, with such limited space, that rule was waived and I sidled through the mass of bodies.

Annay prepared tea and bread for me, while Shermo Donker stirred the boiling pot of meat, bone and the head of the poor sheep, as it bobbed, black-eyed, to the surface. The men were all sitting cross-legged on the ground, their arms stained red, chopping the meat and offal into mince and stuffing the intestines to make long sausages. They muttered prayers for the spirit of the dead animal as they worked and Annay spun the prayer wheel, chanting, '*Om mani padme hum,*' over and over, as the steam from the pot coiled up through the shaft in the tent roof. It is forbidden to fry meat as the smoke generated would pass into the sky and offend the mountain spirits so all meat is boiled.

I watched as the fat and blood were mixed with *tsampa* and a little meat in a huge cauldron. They cut the stomach lining into wide strips then proceeded to make a rich black pudding, spooning the mix on to the textured lining, rolling it up and sewing it together down its length with thick thread. These were then boiled too. The smell of the meat and blood and the thick odour from the floating tallow on the bubbling water filled my nostrils.

When the animal had been cooked, they hung the skin outside on the tent lines to dry and some strips of meat from the roof of the tent to smoke, a nomad delicacy. Then they ate a little while Shermo Donker prepared a saddle-bag full of *tsampa*, butter, fried barley, rice, *jo* – wheat husks – tea, milk and different pieces of fabric. These would be the offerings, gifts from the family to the holy mountain, representing their livelihood.

The rest of the male contingent from the tribe then arrived at our tent on horseback. Gurdo carried a *ndashung*, a wooden spear about six metres high, with a brightly painted flight. He looked like a medieval knight with his lance. The small boys chattered excitedly in the saddle, thrilled to be accompanying their fathers and grandfathers. Tsedup, Amnye, Tsedo, Gorbo and the rest of the men who had been helping with the sheep mounted their horses, and Annay, Shermo Donker, Sirmo and I watched with the children as they made off across the grassland in a procession. The spear protruded from the throng as they disappeared over the brow of the hill into the low cloud.

There had been no room for an embrace, not here. From what I had seen, men and women didn't display affection publicly. I made do with a lingering glance from Tsedup as he pulled his *tsarer* across his face and turned in the saddle.

Without a doubt he fitted in. Despite his years away his face that morning was the face of a nomad, like his brothers': wind-whipped and wild-eyed.

This was to be my first time alone in the family. Annay took my hand and led me back into the tent, chattering soothingly, using phrases she knew I would understand. I had not learnt much Amdo from Tsedup in our time together. Since his English was fluent, there had been little occasion to enter into extensive dialogue with him and he was a reluctant teacher. I knew a few basic words and these would have to do until I mastered the language. So far in Amdo, I had relied on Tsedup to translate for me. Now I was on my own. Annay sensed my discomfort at my inability to communicate effectively and did everything in her power to bridge the language divide. When she offered me tea she took an imaginary bowl in her hand and slurped enthusiastically from it. 'Namma, *ja'n tong*!' she implored with wide eyes, then laughed like a girl when I understood. She urged me to eat, made sure I was comfortable and pampered me. It would be easier than I thought to let Tsedup go and simply enjoy the women's company. To my surprise, once away from their menfolk they were chatty and bawdy. Where before they had remained demure and restrained, they now cackled like banshees and slapped their thighs as they went about their tasks in a more leisurely manner. Shermo Donker and Sirmo drew me into their confidence and teased me. 'Shermo, do you miss your husband?' they giggled.

'No, I don't!' I exclaimed, and we all fell about laughing.

On the second day I was feeling more independent. I had spent the night in our white tent with Dickir Che, the oldest of Shermo Donker and Tsedo's girls. She had chattered animatedly to me as we lay drowsily in the dark and sang at the top of her voice when she woke. Unlike some of the young girls, whose voices rang out in a resounding tremolo, Dickir Che shouted her Amdo song like a military drill. It was a rude awakening, but she was happy and I was loath to silence her. She began the day by examining every item in my wash-bag, including a tampon, which I told her was for putting in your ears if they hurt. I immediately regretted telling her this. It would be just like her to catch an ear infection. Worse, she might recommend them to my father-in-law. Visions of Amnye walking round with strings dangling from his ears entertained me for a while.

It was becoming clear to me that privacy was a scarce commodity in the grassland. Usually my first lavatorial exercise of the day was most prized, since it was the only time when I could be alone in the riverbed. At all other times in the day I was accompanied by at least three other children, who had been instructed to follow me in case I got eaten by the dogs. But I was becoming more confident and was not afraid of them. Actually the children only wanted to get a glimpse of my white behind, but I knew their game and used my *tsarer* cleverly as a mini-tent, hoisted round my hips to avoid their eyes. The family were fascinated by my white skin and found it inconceivable that their own brown-nut colour was attractive. They laughed incredulously when I told them that people back home covered themselves in oil and lay virtually naked under the sun in order to look like them.

There was certainly no escaping Dickir Che that morning. She thoroughly inspected the contents of my rucksack and told me my clothes were too dull. 'You should wear pink, like Mother,' she instructed. Then she followed me to the riverbed, carrying my soap and towel like a diligent maidservant and watched me studiously as I washed, copying every action and laughing at me. The nomads thought my method of splashing water on my face strange – they scrubbed theirs with a soapy towel, a Chinese habit. But when Dickir Ziggy, Dickir Che's younger sister, and Sanjay, her tiny brother, came running from the black tent to join us she narrowed her eyes to angry slits and scolded with such ferocity that I was taken aback. When they tried to join in she shouted at them to leave us alone. She seemed to have adopted me and was not going to share me easily. I urged them all to cease their argument and we all made our way to the tent, in a babble of competitive chatter, 'Ajay Shermo, Ajay Shermo . . . Aunty, Aunty . . .', a girl clinging to each of my hands and Sanjay clutching my skirt.

That day I lay in the sun with Annay under the raised edge of the tent flap and spoke to her, as best I could, about what it had been like for Tsedup in England without his family. There was a lot of elaborate gesticulation but we managed. She told me that she had been very ill while he was away and that she had cried on most days for her son, not knowing what had happened to him. The worry had affected her health: her eyesight had deteriorated and she frequently complained of aches and pains. As I looked at her wizened face, watery green eyes tugged down at the corners and her wiry grey hair, I knew that his absence had aged her. I told her that Tsedup had always talked of them all, so much so that I felt as if I knew them without having met them. I had witnessed his suffering for years and now I was hearing what before I could only imagine she had felt.

Annay told me that now that she had met me and my parents she was happy for her son to return to his life in

England, when it was time to go. I was touched by her ability to confide in me, immediately struck by the knowledge that, despite our cultural differences and my pathetic language skills, we had developed a bond. I was family. I was her *namma*.

On the third day the men returned from the holy mountain. At the sound of approaching horse hoofs we ran out of the tent to greet them, and Tsedup, his father and two brothers dismounted outside. The rest of the men in the tribe dispersed to their own family tents where the hues of their wives' bright shirts signalled each welcoming party. It was good to see Tsedup again. He had lost the slate shade that the English climate had given his skin and it shone like mahogany. His hair hung blue-black and tousled around his shoulders as he stood before me in his *tsarer*, grinning broadly at me. 'I missed you,' he said. It was the only indication that he was not entirely the nomad he resembled. I was glad that our intimacy had not suffered in the face of normal macho behaviour – his brother, Tsedo, walked past Shermo Donker without so much as looking at her. In fact, our words were now like a special secret since no one could understand what we said.

When we were all settled inside, Tsedup produced the video camera he had taken with him and we all settled around its tiny screen to watch the film of their trip. Everyone was fascinated by the camera, but the women were particularly keen to watch; they had never been present at the ceremony that had taken place and clustered around the machine excitedly, awaiting their turn. The men, of course, saw it first.

The screen revealed their journey in miniature. First came the procession of hundreds of men on horseback to the offering site from their base-camp of white tents. They moved silently and ceremoniously through the summer flowers of the valley and alongside a rushing stream, the horses snorting, their bridles clinking in the sunshine. There were small boys, old men and young, some with hats on to protect them from the glare, some with rifles strapped to their backs. Many carried the *ndashung* with *darchok*, prayer flags, tied to the end, balancing the enormous lance across their laps or standing it upright in the saddle so that it pointed skyward. They formed an orderly line that snaked up the side of the mountain to the ridge of the offering site where the *shogshung* stood. The *shogshung*, or staff of life, marked the site of the mountain worship. It was the most important symbol of the mountain deities and its base had been buried in the ground along with *hdir*, treasure, sacred offerings to the earth contained in colourful cloth bags, which, at the time of their burial, were placed with extreme care in exactly the right position so as not to offend the gods. Against the main staff leant many *ndashung*, forming a tepee-like shape of spears, festooned with hundreds of prayer flags from years of offerings, tired and grey with exposure to the elements, flapping in the wind. Along the ridge stood another ten spears placed at intervals of about five paces, again covered in prayer flags. The men assembled beneath the *shogshung* and placed their own offerings of prayer flags in a pile on the ground before three monks. They sat quietly as the monks consecrated the offerings, purifying them before they could be displayed before the gods. The tip of the *shogshung* glinted in the sunlight and nothing but their rhythmic chanting and the wind could be heard. It was the calm before the storm.

Suddenly, the crowd erupted into a riot of whooping and shrieking. Gunshots split the air and a blizzard of white snow clouded the blue sky as they tossed thousands of wind horses into the valley in fistfuls. They called the mountain's name, 'Amnye Kula! Amnye Kula!' over and over, and shouted their own messages to the gods, personal appeals for protection from the mountain spirits against their enemies. Gondo cried, '*Har jalo! Har jalo! Har jalo!* May the spirit win!' as he cast his own paper to the wind. The chief, Tsenach, bellowed his own guttural eulogy, an enormous silver hoop swinging from his ear. Above the cacophony the deep resonance of the conch boomed out, as a monk blew into the shell and brass bells tinkled. They heaped the offerings of *tsampa*, rice, cloth, butter and milk that they had brought on to a huge bonfire beneath the *shogshung* and erected the new *ndashung*, stringing the prayer flags from spear to spear along the ridge and ropes tufted with *merdach*, spun sheep's wool, and *kacher*, long sheep's hair. Each man circumambulated the ridge three times on his horse and the ritual was complete. The ground was littered with thousands of wind horses and still they spiralled densely in the smoke from the fire. It was like a war.

As I watched, I could imagine it happening hundreds of years ago. The timelessness of the scene was disturbed only by a T-shirt or the flash of sunglasses here and there. Apart from the lull of the monks' earlier intervention it had been so wild, as if the men were fearlessly exposing their souls to the mountain. I had never seen such an uninhibited display of worship and was astonished to have witnessed such primitive, raw energy in the men that now sat passively around me, sipping tea.

And, of course, it had been their practice for hundreds of years – thousands, some locals said. For the Amdo nomads still embrace many of the original shamanistic and Bon disciplines of Tibet, despite their acceptance of Buddhism. In fact, Tibet was one of the last Asian countries to turn to Buddhism and the distinctive characteristics of the Tibetan variety developed in response to the strength of shamanic influence. Tsedup's father explained that their gods are divided into the protectors of nature and the protectors of religion. What I had just witnessed was a ceremony to propitiate the gods of nature.

Because of the hostility of their natural environment, it has always been the nomads' religious preoccupation to tame the land. They place great importance on optimising good luck and minimising bad luck by propitiating the gods that determine their fate. I knew that, in shamanic terms, there are three realms of existence: the sky, the earth and the subterranean. The gods live in the sky, serpent spirits live in the earth and humans live on the earth in between. The elemental nature of each domain is also important: the sky representing space, air and fire; the subterranean realm, earth and water, and all the elements being present in the middle realm.

The most powerful sky gods are those who live on the mountain peaks. These warrior-like gods, called *nyen*, are violent, territorial lords, who require propitiation with complex ritual and offering such as I had just witnessed. Amnye Kula takes the form of a man carrying a spear and riding a white horse, but others take different forms: for example, the mountain god, Archa, close to Tsedup's brother Gondo's tribe, takes the form of a snake.

The most sacred mountain for all the people of Amdo is Amnye Machen. It is considered the Mount Kailash, Kang Rimpoche, of eastern Tibet and its range rises out of the Amdo plains for 125 miles on an east–west axis. Amnye

Machen, the mountain god, is lord above all lords of the earth of Amdo. His name means. 'Ancestor of the Amdo People', and he is the greatest and wildest of the mountain gods. But as well as these masculine, warrior gods, there are also female sky goddesses, *dakinis* or *khandromas*, who have an elementally malign nature and are said to eat man's flesh and afflict him in his sexual relationships.

The demi-gods of the subterranean realm are serpent spirits, both male and female, called *lu* and *luma*, the spirits of earth and water. In contrast to the mountain gods, who rule with patriarchal authority, the serpent spirits have a sensitive, female nature. They live in the earth, in the rocks, in the lakes and streams. They are black, white or red guardians of ecological balance, preventing human interference with the earth. Precious stones belong to them, and the power of a coral or turquoise stone, so important to the nomads in their traditional dress, is deemed auspicious or inauspicious, depending on its guardian serpent spirit's satisfaction with how it was mined and how it has been looked after. According to shamanistic belief, the mining of gold or iron is offensive to the serpent spirits, like stealing from them. Even digging a hole in the ground could risk offending them, and Tsedup told me once that his mother would not leave one tent peg in the ground when they moved to new pasture, for fear of wounding the earth. With all this in mind, it was hard to imagine a more devastating proposition than that which was presented to them when the Chinese began gold-mining recently on a holy mountain in Machu.

The middle domain is inhabited by minor gods, more intimately related to humans and their daily domestic life than the mountain gods and the serpent spirits. They have specific functions and include home gods, who provide protection for the family, a god of horses and of cattle. All of these gods need to be appeased to ensure the success and well-being of a nomad family and its herds in this hostile environment. The rituals are said once to have included animal sacrifice or *marcho,* blood offering, but when the influence of Buddhism prohibited this, ritual fire-offering or *garchot,* non-blood offering, became the favoured method of propitiation.

The shamans also believed in 'pegging' the earth. This ritual, which was adopted by Buddhist yogis, was employed to control the earth and render it submissive. The *ndashung* that marked the tops of holy mountains were to bind the earth and spirit powers, taming them through penetration. The mountains themselves are said to peg the earth like nails or *phurbas,* ritual daggers, piercing and securing it. On a human level, the *chortens,* stone monuments, I had seen upon entering Amdo were like symbolic mountains suppressing the demonic forces beneath them.

The other major pre-Buddhist religious influence on the Amdo nomads was the Bon religion. Even after Buddhism had replaced it, it still maintained a hold on people in areas as far away as Amdo, which had always enjoyed strong separatist tendencies, especially among the nomads.

The Bonpos also believed in taming and placating the spiritual powers of the environment, gods, demons and spirits. They were devout ritualists who, like the shamanists, sought to keep the old Tibetan gods favourably inclined to human activity. Before the Buddhists transformed the gods into part of the Buddha-dharma, the Bonpos were propitiating them and using their power to maximise human luck. As with the shamans, they focused on the earth-lords and serpent spirits, who controlled the fertility of the land, animals and their own human power, which is why it was so important to placate them.

Another Bon ritual still practised by the nomads included divination, which took many forms. Tsedup had told me that his father would sometimes burn a *sockwa*, the shoulder blade of a sheep, and foretell future events in the cracks left on its scorched surface.

I had learnt all of these things from Tsedup. I remember him telling me that he had never understood the need for western mountaineers to 'conquer' mountains. For him it was tantamount to hubris. He once saw a documentary about Hillary and Tenzing's ascent of Cho Mo Langma or Mount Everest, as it is called in the West. As they reached the peak, Hillary laid claim to his defeated giant with the arrogance of a big-game hunter, while Tenzing humbly gave thanks to the mountain spirit. A mountain may be tamed and worshipped, but never conquered. Even then, Tsedup's reaction to that TV documentary had seemed to me like a lesson in ecology.

Now, it was fascinating to be witnessing the propagation of these ancient rites. But as I pondered what I had seen, it struck me that I had had no relationship with the land. I'm sure that if I had grown up in the Scottish Highlands or on a ranch in Wyoming I would at least have felt a oneness with the environment, but perhaps, even then, not in the same way. I was a suburban girl. The land, the subtle transition of the seasons, the smell of the earth and real dirt right down in the skin were strange to me. Apart from the joy of a country walk, I had had no previous experience of *belonging* to nature. These people belonged to the land and respected it with astounding, to me, reverence. Their understanding of the transient nature of life was intrinsic, acknowledged, respected, digested. It was at the heart of nomadic life, along with the acceptance of the swift and unpredictable passage of life and death.

I learnt not just to look, but to *see*. As I walked in the grassland the next day, I beheld the indefinable strength and solidity of the omnipresent mountains, which seemed like benevolent ancestors contemplating with amusement the scurrying descendants beneath them. Their sunny slopes betrayed a more sinister aspect and their shadows seemed darker. They held curious forms. To the north, they resembled slumbering figures with hulking shoulders slunk into the pit of the land; their valleys and ridges, flesh folds and backbones rolling over and into each other, settled and still. To the south, they receded in waves, peak after trough, until the last visible tips faded into a dusky blue, leaving us behind in their wake. I had never had a true sense of scale until I came here. How frail the tent appeared against this background. Nothing more than a wind-teased flap of black fabric supported by spidery legs that could scuttle away in an instant.

This was my home.

# SIX

## *Visit to the Sky Man*

We had been in Machu for almost a month when we were summoned to the police station. It was the moment we had both been dreading. Leaving the country surreptitiously, as Tsedup had, could incur a serious penalty or worse. We had heard of others who had returned and been temporarily imprisoned. We had no idea what to expect. I said a silent prayer the night before that no harm would come to him.

The next morning we pulled into the forecourt of the police station, which was the first building on the tarmac road into town. It was of the usual concrete variety, three storeys high, glass-fronted, with the scarlet and gold emblem of the police force hung above its pillared entrance. The third floor was shielded by a large net curtain and was reserved for karaoke parties. The place breathed boredom. Apart from a builder toiling leisurely in the corner of the yard, there was no one in sight. We got off the bike and I followed Tsedup up the steps into the cool of the entrance. It smelt of dust, and I was surprised and momentarily delighted to see Tashintso. She sat in the dark reception room behind a sheet of glass on which were written various scarlet characters in Chinese and Tibetan. She wore her conscientiously pressed dull green police uniform, and a coquettish smile. '*Cho demo*,' she giggled in greeting, as we took seats in the black plastic armchairs opposite her kiosk. Beside her sat another young woman, identically dressed, who smiled shyly at me from beneath her permed fringe. A pile of paperwork sat neatly at the side of their desks, which were otherwise bare. Tashintso came round from behind the glass partition and said something to Tsedup, then she disappeared out of the door and I could hear the clump of her heavy high-heels down the corridor.

'Will they want to see me?' I asked Tsedup, taking advantage of the last few moments alone. 'I have no idea what to say.'

'Just leave the talking to me,' he said.

But I wasn't reassured. What if they wanted to see us separately? It was like our interrogation at the High Commission in Delhi all over again, but this time more serious. However, I hadn't realised that I would be excluded from the grilling, simply because no one spoke English. A few minutes later Tashintso returned and signalled for Tsedup to follow her. He left, and I sat chewing my lip and studying a calendar with a picture of a tree in blossom beside a lake. The scene did little to pacify me and I imagined that the young policewoman sitting across from me would confuse the thudding of my heart with the thumping of her rubber stamp on the crisp white sheets before her. The main responsibility of the office appeared to be the endorsing and renewing of identity cards for the local population. She stamped face after face. The blood pulsed in my eardrums. My palms stuck to the chair.

Soon Tashintso returned and put on the kettle to make me a cup of tea. It seemed a ludicrously civil thing to do at the time and I felt slightly more at ease. She beckoned to me to come round the back of the screen into their small section where she drew up a chair for me and then pulled out her knitting from the drawer under her desk. As if this were a signal, the other policewoman stopped her stamping and took up her needles from a stool by her knee. Then Tashintso struck up a conversation with me as the pair of them clicked away. She was fashioning a brown tank top with a rather intricate pattern for her husband, and her partner was putting the finishing touches to a fluffy blue jumper for her baby son. The corridors were silent and Tashintso's sporadic giggling and the relentless tick-tick of the needles echoed down the halls. I wondered in what deep recess Tsedup was cornered and strained my ears for a voice. But I heard nothing, except the twang of a plucked guitar string in the karaoke room upstairs and a gurgle as the kettle began to boil.

Tashintso poured us tea and distracted me effectively with idle chatter for some time, until I became increasingly aware of the surreal quality of our situation. There was I, a western girl in full nomad attire, sitting opposite two Tibetan women knitting in police uniform. Whenever their superior passed the office they deftly concealed their handiwork and stopped giggling. Upstairs a policeman was practising the guitar for the evening's party, while I imagined my husband in a cell suffering interrogation under a stark lightbulb. I began to laugh, only gently, of course, but it helped to relieve the exhaustion my anxiety had inflicted and I was grateful for the moment of irony.

After two hours and several cups of tea, Tsedup emerged. He looked fine. He asked me for our passports, which he gave to Tashintso, and spoke a few words to her. Then they laughed and I realised that everything must be all right. 'Come on,' he said. 'Let's go and get some food.'

In the Formica back room of a restaurant we slurped our noodles and he told me what had happened. The sergeant was Tibetan and very amenable, although curious. Once he had established that Tsedup had no political motivation, they had shared tea and enjoyed a long, convoluted discussion about life in the West. Tsedup had paid a small fine and his file had been closed, the 'black mark' removed. The sergeant had even been generous enough to offer to assist us with extending our visas, which we had feared would be impossible here. I was speechless and euphoric all at once and, since we were in a private room with only the buzz of the strip-light for company, I jumped up and hugged him.

We had been spared the third degree and I felt lucky that day. Police dominance of the local community was widely known. But I discovered that later, although policing the population was the responsibility of the local force, there were other important figures in the nomadic community who played a part in maintaining social order.

Tsedup's step-grandfather, Azjung, 'uncle', was something

of an *éminence grise*. For the nomads of Machu, his role was greater and his title more hallowed than any state authority could bestow upon him. For Azjung was a Sky Man.

Nam Nyeur, Sky Man, or ancient man, is the name given to an old person by their people. The title is not appointed, but means that that particular person has come to represent the last of a generation. They bring the past into the present with their story-telling and have remarkable powers of recollection. Since the nomads have no written history, it is the responsibility of the Sky Man to continue the oral history of a people. He *is* the text. The tradition carries with it enormous responsibility in terms of morality, for it is the Sky Man's duty to resolve domestic disputes among tribes by his wisdom. Most tribespeople carry the stories of their forefathers with them and retell them throughout their lifetime to the next generation, yet Azjung carried between five hundred and six hundred years of stories passed on orally from generation to generation. He was considered particularly sharp and could mediate to solve problems with a superior knowledge of historical precedents, selecting and recounting exact times in history and relating the stories of past events to clarify and resolve a present situation, so that the grieving or avenging parties may know how to follow the right path. He also had the power to set new precedents for future reference, providing the disputing parties both agreed to his proposal. This was nomad law.

Of course, if a story was very old, it might take on mythical proportions, accruing layer upon layer of embellishment from circling around the people of this land. The exact words of a particular figure in a tribe's history could be invented and reinvented, along with their emotions and thoughts, for that is the nature of story-telling. A story-teller must have an audience and the audience must be amused.

Nam Nyeur may also be female and the nature of a woman's wisdom and story-telling may be of a different nature altogether. Whereas a Sky Man tells of conflicts in battle, disputes over territory or livestock, a Sky Woman usually has a female audience and her stories provide more of an insight into intimate relationships. Thus she may tell of marriages, love or family concerns and disasters, and just as the old stories of the Sky Men assume mythical proportions, so the tales of the Sky Women are, in their turn sometimes romanticised. For that is often the nature of women.

On the afternoon of the interrogation we visited the Sky Man. He and Tsedup's grandmother, Ama-lo-lun, lived at the monastery with Tsedup's brother, Cumchok, and his nephew, Tinlee, who were both monks. The monastery stood at the top of a hill above the town at the end of a winding track; it was small in comparison with the palace of Labrang, yet still elaborate enough to suggest its spiritual significance in the community. It sat among a jumble of small dwellings ramshackle and tumbledown, inhabited by the monks, the whitewashed walls propped up by tree-trunks stripped of bark, each with a wooden door, leading to quiet courtyards, books and rooms of contemplation.

We stopped outside one such door in the labyrinth, and as we pushed it open a small brass bell tinkled above our heads. The sound was not enough to alert the tiny aged figure who knelt on the veranda opposite, bent over like a dried piece of leather. Ama-lo-lun continued sorting through a pile of dried flowers, oblivious of our presence, her careful handling of the blue and yellow blooms interspersed with prayer. But as we crossed the bare courtyard and came up the dirt path towards the wooden house we called out to her and she lifted her head, not knowing us for a moment, her pebble eyes squinting. '*Sou ray*? Who is it?' she exclaimed, and then as we came closer she remembered: the One Who Is My Heart.

She cried out Tsedup's name and we helped her to her feet as she clucked in appreciation and led us back down the steps of the beautifully made house. It had been built for Cumchok at Amnye's instruction, but Azjung and Ama-lo-lun had their own small hut to the side of the courtyard. It was meagre by comparison: small, with a turf roof and a dirt floor, a sleeping platform, a stove and one window, glassless but covered in dusty plastic, which had weathered and torn at the corner. Dust had settled deep into the skins on the bed and the pots hanging from the wall were soot-stung and blackened. I smelt dried meat, earth and strong tea, as the dented kettle steamed and the fire crackled and spat out the husks of dried grass from the dung. They seemed to have only the barest necessities, a habit that had lingered, no doubt, from two nomadic lives. It is customary now for elderly nomads to settle in a house when their bodies can no longer endure the hardships of weather-beating and work, but a roof over the head does not quell the nomad spirit. Azjung and Ama-lo-lun looked every bit as wild as they sat on the dirt floor in their sheepskin *tsarers* and served us the bitter, black tea. They were exactly as Tsedup had described them when we were in England. In the years while we waited for his documents he had feared that they would die before his return, but it had not been too late and that day, watching them together, I was moved.

Despite his years, Azjung was a remarkable-looking man: his old skin was taut on his skull, like stretched hide, over cheekbones smooth as stone; beneath his shorn head his brow was as square as the thin line of his mouth, and as he turned to lift his bowl I saw that his nose was not flat at the bridge, as many Tibetans' are, but ridged and aquiline, almost aristocratic. He smiled at me and the deep sockets of his eyes were filled with a dark sparkle.

Ama-lo-lun sat before us fingering her prayer beads, her lips moving rapidly as she mouthed her silent mantra. Her shock of dreadlocked grey hair was woven into two miniature plaits, one on either side of her neck, which protruded rakishly like two stick antennae. Around her neck she wore a tangle of religious adornments: a string of ivory prayer beads, a small, faded silk purse containing blessings, and a piece of frayed, luminous green ribbon given to her by a lama. Her *tsarer* seemed as old as herself, a crush of matted sheepskin and faded trim, beneath which she wore a soiled, bottle-green sweatshirt turned inside out. Her small face was a lattice of furrows and her green eyes burned, keen and sharp, darting from face to floor to space, observing everything and missing nothing. Occasionally she would laugh, a curiously girlish outburst, and punctuate each sentence, each pause between sentences, with 'Oh, yeah,' muttered through toothless gums.

The Sky Man spoke to Tsedup in a low voice while bent double over the prayer beads that he fingered slowly and methodically in his big hand. His sunken cheeks filled and puffed out the words in a throaty resonance. He had a presence, as if time itself had settled around him like a cloak. Azjung was not only a man with a good memory, he was living history. He listened carefully to his young relative and gave ponderous, methodical answers, smiling benignly. He wanted to hear about the West and Tsedup told him.

Occasionally he laughed huskily at something ironic or surprising, relishing this new knowledge and storing it for future reference. New stories from a new world.

As they sat talking by the fire, which belched out a small cloud of smoke now and again, I felt humbled by the spirit of this old couple. They had enormous dignity, and it struck me that, because of the importance of oral tradition here, they had attained the respect they so rightly deserved. It was clear that the more old people talked, the more others listened. Their wisdom could directly affect the morality of a society and they were therefore placed at the top of the hierarchy and were profoundly revered. I had always felt that there was so much more I could have learnt from my own grandmother. I had tried to suck up her words as we sipped tea from china cups, the clock ticking on the sideboard, the dog snoring in the chair. She was my history. But, in the West, the war stories of a pensioner are often discarded as of little consequence. The young audience are too busy to listen, too bored by the past. In a fast-moving world there is no time for stories, no fire to tell them around. And the spark of imagination died with TV.

Tsedup listened respectfully to the old man, laughing with him, debating, learning. Sometimes they fell into quiet, intimate discussion, and I could hear the steady chink of the prayer beads and the squeak of Ama-lo-lun's prayer wheel as it spun in her bony grip. She smiled at me with such warmth that I was reminded of my own grandmother. They shared the same strength of character honed from years of experience, both diminutive but powerful women, their bodies decrepit but their minds alive with wisdom, defiance and raw energy. My grandmother had loved Tsedup because she sensed his respect for her. When she died, he telephoned his family to tell them. They asked for her name. He told them Lily. I could hear them pronouncing it tentatively down the receiver. Then Ama-lo-lun and Tsedup's mother came to this monastery and asked the monks to pray for her spirit on its journey to the next life. One hundred butter lamps were lit for her here on this hillside. A life that had begun in 1910 in the depths of suburban London, had ended with a tribute by Tibetan nomads on the Roof of the World. It was memories such as these that made the polarity of our cultures and their fusion seem even more remarkable.

Before we left, Azjung took a small felt holdall from inside the musty cupboard. Tied carefully inside it was a small polished bowl made from a light substance. He said he didn't know whether it was wood or fungus. It had been in his family for four generations and his ancestor had paid for it with a yak. It was obviously of value. A Tibetan's prize possession, along with the obligatory knife and tinder box, is their own bowl, so it was a great honour when he pushed it into Tsedup's hand and told him to keep it.

We closed the wooden door behind us and heard the familiar tinkle of the bell. Time had stopped in the dark dust of that hut. I could still hear the voice of the Sky Man and it was no longer a simple resonance, a vibration on the dirt floor and soot walls, but the echo of a thousand forefathers in my ears.

# SEVEN

# A Woman's Work

It wasn't an echo, but a snorting and snuffling that woke me the next day. A yak was licking the side of the tent, its tongue rasping against the coarse canvas. I beat the moist imprint of its muzzle with the back of my hand shouting, '*Sshtoo!*' as I had been taught and it thundered away with a snap of the guy rope that continued to vibrate in a dizzying drone. I lay for a few moments, feeling the warmth of our bodies, watching my spiralling breath. Then, pulling my sheepskin *tsarer* loosely around me, I stood up on the damp grass and shucked on my shoes. It was six a.m. and nature was calling.

Outside was silent, apart from the odd sheep bleat and yak grunt. I crouched, shivering, in the frosted grass by the stream's bank and watched dawn laying down her palette of rose, peach and gold, the low cloud suspended over the Yellow river. It was a rare moment: there was no one but myself and the animals in sight. Behind me our flock of sheep lay sleeping in a large orderly circle on the grass. They were nothing like the sheep I was used to, more like goats, lithe and leggy for scaling the mountain slopes in winter, with thin snouts and long, twisted horns. Their summer fleece was dense and thick shanks of winter wool hung from their sides. Even their bleating was different, a comical refrain, like a man pretending to be a sheep, we decided. Beyond them, the yaks and their calves lay drowsily pegged to the ground in rows, shifting in their churned-up mud-bed. They were hardy beasts, incapable of surviving at low altitude, but perfectly equipped for life on the plateau and its harsh environment. But I knew nothing of that harshness: I had tasted only the balmy summer of stark light, cold nights and sharp morning frosts. The odd day had found us huddled round the fire in the tent as the rain lashed wildly and dripped through the sooty fabric, but I had not yet felt the thrust of a chest-thumping gale. That was to come.

I stood staring up at the platinum moon, heavy and perfect-round, like a medallion in the deep azure pool of the western sky. When I looked down again Shermo Donker was standing by the black tent. She didn't call to me, just smiled. However, she had little time to pause and admire as it was time for the first milking, and she bustled off towards the yaks in the laboured gait characteristic of nomad women, her gumboots scuffing through the wet grass. Rather guiltily, I bustled back to my bed, confident that I would be with her for the lunch-time milking. It wasn't as if anything was expected of me and the other women showed no resentment towards me for being different. In fact I was thoroughly spoilt, but I was keen to show willing. At a reasonable hour, of course.

But as I lay listening to her shouting to the children to get up, I felt a gulf between us. What was it like to belong to a place like this, as she did? It was impossible for me to know. I was too different and had seen too much of the world. Her vision and mine seemed irreconcilable and I tried to imagine what it would be like to share hers. She had been born into this tribe. Sometimes women or men married into other tribes, like Tsedup's brother Gondo and sister Dombie, but through marriage to Tsedo she had secured her future here. She had only left Machu to go to Labrang a few times, and as a child had joined her family on a pilgrimage to Lhasa, but apart from that she had never left this place. Generally nomad women do not leave the tribe much, as they are so busy with their chores. I wondered how it felt to live a life that, to me, seemed so predictable, in a place where you knew everybody. You knew your place. In some ways I was envious of her. The security and communality of this life was a far cry from the mutual isolation of the equally routine rat-race back home in London: the slow shuffling of aliens in an underground tunnel on the way to an office full of gossip, shrill laughter and telephones. It was a world away now.

I felt as if I was standing on the outside looking in. It wasn't just the way I looked that set me apart, it was the knowledge that they had grown and lived together all their lives. What was it like to be part of a tribe of people that you have known all your life? I supposed it might be claustrophobic, but they didn't think like that. For them the tribe meant comfort, safety, identity and stability. The more I thought about it, the more attractive it sounded. I resolved to try to bridge the gap between us by attempting to help more with the workload, before snuggling down again beneath the sheepskin.

Later when I emerged from the tent, the milking was over and Shermo Donker and her two daughters were bent double, spreading fresh dung on the ground. They used their bare hands, grabbing fistfuls of excrement, which they slapped on to the grass and smoothed out with their palms in a thin layer so that the sun could bake it to a crust. This was one job from which I was quite happy to abstain, but shit was fuel and fuel was life to them, and they rinsed their hands in the stream then came in for breakfast.

Inside the tent the family met around the clay fire, where a steaming pot of broth threatened to overflow as its tin lid danced up and down. It was customary for them to wait for Shermo Donker to finish her milking so that she could serve us our breakfast. But today there were complications to the smooth running of the family rota. Sanjay, her little boy, was wailing heartily due to some mishap and would not be comforted. He lay prone on the dirt floor, occasionally raising his matted head to gasp for air through a film of snot and tears, his protruding lower jaw jutting out rigid and determined. Amnye was cooing 'Babko, Baddo . . .' in his tender voice, reserved for the children. According to Tsedup he had a series of different names for them. He was an adoring grandfather and especially pampered Sanjay, who slept inside his *tsarer* with him most nights. But today Sanjay was having none of it.

Tsedo was simultaneously laughing at his son and attempting to suppress Sanjay's tears with a few of his own comforting words, though they were delivered somewhat gruffly. It was not common for a father to demonstrate his affection too much for his own child, that was left to the grandparents. Tsedo appeared redundant, embarrassed at his son's tantrum but amused, too, which I found a little cruel. He was a young man, two years Tsedup's senior, with unusually delicate features, a calm stare and an air of gentility, which was frequently punctured by bouts of wicked sarcasm and fits of rasping giggles. He looked older than his years, weatherbeaten and lined, skin scorched, hair tousled, and was incredibly clean for a nomad. He always had a new shirt on, and often glanced in the mirror. A formidable horseman, he had been the dashing prize-winner among the nomads in his earlier years, famed for his agility, with a history of shooting targets from the saddle and plucking flowers from the ground with his teeth while galloping. A nomad girl's dream.

His wife threw him nervous glances from her side of the tent. It was time to defuse the situation. She scurried round to the men's side, placed one hand firmly on her son's collar, the other on the waistband of his soiled trousers, and wrenched him perfunctorily from the floor, causing him to choke then renew his vocal assault. She carried him to the other side of the fire as Amnye urged her not to use such force, Tsedo swore and Annay, who had remained deferential up to that point, began to laugh her peculiarly girlish laugh. Then Shermo Donker lifted her blouse and pushed Sanjay's screaming mouth on to her shrivelled breast.

She held his head there in her vice-like grip, as he kicked and resisted, then gradually he became limp, quietened and began to suck.

I knew that Tibetan mothers usually suckled their children for a year or two – but a six-year-old boy at his mother's breast! I was stunned and fiddled with some loose stitching on my shoe, while struggling with an astonishing sense of the impropriety of the act. I was amazed at the feeling that it aroused in me. I had always been a liberal sort of girl, hadn't I? Was it not the most natural form of comfort in the world for a child? These people clearly thought so.

When Sanjay had nursed long enough, he slunk, subdued, from his mother to his grandmother. She embraced him and I watched, astonished, as he lifted her shirt and nuzzled into her aged breast, sucking again. She smacked his head lazily and told him off, but her protest was weak and as she let out a long, contented sigh I could tell that she was happy with her maternal role.

When the last bowl had been licked clean, the men smoked awhile, the children ran off to play and Shermo Donker heaved the huge pot of the morning's milk on to the fire to boil. The daily milking process was central to the nomads' survival. From the milk they churned butter and made yoghurt and cheese. While the milk boiled Shermo Donker set up the *turnkor*, churn, comprised of various components, which had been dismantled and cleaned the day before. It was a wooden box with a metal basin on top and a metal funnel, containing rotating discs, with two spouts protruding from each side. On top of the funnel was a metal bowl into which the milk was poured and around it was tied a thin piece of muslin, to sieve the milk and trap yak hairs and grass. On the side of the box was a handle and when the milk had boiled Shermo Donker sat on the floor beside the churn, began to pour in the milk and turn the handle vigorously. As the milk passed over the rotating discs and was separated, the cream dripped in a thick stream from one spout into the metal basin and formed pools on top of yesterday's solid yellow butter. From the other spout the skimmed milk rained into a wooden pail at twice the speed and formed a moussy white froth on the surface. She had milked forty yaks that morning and, not surprisingly, after a short while her arm was aching with the effort of turning the handle. I offered to take over, much to everyone's delight and amusement, and took her place as she went off to some other task outside. I began earnestly turning the handle, a little faster than her at first to prove that I was capable.

Tsedo congratulated me. 'The Amdo *namma* knows how to do her work,' he called, over the whir of the machine.

But as soon as they had all resumed chattering I faltered with the effort of my task. It was a lot harder than I had thought it would be and soon my neck muscles had stiffened into a twingeing knot. Still I smiled and declined the offer of a rest from Tsedup's father. I had to show them I could do something. If dung-spreading wasn't on, then surely milk-churning was possible. I feigned ease and focused on some faraway mountain beyond the open tent door. This had to get easier. In a week I'd have it nailed.

When most of the milk had been separated, Shermo Donker poured the remainder of the cream into a bucket and covered it over with an old sheepskin. She placed it in a dark, cool corner of the tent where it would quickly ferment into yoghurt. She relieved me and praised me, and I rose to my feet as graciously as I could with pins and needles cascading through my legs. If I could have disguised the discomfort, I would have proved my worth. But I was unable to put a foot forward. I just stood resignedly right in her path, as she laboured under the weight of the huge pot of skimmed milk, which she wanted to place on the fire. I gestured to my feet and looked pleadingly at Tsedup for help with an explanation. As he spoke the whole tent burst into hysterics. I would have to be content for now with my role as the incompetent foreigner.

I left the cheese-making to her and breakfasted while she boiled up a pulp from the milk then strained it in a mesh bag. She crumbled the curds thinly on to a plastic sheet outside to dry in the sun, then poured the whey into a bucket for the *tzorgin*, half yak, half cow, who awaited this treat outside the tent each day. He was drinking it as Sirmo and I left to wash the clothes.

We walked to a stream in a valley between two mountains, she carrying the load in a wicker basket on her back. Then we sat in the sunshine and scrubbed in the warm flow of fresh water as she sang Tibetan songs in her sweet, husky voice. '*Yucka*!' I proclaimed. 'Beautiful.' As she laughed modestly, the tiny, silver chains on her earrings jangled on her shoulders. Then she urged me to sing an English song for her. This didn't feel as awkward as performing in front of the audience at the karaoke bar in Labrang, but I was running out of ideas for good tunes. It seemed so humiliating when the Tibetans had so many lovely folk songs. Most of the chart hits at my disposal would have been a bit too progressive for nomad ears. Progressive or downright ugly, I wasn't sure. I found a compromise in Simon and Garfunkel. Like the Beatles, they were the least offensive and most melodious examples of contemporary western music I could muster, and I remembered that Tsedup had liked them when I first met him in India. I sang the first lines of 'Kathy's Song'. The words, on the breeze of that wild land, appeared more and more uncannily inappropriate, since they were about rain drizzling on a house.

It was a scorching day and I hadn't lived under a roof for a while now. It was only when I got to the bit about England being where my heart lies that I became most acutely aware of the irony of my choice of song. Did my heart lie in England now? As I gazed at the rugged, infinite expanse of grassland and to the dizzy heights of the rocky mountains behind, I realised that I loved this place, and that these images would endure even when I was tramping the drizzly streets of London. I remembered when I was in London trying to imagine what it would be like to be in the vast spaces of Amdo. Would I feel small? Insignificant? Now I was here, I knew that there was a kind of symbiosis between man and nature and, rather than feeling excluded or exposed, I was simply part of the landscape, like the yaks.

Sirmo had become my closest friend. She was twenty-one and more adept than anyone else at interpreting my Tibetan. We were able to chatter away quite intimately together. She was different from the rest, more of a rebel, and although she performed her duties with all the strength and ability of the other women, there was something about her that suggested a reluctance to conform. It was because she had been to school. Like Tsedup before her, she had expressed a desire to be educated when she reached puberty; a rare thing for a nomad girl. She had been a good student but had only stayed at school for four years. I had heard Tsedup telling her off many times for leaving school so soon. He was an avid proponent of education, and he hadn't understood why she had left. However, she had been knifed, and the scar still showed on her arm. Amnye had been vague about the circumstances when he told Tsedup, but apparently a schoolboy had done it. She had never gone back after that. She had resolved to live the nomad life and be a good nomad woman, but I thought perhaps she was bored. It was only a guess, but sometimes I could see the thirst in her eyes. In the evenings, if Tsedup stayed in town and Dickir Che was sharing my bed, she came to our tent to tuck us in. She would sit by the candle and read Tsedup's Tibetan books until she was missed in the main tent, when she would rush back to her duties. The older women were always urging her to marry, but she was secretive about the affairs of her heart. I suspected there was somebody, though. She was quite a catch.

When we had finished wringing the clothes, we made our way back to the tent. She laboured under the weight of our sodden washing, which she insisted on carrying, even though she had damaged her back the day before trying to catch flowers in her teeth while on the back of a galloping yak. She had the exquisiteness of a princess and the guts of a spirited boy. I guess that's what I loved about her most. But I had yet to discover her true bravery. For now we paused in the long grass for a cloud of flies to settle on us, while she rested. She took my hand and stroked the skin of my arm. '*Yucka*,' she said, then guided my fingers over her own callused forearm. The skin was tough and ingrained with dirt, the joints of her fingers swollen, their nails buckled and dented. They were working hands.

Back home the children and I hung the washing on the

tent lines to dry. They were fascinated by my knickers, which they examined and shrieked at with amusement. It was the number that amazed them most. 'Eight pairs!' They giggled. I hadn't thought that eight pairs of knickers might be excessive for six months.

Then they started jumping around me shouting, 'Karee Ma, Karee Ma!' dragging me excitedly towards the yaks. It was lunch-time milking and White Face was waiting. This was to be a first. They guided me to my yak and sat me down on a tiny wooden milking stool at her side. Then Dickir Che gave me a quick demonstration, and the milk gushed out over her tiny hands. I hugged the side of that beast, whose stomach gurgled next to my ear, squeezing and pulling as instructed, then yanking and tweaking for greater effect, but somehow only a squirt fell into my pail. The children laughed and I persisted. I wasn't much of a milkmaid. Milking was a mystery. The night before last, Annay had wanted me to eat rice and milk so she led me to a yak while I carried her bucket. I was startled when she lifted its tail, matter-of-factly placed her mouth on its bottom and blew hard. Then she proceeded to milk. Even Tsedup could not tell me what that had all been about.

After a lunch of *tsampa* and yoghurt in the smoke-filled tent, we went to collect the dung. They showed me how to pile the crusty pieces into small mounds with a short rake and a brush of twigs. Then we filled the *seeto*, wicker baskets, and hoisted their string handles over our shoulders so that they sat on our backs. The women and the two little girls did this with ease, but I could barely lift mine. I was amazed at how heavy dung was. I was even more astonished at how strong the children were. I was no match for them. Bent double, we carried the baskets back to the tent and swung their contents on top of the dung heap in the corner. We continued backwards and forwards in this way until all of the grass around the tent was cleared of yesterday's dung. I was exhausted, but the heap in the tent looked impressively large. Annay would be pleased when she saw it later. A big dung pile was the sign of a good *namma*.

Later that evening I helped with my favourite job, tying up yaks. This was a battle of wills since these wild animals are loath to be tethered. I heaved at the rope around their necks, coaxing them on in my pidgin Tibetan, although English would probably have done just as well, dragging them through the mud towards the long rope pegged to the ground. A quick flick of a knot and each one was secure. At first I was given charge of the calves with the children – the family were afraid I might be gored by the adults' horns – but I had since graduated to dealing with a tonne of fully grown yak. The only thing I had to look out for was their hoofs. I had often been trampled on. I stood perspiring in the twilight, as the smoke from the tents ghosted gently through the regiments of grunting black beasts, and stared at the silent silhouette of the holy mountain behind our camp. This was the best time of day. The family would all assemble again soon. This woman's work was done.

Annay took my hand and led me to a convenient spot of grass and we squatted together in the moonlight. My dear mother-in-law didn't bat an eyelid as we sat farting together under the stars and, to be honest, I enjoyed the intimacy. As we walked back to the tent, the children's laughter drifted to us on the night air, with the clatter of cooking and the crackle of the transistor radio. A horse whinnied in the dusk-light and I heard a pained snort. A yak was sick with what looked like a festering leg. It was in obvious pain and couldn't move, but we were powerless to help it. I guessed its days were numbered. Today's lame yak was tomorrow's meat here. That was life.

# EIGHT

# *The Buddha Boy*

T oday's meat was indeed yesterday's lame yak. Despite our efforts, the beast perished in the hot sun. Tsedup and I had fed it a huge dose of human antibiotics and dribbled milk into its mouth in desperation. The children and I had even held an umbrella over its head to ease the glare of the midday heat, but the yak knew it was dying. It grunted pathetically as the dogs sniffed around it.

When it had died I went out to look at it for the last time. Unlike these people, I was unaccustomed to seeing death. I had only seen my mother's dead bitch. We buried her solemnly beneath a cherry tree in the back garden. The yak was still warm, and as I gently stroked its head I muttered, '*Om mani padme hum.*' It is better to die than to suffer, Annay said. As far as she was concerned, its soul was on its way to the next life. She prayed as she skinned it with the other women.

From the day that Tsedup had run away, Annay had stopped eating animals that had been killed, and only ate those that had died naturally. She had prayed that her son would be protected. But even now that he was back, she would not revert to her old ways. Sometimes she had to rely on the generosity of another family in the tribe whose animal had died. But these treats were only occasional, and her diet was poor. Tsedup was always remonstrating with her for not looking after her health. But she was stubborn and not even he could change her mind. Annay was a devout Buddhist. Her virtuous actions were symbolic of her religious devotion and compassion for all sentient beings. She sought empathy with the world and a deeper level of understanding for the life around her. She knew that each of her actions had an outcome. If she showed compassion, the outcome would be positive; if she committed a harmful act, the outcome would be negative. Every day she experienced the world at an emotional level and compassion was her primary motivation. With every good act that she performed, she was increasing her own good karma and achieving merit, *sonnam*. The ten main meritorious actions of Buddhism are not unlike the Ten Commandments: one should not kill, steal, conduct inappropriate sexual activity, lie, gossip, swear, sow discord or be covetous, malicious or opinionated. Annay was in line for a glorious rebirth.

That evening, we made mincemeat of the poor yak. Amnye, Tsedo and I fashioned *momos*, the tiny steamed flour parcels, which were the nomads' delicacy. They laughed at my squashed efforts as they placed their own creations, like perfect poppy buds, on the floured board. Later, I tried not to think of the ethical implications as I munched gratefully, delicious hot juice dribbling down my chin. Now and then each person breathed their prayer through greasy lips, as in the corner of the tent the black hide hung limply over the basket of meat.

As we talked in the firelight, Shermo Donker made butter. Tomorrow the tribe would be honoured by the visit of a lama. The butter was to be our family's offering to the monastery. She kneaded it in a bowl, squeezing out the excess liquid; it squelched and oozed lusciously in her fingers. Then she slapped and patted it into cylindrical shapes; perfectly smooth. She continued until long after the children had fallen asleep, the fire had died, the dogs had ceased their howling.

Despite the imminent arrival of the lama, Tsedup had resolved to go to town. The next morning, he sped off with his brother, Tsedo, on the motorbike, scattering sheep, his mother shouting after him, 'Come back tonight! Namma needs you!' Tsedup waved and disappeared in a dustcloud on the far track. I had discovered his fondness for town life, which was strange since I had always thought he would be a true nomad. But I hadn't known how much young nomads loved the town. These days, it was the place to be. And it was normal for nomad husbands to leave their wives sometimes, in favour of carousing with friends and a hotel bed. I missed him when he didn't come home at night and Annay knew it. Yet I tried to suppress my possessive urges. He had been away for nine years and I wanted him to feel alive again. I was just going to have to bite my tongue. One thing was for sure: through sheer necessity, my Tibetan language was improving and I was becoming a more competent *namma*.

Soon a figure appeared in the shimmering heat. Tsedup's grandmother was ambling over from Rhanjer's tent with her stick. She had walked six miles from the town to stay with his family, as she often did in the summer months. Tsedup's oldest brother had been raised by Ama-lo-lun and Azjung. They had never been able to have a child of their own – Amnye was the product of her previous marriage – and as a boy Rhanjer had been so idolised by them that his grandmother had gradually prised him away from his parents. Subtly he had become a permanent fixture in their tent. It wasn't that Tsedup's mother and father had not wanted him; this practice is quite common in nomad families and usually there are so many children that they are willingly shared between grandparents and parents.

Ama-lo-lun had come to help with preparations for the lama's visit and soon settled into deep-frying twists of golden bread in a wok, heavy with oil. She recited her prayers rhythmically as she turned the bread in the oil with a stick. Tibetans did not pray in the way I understood. Ama-lo-lun was not asking for anything, or thanking her god. She was probably just using the prayer for dedication of merit, part of every devout Buddhist's practice. 'May any merit attained through this practice be dedicated to the enlightenment of all sentient beings.'

As she repeated her refrain, she strained the doughnut morsels and placed them on an upturned metal lid. The fire was bright, the tent dark and clouded with dung smoke. Above her hypnotic chants and the bubbling oil, the milk-churn whirred, as Sirmo turned the handle. Meanwhile,

Annay rolled out dough on a wooden board and cut it into small rectangles, slitting each piece in the middle and weaving it into shapes, ready for frying. We were silent, listening to the prayer, which seemed infinite.

Suddenly, through the drone of incantation we heard a jeep engine. Shermo Donker came running into the tent, a flustered look on her sun-blistered face. The lama was here. 'Hurry! Hurry!' she barked at the children. She pulled me outside, and I caught a brief glimpse of the holy man's vehicle as it pulled up next door before she spun me inside our white tent. I felt as if I was being hidden from him. Were they ashamed of me? I would surely be a most bizarre spectacle for the lama. For a moment I felt disappointed. But Shermo Donker soon began rummaging through an old rice sack and produced a fistful of *kadaks*, the white silken prayer scarves.

'Your *tsarer* needs retying.' She smiled and I realised that she was about to help me smarten up. She was the expert and I had to look my best. She handed me the prayer scarves and fussed around with my costume, until I was bound tight enough for her satisfaction. In a gentle, motherly gesture, she licked her thumb and smoothed away some mark on my face. '*Yucka*!' she said, then tugged at my arm and propelled me towards the main tent. We distributed the prayer scarves and Sirmo and Shermo Donker retied their *tsarers*, combed their hair and put on their best jewellery. I helped the children into their best clothes. Their *tsarers* were only marginally less soiled than the clothes they had been wearing, but it was an improvement, and once I had tugged at their hair with a comb, we all set off.

Jerko's tent was on the other side of the stream. It had always been there and it always would be. Each summer when the tribe reassembled in the river valley, all of the tents were always in exactly the same position. Tsedup's father and Jerko seemed to be the luckiest ones. It wasn't a question of status, although they were both prominent figures in the tribe, just the way things were. Being closest to the stream, those families were in the most convenient position for collecting water and washing clothes. Their women were more fortunate than the others, who toiled across the grassland with their water vessels. Our tent was also the closest to the track, so anyone arriving at the tribe would call there first. We were always the first to know who was coming, which was an advantage when the trucks came from town, selling fruit and packet noodles.

Jerko shared the family name, Kambo-Wasser as he was Amnye's illegitimate brother. The two had the same father. Ama-lo-lun knew about it, but it didn't seem to have been a problem for her. That kind of nocturnal liaison was not uncommon in the grassland. The Kambo-Wasser lineage was centuries old and their ancestors had origins in Kham, the province south of Amdo. The people of Kham were notoriously fearsome warriors of gargantuan stature, which explained Jerko's appearance. He was the tallest man in the tribe, with enormous square shoulders and a square jaw. His son, Gabo, was the strongest man, a prize-winning wrestler. The hallmark of a Kambo-Wasser man was his shoulders, which Tsedup had inherited, although Amnye was of a muscular but slighter build, more like Ama-lo-lun's family.

Outside Jerko's home, we joined the rest of the tribe. The lama and his retinue were hidden from our view within the dark confines of the tent, although the front flap had been raised and we could see some magenta-robed monks sipping tea. Jerko's family had laid out low wooden tables, which were overflowing with plates of *momos*, meat, apples, sweets, soft drinks and Ama-lo-lun's golden bread. The guests sat cross-legged on tufted Tibetan rugs, decorated with elaborate patterns, and I could just make out the golden glow of the butter lamps and the *thankas* they had hung on the sides of the tent. Outside the tent entrance they had prepared a throne, which was covered in silk cloth, for the old lama to sit on when he gave his blessings. Around me, the crowd mumbled in anticipation. The young girls wore elaborate headdresses that cascaded down their backs in a shower of coral, turquoise and amber. They had donned their best silk shirts with stiff gold brocade designs especially for the occasion and stood in a group, giggling and whispering, shyly nibbling the tips of their fingers. The old women cooed their satisfaction with my traditional costume and took my hand now and again, squeezing it affectionately. 'Amdo Namma,' they said gently, looking up at me with kind eyes.

The sun was growing fierce in the cloudless sky. The prairie lay scorched, the iridescence of the summer flowers lessening now to patches of yellow and lilac here and there. The Machu river shone back at the sky, the same pure blue. A raven looped lethargically above my head and made for the craggy heights of the mountains in the distance. I stayed close to Sirmo and watched for clues about protocol. Most people had begun to prostrate. I watched Shermo Donker push her palms together, then touch her forehead, her throat and her heart. Then she lay prone on the grass, her face buried in the dry stems for a moment before she rose and repeated the action. She was paying homage to the lama by practising the Buddhist form of obeisance. He was the embodiment of Buddha-body, speech and mind; the superior object of prostration. He was a sacred teacher, who had made a vow to serve all sentient beings and through his own actions could demonstrate the Buddha's teaching and give the Buddha's blessing.

Now, even the old men and women of the tribe were stretched out humbly before the empty throne, rising and falling like a Mexican wave. I felt self-conscious. I wasn't a Buddhist, but I had a great respect for their beliefs, and just as Tsedup had never stood up in church when everyone else was kneeling to pray, I wanted to honour this code of conduct. I had never been fit, however, so I was in trouble by the fifth prostration. Flushed of face and panting I was forced to stop, while next to me Tsedup's octogenarian grandmother was still going strong. I had due cause to feel inadequate – but, then, she was driven by a profound sense of devotion. I was not. She awaited the appearance of the sacred old man with all the eagerness of a child.

Except that *he* was a child. When he finally emerged from the tent, I was shocked to discover that the venerable lama was no more than five years old. He was dwarfed by his entourage of monks, who ushered him to his throne, lowering their heads in respect. His head was freshly shaved, his body draped in layers of miniature yellow and magenta robes, and when he climbed up on to his throne, his tiny Tibetan boots dangled over the edge of his seat. He gazed impassively at the throng before him and squinted in the midday glare. As the monks began chanting their prayer, we were all made to form an orderly line to receive the lama's blessing. One by one, the tribe approached him, bowing in supplication, holding the *kadaks* in their outstretched arms. He touched each of their heads and placed the scarf around their necks. I had been shocked when I met the thirteen-year-old lama Jarsung in Labrang, but nothing had prepared me for this extraordinary event. I was just as perplexed to see him as he would be to see me.

As I approached him I wondered what on earth he would think of me. Five-year-old children here usually stared and pointed when they first saw me but, of course, that would be an inappropriately extravagant display for such a sacred being, even if he had wanted to show his surprise. As I got nearer, it was impossible to keep my head lower than his as he was so small. I knew it was forbidden, but I was curious to look into his eyes, to see what lay within that face. As his tiny hand touched my head in blessing, I chanced a glimpse. He sat inert, staring with the intelligence of a scientist at my yellow hair. Like Jarsung, he had a seriousness about him that betrayed his inner self. His child's body was just a shell. I felt unnerved, as if he had the power to look into my soul.

He placed my *kadak* delicately around my neck, and in that moment I experienced an almost tangible sense of the magic and mystery of this place that I had come to love. I felt distanced, unable to understand it, as if the country itself defied being fully understood. It was a place of the unknown, of the fantastic, the impossible; a strange sanctum, whose very landscape was riddled with symbolism and whose holy men possessed superhuman powers. I looked away and moved on obediently, collecting my knotted protection cord, *shugndot,* from the monk at his side, as the lama bestowed the next Buddha blessing. Free of their religious obligations, the small children were now frolicking and rucking in the grass, splashing in the stream, falling in dung, shouting and laughing, hitting and pinching. Sirmo and I chided them as we walked back to the tent, but as I took one last look at the holy child climbing into his jeep, which was full of butter, I was happy at their wild freedom.

There was a feeling of elation in the tribe after the blessing, like the post-Communion camaraderie of a Christian congregation. There had been a washing of the soul by a 'wave of grace'; for that is what the word blessing, or *shinlab*, means in Tibetan. I watched the nomads return to their tents and the lunch-time milking.

That day I had witnessed their devotion to Buddhism, not in a monastery but at home. It was remarkable to have been outside, under the blistering sun and the dome of the sky and to have been part of their worship. I had seen evidence of their shamanic practices before, but this had been different. For me, that day revealed the nomads' piety, humility and their veneration of the lama, the symbol of Buddha.

In Amdo, the Buddhist deity predominantly worshipped is Lhamo. She is depicted with a fierce blue face and riding a mule. Amnye had explained that one could pray to her in a manner different from the practice of 'calling upon' the spirit powers of the earth and sky. In the mind of the nomad, Lhamo may be helpful after death, which none of the shamanic gods are. Equally, Chenrezik, the bodhisattva of compassion, may assist after death: his role is to delay his own entrance into nirvana – the ultimate Buddha state, which precludes all possibilities of reincarnation – until every sentient being has been released from the wheel of rebirth to accompany him. I had heard his mantra '*Om mani padme hum*' muttered everywhere, as a means of supplication for his blessing. Indeed, the Dalai Lama is his incarnation: 'He who gazes upon the suffering of the world with tears in his eyes.'

The preoccupation with death and rebirth appeared to form the crux of the Buddhist mindset. It seemed to me that the nomads took refuge in Buddhism as a means of understanding and conquering death. I had realised the clarity with which they accepted the impermanence of life. I had seen the strings of white prayer flags fluttering on the opposite bank of the Machu river and knew that it was a water-burial site. I had heard the terrible tales of the tribeswomen performing sky burial for their dead men on the mountain.

But the process of dying I had heard about seemed as mystical as the shamanic rituals. Certain mystic initiates are capable of maintaining a lucid mind during the dissolving of their personalities. They can even pass into the next life fully conscious. An ordinary man, however, is guided down the path of death by a lama. He explains to the dying man the nature of the journey on which he is about to embark and reassures him. Then the lama's task is to command the spirit out of the top of the man's head with a cry of '*Hik!*' followed by '*Phat!*' The disembodied entity may then begin its journey through a series of visions, guided by his character and past actions. This is the intermediate state, *Bardo.* After three days, when the lama has induced the spirit to leave the corpse and abandon its attachment to the world, the body is tied up and carried to the sky burial site. It is dismembered, the organs removed, the limbs cut off, the bones pounded to powder with rock. The dead man's body is a last generous offering to the other sentient beings of the earth: the vultures, wolves and birds. Or the fish who consume a waterborne corpse.

After death a person embraces a new life. If they have accumulated enough merit they will be a good person. If not, they may come back as an ant, or worse. Annay was always careful where she trod. Whatever their state of rebirth, the dead person's name is not spoken in the same way again. I had referred to a late relative of Annay's by his name and had been corrected. I had also seen photographs with faces scratched out. Although the younger generation, more familiar with new technology, accepted pictures of the dead, it seemed that older nomads were unsettled by them and preferred, as they always had, the vividness of a mental picture. I wondered what Amnye and Annay had thought of the pictures I had shown them of my grandmother.

I realised that the intricacies of the Buddhist doctrines were not the main preoccupation of devout people like Annay and Ama-lo-lun. It appeared, as with most nomad women, that their main preoccupation was with living a compassionate existence, reciting the mantra, visiting the monastery. They saw the lama as being like a god, representing the Buddha, and I recognised the importance they attached to the offerings they made to him. Buddhism had brought the nomads morality and spiritual liberation and they worshipped the Buddhist deities, but I knew that the tribesmen's hearts were more closely bound to the mountain gods. Annay was always scolding Amnye for not going to the monastery often enough, but a nomad man needs to feel invincible: he calls upon the mountain warrior for his own protection, in battle against his enemies or the elements. The younger men, like Tsedup's brother Gondo, were especially reliant on the protection of the mountain gods. Gondo would climb Archa and scream to the wind over his fire-offerings for success in gambling. There was no place for a lama in these matters. If Gondo sought refuge in the holy man he would be entering a moral debate and would probably be encouraged to cease his negative actions. The mountain gods were not morally judgemental.

I had been privileged to listen to both the soft murmur

of a mantra and to the war-cries of wild men on a mountain peak. If the nomads could live with this rich contradiction, so could I.

# NINE

## *A Trip to Town*

It was the first day of autumn, a sad day. Tsedo and Amnye were in serious discussion over breakfast, their conversation riddled with numbers. They were talking about the herd. Today the annual head count was due. Each family member was allowed by law to own only ten yaks, twenty sheep, and half a horse. Though what a nomad could do with half a horse, I had no idea. There were eleven family members in Amnye's tent and now he had a dilemma on his hands. According to his calculations, he had too many animals and today he would have to sell ten yaks, thirty sheep and four and a half horses to the Muslim slaughterers.

It was a difficult task deciding which ones should die. Many had been promised a safe life by the family and could not be sold. My yak, Karee Ma, was one such lucky beast. They knew each animal's name, and I listened as they recited the roll-call and determined their fate. It seemed inconceivable that every sheep could be so clearly identified, since they all looked more or less the same to me, but it added poignancy to the proceedings. Hardest of all to judge was which horse should go. The nomads loved their horses. When I had met Tsedup, he had told me that his family had fifty horses, five hundred yaks and a thousand sheep. But this was only a memory. He was shocked to discover that while he had been in England, the government had introduced new laws to control land division and livestock ownership. The vast herds that used to roam the great grasslands for hundreds of miles were now depleted and had been sectioned off by barbed-wire fences.

At this time of year, the only contented people were the slaughterers. With every nomad bringing animals to town to sell, they controlled the prices. The market would be saturated and such competition meant no profit for a man like Tsedo. For him, there was nothing to be gained but a few paltry yuan. In fact, it was difficult to see how the nomads made their money. I knew that Amnye received a small salary for his post as local councillor and that must have been the family's major source of income. They were big producers of cheese, wool, leather and butter, but they seemed to use most of this for their own subsistence and didn't appear to sell much. The butter was part of their staple diet; any surplus was stored in the family tent, in a skin-covered wooden box for the winter, donated to the monastery, or used to make butter lamps for the altar in the tent. The sheepskins were kept for making *tsokwas*, the thick winter *tsarers*, and the wool was spun and woven into *dobshair*, the textile hanging used to cover the items stored at the back of the tent, or felted to make mattresses, clothes, saddle-blankets or *dalin*, saddle-bags. The cheese was eaten or stored – it was so hard it didn't go mouldy. Sometimes it was traded for fruit and noodles when the Chinese entrepreneurs' three-wheeled truck brought provisions from the town to the tribe. The yak wool was spun and used for weaving the tents and braiding ropes. Only the occasional yak hide and some sheep's wool had made their way to town, as far as I had observed.

I had recently watched the men complete the shearing. They rounded up the sheep into a corral, which had once been 'houses' for the nomads during the Cultural Revolution. The ugly stone and concrete constructions looked like small railway arches, about twenty in a row. They punctuated the landscape all over Machu, like lines of abandoned gravestones. I found it difficult to believe that these tribal nomads, whose home was the land, had been forced to inhabit such dungeons. But today they had a new function. I had watched the sheep bleat and riot with brainless terror beneath the arches, as the men grabbed their horns and wrestled them, one at a time, to the ground. A man or boy stood on the horns while another sheared swiftly with huge scissors, sharpened with spit and stone. Once the wool had been cut, it was flung on to a huge pile and twisted into long skeins, while the sheep fled, bouncing comically into the air.

The family lived comfortably with none of the trappings of a materialist culture. They had a tape-recorder and sometimes bought cassettes of Tibetan music. Occasionally they bought new clothes or shoes, but normally it was the food and essentials with which the animals could not provide them: wheat or barley flour, rice, cabbage, spring onions, chillies, apples, oranges, watermelons, sugar, salt, matches, candles and, of course, tea. The nomads were big tea-drinkers. That was something we English had in common with them. In fact, it was so important to the nomads that in the nineteenth and early twentieth centuries, tea was compressed into bricks and used as currency. I had seen and tasted this brick-tea: it was a powerful brew made from the coarse leaves and twigs of the shrub, which had been steamed, weighed and squashed so solidly into bricks that it had to be ripped apart with some force. The Amdo nomads did not drink butter tea, as their Lhasa neighbours did, but occasionally they added milk to the black broth in the kettle. All of the family's provisions were bought by the sackload and stored at the back of the tent, apart from the vegetables, which were kept in a tin box in the corner and the fruit, which was devoured within half an hour. They always gave me a pile of apples to hide for myself before the children finished the lot.

They had few possessions and the ones they had were given away freely. If you admired something, they offered it to you with no qualms. Their Buddhist philosophy taught them the value of non-attachment to material possessions and I could see this clearly in their generosity. But the nomads also didn't like to be swindled by their Chinese neighbours and were shrewd at bartering. When it came to the animals, a man like Tsedo was no fool. He would try to make as much as he could from the sale.

The next day he left early with the doomed beasts. Sirmo, Shermo Donker and I were also bound for the town, but our trip was to be less harrowing. We girls were going shopping.

Since the women were rarely away from the tribe it was a treat, and in contrast to the sober mood the herd count had induced, we were all in high spirits.

After breakfast we dressed in our finery. It was important that we looked our best to go to town. Sirmo and Shermo Donker scrubbed their faces and rubbed lotion into their ruddy cheeks. They moistened their hair with a highly perfumed balm and combed it long and flat, until it shone with greasy brilliance. Then they wove it into two plaits, one over each shoulder and tied the ends together, before flicking it over their heads, down their backs. They rummaged around at the back of the tent under the plastic sheet and pulled their best *tsarers* and silk brocade shirts out of an old rice sack. These were never used for work. In contrast to their everyday clothes, these were vivid and lustrous. I watched them tying their sashes. Although she was tough, Shermo Donker was so petite I found it difficult to imagine that she had had three children. As she pulled the fabric tightly around her waist, I noticed that her hips were no bigger than a girl's. By contrast, Sirmo was taller and more voluptuous. Her full breasts quivered beneath her thin shirt as she deftly rearranged the tucks and layers of her *tsarer*, checking her back, measuring the front, until she was satisfied. They polished and put on their best shoes and, finally, retrieved their jewellery from a wooden box and strung the coral beads around their necks. Shermo Donker's necklace was a family heirloom given to her by her mother. Between the coral, there were enormous amber orbs, the size of cricket balls. Tsedo had lent me his coral necklace that day and I wore it proudly and conspicuously over the top of my red silk shirt. We giggled at our new-found splendour.

They saddled the horses and helped me to mount. I was

riding with Shermo Donker on Amnye's white horse, and Sirmo had the grey. They had placed a piece of foam mattress on the horse's rump for me to sit on and, for now, it felt comfortable. I put my arms around my sister-in-law's tiny frame and we set off at a gentle walk, the children running alongside laughing, the dogs barking. It was a bright, hot day. The crisp grass crunched beneath the horses' hoofs and skylarks started from their nests into the blue sky. In the distance, the rocky summit of Kula stood jagged and stark above us. We made for the road, stopping at the gate for Sirmo to dismount and let us through before closing it again behind her. If nothing else, the fences kept out the wolves. The nomads had strung pieces of fabric tightly over the gate to cover any holes the predators might squeeze through, and Sirmo was careful to replace them exactly as before.

Then we discovered we had an addition to our party. Cherger, the dog, had followed us to the boundary of our encampment, and when Sirmo ordered him to return to the tents, he stood obstinately wagging his tail. As we continued through the grassland, he trotted loyally alongside us. He was obviously familiar with the six-mile journey and fancied a day sniffing out a different environment. But when he heard a bus's engine he started barking. The white vehicle had turned off the dirt road from town and was now bumping over the pot-holed track through the grass towards the tents. As it neared us, I peered curiously through the tinted windows and was astonished to see the excited faces of a group of Chinese tourists. They were pointing at us, laughing, taking snapshots. I was filled with dread: they were on their way to the tribe.

I turned away and ignored them. The girls did the same. Tsedup had told me about this sort of thing. He remembered them coming when he was a boy. They had parked their bus in the middle of the tribe and flashbulbs flashed. Then the rain had come and they had sought refuge in Jerko's tent. The nomads hadn't understood why they were in the tribe, but had let them in and served them tea anyway. They had sat on the wooden *gamtuk*, containing the family's *tsampa*, and hung their socks over the fire to dry, both sacrilegious acts. They had not realised their errors, but Jerko's wife had been furious.

A few weeks ago I had witnessed other curious visitors to the tribe. Sirmo and I had been washing clothes in the stream, when a jeep pulled up and a voice cried, 'Hi, there!' It was an American accent but I didn't know the people inside. I had felt a curious sense of loathing and had turned away as two Chinese men got out and walked towards us, followed by a Tibetan, who had smiled in embarrassment at us and given a half-wave.

'Do you know them?' I had asked Sirmo.

'I don't know the Chinese. I know the Tibetan,' she had replied.

From their dress I had realised that they were not from America but were English-speaking tourists from one of the big Chinese cities. The Tibetan was their guide. Judging from the size of the lenses suspended around their necks, I knew what they had come for. They had instructed the guide to ask Sirmo if she would stand by her horse so that they could snap her. I had felt her reluctance as we sat huddled together in our *tsarers* and I did not want her to perform for them. She told the guide that she didn't want to be photographed so they had reluctantly taken a few pictures of her horse, said goodbye, then driven off to photograph the rest of the tribe.

I had been galled by their blatant voyeurism and insensitivity, yet found myself struggling with my identity. Was I a hypocrite? I had been photographing the family and the tribe at odd moments in their beautiful, traditional costume. I knew they were photogenic. I knew they were a curiosity, part of a world that we 'civilised' nations had lost in the frantic race for development. In that respect I knew I was no better than these tourists. But somehow it was different. I was a part of things, and not just objectively pointing a lens at *something* beautiful. I was trying to capture *someone*, a member of my family, whom I respected and loved. They had made me a part of them and I was honoured.

That morning, the vulgarity of the tourists' actions had made me feel more of a nomad than I had felt before. Yet I would never be one. I was under no illusions. I was a westerner living the life of a nomad. There was a big difference.

The tourists were soon forgotten and we strolled on horseback through the dandelions, fording pebbled streams and laughing at the prairie dogs, who stood alert, yapping on their hind legs, then scurrying into their burrows. Below us, to our right, the river meandered through the sun-dazed valley from the eastern horizon. On either side the mountains slipped to the valley floor and a white spray of cloud flecked the otherwise blue-blank sky. The dog trotted amiably at our side as we chattered in the saddle. We passed an old man on horseback, who smiled, and a couple of young boys on yaks, who nearly fell off when they saw me. Shermo Donker started to tease Sirmo. It appeared that she did have a loved one, after all, but she was not giving anything away. We pleaded with her to tell us, but she just smiled coquettishly from beneath the brim of her hat. The only details we could extract from her were that he was beautiful and he wore a big earring. I wondered if she was hoping to catch a glimpse of him that day.

Soon we rounded the brow of a hill and saw the town spread out before us in the distance. It was low-rise, clinging to the valley floor, its tiled roofs packed together. Only the post office stood sentinel in the crush of concrete, the sun blazing brilliantly on its blue-glass façade: a symbol of progress. To the north of the labyrinth of squat buildings, stood the scarlet archway built by the Chinese to signal the entrance to the town. Tiny trucks trailed dust along the gravel road into the distant mountain valleys. We trotted down the track on to the flat pasture. It was two hours since we had left the camp. The dry heat of the midday rays toasted our cheeks, as the flies droned and the horses swirled their tails.

At the first set of dwellings on the outskirts of the town, Shermo Donker and Sirmo pulled up beside a mud wall and dismounted. They helped me down from the saddle and I slumped, numb, to the ground. '*Tsanduk errgo?*' Sirmo asked, squatting in the ditch. I joined her, hitching up my skirts, then took the horses' reins so that Shermo Donker could relieve herself. This was an important pit-stop, I soon discovered. A trek across the grassland could play havoc with a girl's clothing and it just would not do to arrive in town without first smartening up. The next few minutes were spent nipping, tucking and tying until we all looked like new again.

We rode in like a scene from a Western, two abreast on the sandswept road, high in the saddle. The town was a dusty ramshackle of shops, restaurants, a market and street stalls all plying their trade. The buildings were concrete, some white-tiled, like a bathroom, some painted white with green and orange decorative borders under their eaves. Their doorways were crowded with goods, and people spilled out of watch-menders' and carpet-vendors' on to the pavements. A gang of Chinese schoolchildren in blue and white tracksuits ran from the gates, shouting hello. Nomads riding yaks jostled Han Chinese on bicycles. Sharp suits cruised on motorbikes through flocks of sheep. Muslim women bartered in black headdresses over wheelbarrows of fruit. Monks sat begging in burgundy robes at the market entrance, chanting prayers. Chinese pop and traditional Tibetan music pumped out from every doorway, while a shooting range emitted a relentlessly mundane, electronic refrain – *Kwan ying, kwan ying, kwan ying, kwan ying*.

We moved through the cacophony and came to rest at the crossroads in the centre of town. There we tied the horses to a telegraph pole and hobbled them as a small crowd began to form around us. I was obviously something of a spectacle: an old nomad couple cooed their satisfaction with my costume, grinning through blackened teeth; a group of Chinese workers in blue suits and caps stared, expressionless; a young nomad woman with fat, rosy cheeks and jangling earrings jabbered at me, throwing her hands in the air and squawking with delight. Shermo Donker took my arm and guided me across the road to a restaurant. We dived in as she cussed the dog, who was still following us. He lay down on the pavement to wait. Safe inside, she shouted for a jug of water and the Muslim waiter filled her bowl. As he walked back to the kitchen, she called, '*Arro! Tangwan!* Oi! Waiter!' He turned and she quick-fired her order in Tibetan while Sirmo gave hers in Chinese. I ordered a bowl of *tanthuk*, gesticulating the action of flicking dough pieces into water.

Sirmo translated. The restaurant was one big room with Formica walls and four tables. A mirror spanned one wall and a bar stood opposite. The sunlight filtered through the net curtains and formed doily patterns on the yellow linoleum floor. A couple of nomads stared, unblinking, at us as they slurped their noodles and smoked simultaneously in the corner. Off the main room were four doors leading to smaller, private dining rooms. This was a common feature of Chinese restaurants, as most people preferred to eat discreetly, especially the officials, who would carouse for hours. But there were no restrictions and anyone could relax in seclusion with friends or family.

As if on cue, the door to one of these rooms opened and Tsedup walked out. He was wearing his *tsarer* and a cheeky grin of surprise on his face. I had not seen him since yesterday and was amused to find myself blushing with pleasure at the sight of him. He was followed by his younger brother, Gondo, and as they were both a little bleary-eyed, I concluded that they had probably been ruminating over a bottle of rice wine in the confines of their shady room. There was a lot to catch up on. They sat with us for a while, smoking and teasing us, as we devoured our food. Then they paid for it quietly, and left to wander the streets. I felt like a young girl who had bumped into her boyfriend. It wasn't the done thing for men and women to hang out together here. Even if I had wanted to, I wouldn't have gone with him: today was our girls' day out and I had no intention of deserting the side.

When we had finished and Shermo Donker had licked her plate clean, we stepped out into the street. Shopping was a serious business and these women were no different from me when it came down to a bit of retail therapy. Soon I was being steered from shop to shop as they examined, prodded, poked, measured and tasted. They were like methodical housewives in the January sales. No shopkeeper was going to get the better of Shermo Donker. She was a seasoned professional at bartering and pulled me away from any purchases she deemed unreasonable. She knew the Chinese traders were out to make a fast buck from someone like me. They ushered me into their shops, eyes glinting, rubbing their palms together. Everywhere we went people asked the same questions: 'Is she married? How old is she? Does she have children?' She evaded their impertinence with a swift retort of 'She's a *namma*,' implying that I had just got married and didn't have children yet. But the pressure was on. A woman of thirty with no brood was unheard-of. In the street the nomads stared amazed as I wandered conspicuously through the small crowds, feeling uncomfortable. Some old men stood transfixed, staring blankly at me, and I wondered what they were thinking. Some women, who had heard about the English bride, stopped to point and exclaim quite vocally to their friends, 'Look, *namma*!' I was really under the microscope. Most of the old nomad women smiled at me, examining my costume, murmuring, 'Sweet.' I was touched that they acknowledged my attempts to assimilate with their way of life. When they chatted to me and discovered I spoke a little of their language, they were even more delighted. It was strange to them that I wanted to be a part of their culture. In Machu only a few Chinese spoke the Amdo dialect: they saw it as the responsibility of the nomads to learn Mandarin, and the nomads assumed that a foreigner such as myself would demand the same. I was a mystery, a phenomenon, a friend.

Still, it was important to keep moving. If I stood for any

time on one spot in the street, a small crowd would rapidly form around me, a sea of unabashed, staring eyes. It was tolerable for a short time and I would perhaps focus on some distant space or pretend to be absorbed in examining an interesting purchase. Then I knew it was time to move on. But I couldn't blame them for staring: this place was so remote that the locals had rarely seen a western face. Perhaps a handful of tourists each year would venture this far into the wilderness. Also many of the nomads hardly ever came to town as their encampments were often far away, so I understood their bewilderment at witnessing, probably for the first time, a white face, a long nose, eyes like marbles.

We took a break from the shopping in a poky wooden shack, where Shermo Donker barked for three plates of *rungpizz*. The cold ribbon noodles, covered in tofu, chilli, garlic and vinegar, were delivered to our table by a surly Muslim woman. She flung the plates down in front of us and Shermo Donker scowled and snapped at her carelessness. The woman snapped back. *Rungpizz* was the nomad women's favourite afternoon snack and was called 'the women's *tuckpa*' by the men. It was hastily devoured by Sirmo and Shermo Donker, who sucked on the slippery noodles, splattering juice liberally on the plastic tablecloth and wiping their chins with the back of their hands. I did the same, but nearly choked as the hot chilli stung my throat. '*Ka tsag!*' They giggled. 'Mouth hurts.' The nomads had a high tolerance for chilli, which sadly I lacked. I drank some water and paused to catch my breath.

Outside a Chinese man in a cap and blue jacket was selling chickens from a wheelbarrow. They were crushed into cages, piled three deep, squawking and flapping pathetically. A small boy was prodding them through the bars and recoiled,

giggling, when they pecked him. I watched a Chinese customer arrive. The chicken-seller selected some birds and
pulled them from the cages for the man to look at, stuffing
them back when he seemed uninterested. Finally he chose
two birds. The chicken-seller strung them together by their
feet and suspended them upside down from the rod on his
scales. Then the man paid and squashed them into the front
pannier of his bicycle, one upright like a passenger, the
other upside down, and rode off past trucks full of yaks,
driven by Muslim slaughterers. That day, all manner of life
was doomed for the dinner table.

It struck me that the Chinese were especially cruel in their
treatment of the animals. Their methods were at odds with
the concerns of the compassionate nomads. I had witnessed
extreme examples of this, such as the fish outside the post
office. The nomads were appalled by the shallow basins of
river creatures gasping for life at the street-traders' stall.
They saw the fish as sacred. They would buy them from the
Chinese to put back in the river. Of course, the traders knew
this so they continued catching the fish. It was a profitable
business.

The dynamic between the three different peoples in the
town was intriguing. A fragile hierarchy supported a population that seemed to exist only by being tolerant. According
to the local guidebook, the Gannan Tibetan Autonomous
Prefecture (of which Machu was a part) had a population of
600,000, which was predominantly Tibetan, then Chinese,
with the remainder made up of other ethnic groups. The
book boasted a harmony of interests, due to the Communist
Party's policy on minority nationalities in the prefecture and
its open-door policy which, it claimed, saw that everyone
adhered to 'one central task, two basic points'. The central

task was the priority of animal husbandry, which was the major area of production, with cereal growing and forestry as its two sidelines. With 3 million livestock in the area, providing 30,000 tons of meat, 4,000 tons of milk, 1,000 tons of wool, 90,000 pieces of cattle hide and 29,000 sheepskins, it was not hard to see how important the nomads' lifestyle was to the local economy. Yet, on the social scale, as far as I could see, the Han Chinese condescended to the nomads, whom they saw as inferior and dirty. The Tibetans were disgusted by the Muslims' obsession with killing, and thus condescended to them. Meanwhile, the Muslims stuck together and profited from their astuteness for trade.

At the table in the noodle shack, I toyed with a yuan note. Like the guidebook, it celebrated the harmony of races with a picture of a Tibetan woman next to a Muslim, next to a Chinese, and a few words from their different languages. I paid the cheerless waitress with it and she scowled ungratefully.

That afternoon we bought needles, cotton, woven trim, shiny fabric, cooking utensils, a new basin for washing in, hair balm and soap. Sirmo treated herself to a tiny pot of face cream, and she and Shermo Donker bought identical new shoes for the winter. I bought a pink shirt, sweets and *wa ha ha*, small bottles of milk shake, for the children. We stopped at a hoop-la stall that had been set up in a courtyard and threw plastic hoops. Our neighbour won a wok. Sirmo missed a blanket by an inch. She was distracted: looking over her shoulder for a sign of 'the beautiful one with the earring'. It was getting late now and we still had to get to the jewellery shop. Cousin Dolma was waiting.

When we arrived she was standing, like a doll in her Tibetan costume, behind the glass case of treasures and ornate knives, chattering to the Chinese jeweller in her impish voice. She was the nomad women's contact for getting good jewellery made. Today Sirmo wanted her earrings changed to include more silver chains and coral, which Shermo Donker had given her. I had been given a lump of silver by Annay and Amnye to have my own earrings made. They thought it wrong that I didn't have any nomad jewellery. They wanted to spoil me. I chose some small turquoise stones and showed Dolma the design I had drawn up. Then she huddled in conversation with the jeweller, who winced at it through his eyepiece. He nodded his approval. Our new accessories would be ready in a week, Dolma twittered. Would we like to come back for dinner? She had just bought some meat. We declined politely, but walked with her back to the horses.

The streets were dim and most of the shops were closing. A few street-lamps were lit and straggling shoppers toiled home with their wares through the pools of light. Even the monks had ceased chanting at the market entrance. In their place, an old beggarwoman was sifting through a box of rubbish and bruised fruit, mumbling and cursing. We filled up the saddle-bags with our purchases and untied the horses. Shermo Donker gave me their reins and darted into one of the last open shops. She wanted to make the most of her freedom. It was already too late to get back in time for us to tie up the yaks. Indeed, I realised, she had had no intention of being early. Despite her conscientiousness, she was a rebel today.

Eventually we rode off in exuberant spirits out of the town and into the wide open spaces of the grassland. They teased me bawdily about the saddle sores between my legs and all the way home we sang to the sky and screamed the wild cries of the horse-racers, with shameless tongues. '*Ngoo sajer mek*!

You have no shame.' We laughed lustily. Women didn't do this sort of thing. Yet we were alone and who cared? It had been a great day out. We laughed until the sun fell over the snow mountain, until all I could see was the white of the horse's hide as the ground spun beneath me in the blackness. Then all I could sense was the homely scent of smoked dung on the night air.

# TEN

## *Holiday*

There had been an accident. Tsedup was in hospital. I searched Rhanjer's face as he tried to explain. Tsedup hadn't come home to the tent the night before. I had assumed that a day out with his teenage brother had disintegrated into a *piju*-potent sleep as I had stood in the twilight tying up the yaks, looking at the road. I made excuses for them: it was best that they had stayed in the town: Tsedup was a novice motorbike rider and it had probably been too dark to make the return journey.

That night I had a nightmare about a mutilated dog and woke in a sweat to a yak head-butting the tent. As I crept outside into the dawn, it had thundered off with a sharp thwack of the tent rope. At breakfast, we heard the familiar buzz of a bike-engine and I thought it would be my husband. It was not. A messenger had come from town. We should leave now. Amnye said the dog dream had been a sign. I felt sick as I ran to our white tent for my bag.

I sat numbly on the back of Rhanjer's bike. I hadn't really understood much of what he had said to me in the tent. How serious was it? It was so difficult at times like this, not speaking the language. It was easy to get confused or worry needlessly, I reasoned, but a sense of panic was rising in my gut. I felt powerless. At home in England I would be able to cope with a crisis. I understood how to get help, where to go, how to try to make things better. Here I was lost. I was completely reliant on Tsedup's brothers. I knew they were protective and well organised – it was the Tibetan way: when all around you appeared to be chaos, there were always forces at work to pull the whole thing together at the last minute. Everyone relied on each other. I prayed that everything would be all right as we sped along the road above the river valley. The river glistened as usual. The sun shone as usual. But everything might have changed.

We arrived at the hospital to discover that Tsedup and Gorbo had been discharged and were directed to an out-building. That was a good sign, I thought. There was a row of small bungalows under some trees at the back of the hospital, where the doctors lived. The bikes tore up the gravel as we skidded to a halt. Rhanjer and Tsedo led me inside. It was the home of a relative, a Tibetan doctor at the hospital. He was bent double, cleaning some bowls under a dripping tap inside the glass porch. Geraniums stood along his shelf. Inside it was dark. The first person I saw was Gorbo.

He sat in a chair, attached to a drip, his face stitched and caked in bloody scabs. He was wearing an eye-bandage and looked at us sideways through his good eye as we walked in. I gasped. Tsedup sat on a bed to our side, his own face battered and scarred, with black circles beneath both eyes. On the floor, covered by a blanket, lay the inert body of our friend Tsempel. For a moment I thought he was unconscious, but as he raised his head to gasp his greeting, he revealed a lack of front teeth. I was in shock.

'It was dark. Three of us on the bike . . . drunk . . . a concrete block in the middle of the road . . . lights didn't work . . . over the handle-bars . . . thought he was dead . . .' Tsedup was mumbling the story through bruised lips. It seemed that he was all right and I was relieved, angry and sorry for them all at the same time. I wanted to scream at Tsedup for being irresponsible, but I shut up and braced myself for Rhanjer and Tsedo to chastise him instead, as older brothers did. But they all started laughing. Even the doctor was in stitches.

'It's not funny.' I glowered at Tsedup. 'Your brother is bad,' I said to Gorbo.

'*Shagga*. He's good,' he said loyally, grinning through the dried blood.

No one was listening to me.

The men went out and bought some beers, then sat on the steps of the porch as Tsempel lay sedated on the bed and Gorbo slept in the chair. I relented and joined Tsedup and the others when I had cleaned some blood off the casualties' faces. As I drank my beer, Tsedup cast me sheepish glances. Of course I could forgive him. I could forgive him anything when he looked at me like that. I was just thankful that he was alive.

Later that day we brought the two brothers home in a three-wheeled *tolla*. Strangely they hid under their *tsarers* as we drove through the town. I realised it was a ploy to prevent idle gossip. If they were spotted, a rumour might circulate that they had been in a fight. It would be wrong to disgrace the family. Annay and Amnye had not been to the hospital and would be waiting anxiously, I thought. Annay will cry. Amnye will scold. When we finally pulled up outside the tent in the late-afternoon sunshine, they came out laughing with relief. I was having a tough time predicting people's responses. They seemed to make light of everything. It must be the nomad way. Or so I thought.

When I had got over the shock, I realised that Tsedup had precisely five days to recover before our friends arrived. Ells and Chloë were coming to see us from England and we were due to pick them up in Labrang by jeep. Tsedup spent the next few days lying in the tent next to Gorbo; we nursed them and watched their faces emerge from under the purple, green, then yellow bruising. Each morning, noon and night I bathed Gorbo's swollen eye and it gradually deflated from the size of half a tennis ball to normal. He insisted on picking off his scabs, which left his skin covered in pink patches. Then I was given the unenviable task of removing his stitches. He wouldn't go back to the doctor; he wanted me to do it, he said. They seemed to see me as a Florence Nightingale figure. Still, I found that removing stitches was much easier than I had thought and even quite pleasurable. As I worked, I teased him about our friends arriving.

'Your bride is coming!' I said. 'Ells wants a husband. She'll give you a big kiss!'

He recoiled, then grinned mischievously. 'I'll hit her with the lump of steel I use to hit the dogs with,' he threatened. Girls were still a mystery to Gorbo, but he had to appear knowledgeable and stay cool. I knew all about this from having a brother, and Gorbo reminded me of Phil in his younger days. He had the same sharp tongue and challenging twinkle in his eye.

Oddly Gorbo and Tsedup's adventure had brought them closer together. They lay chatting and laughing in the tent together while Annay fussed around them. Tsedup had left for India when his brother was only four and now he was getting to know him. They were proud of each other.

One morning we were invited to Tsedup's uncle's tent.

'You go,' Tsedup said. 'I can't, because it'll make my scars worse.'

'Why?' I said, not quite happy to go alone, and wondering what on earth he was talking about.

'Because I have to bite a chunk out of their fireplace,' he stated matter-of-factly.

I'd heard it all now. 'What?' I exclaimed.

'I can't be bothered to go through with all that,' he replied lamely.

'You and your bloody superstitions!' I stalked off leaving him frowning after me.

But I had been unfair. Later, in more generous spirits, I would learn that it was indeed as he had said. According to nomadic custom, he was forbidden to join me unless he performed the ritual of biting a chunk out of his uncle's fireplace: the *jib*, fireplace, was protected by the family deity, which might be offended by his fresh scars and cause the family bad luck. If he bit the fireplace he would be demanding his rightful protection from the deity; his scars would not get worse and the family would not be punished. When he was feeling better, he performed the ritual at Annay

Urgin's tent next door. He entered, and before he said a word, he knelt down and bit a piece off the front of the clay fire and spat it into the ashes.

On the fifth day, when Tsedup was sufficiently rested, we rustled up a jeep from the mayor of the tribe to take us to Labrang. Ells and Chloë wanted to sample a couple of weeks of nomad life for themselves. They had been Tsedup's English teachers when in India and were among our closest friends – and I was looking forward to having a girlie chat. I sat in the back, bouncing through the landscape. We moved through lush green mountains to arable lowlands, where farmers were busy harvesting, past rows of *momo*-shaped barley bundles, beside which men and women scythed the crops and sat under umbrellas in the hot sun. We drove through villages of clay built hovels and changed down a gear to negotiate the mass of yellow straw spread on the road by the farmers. Meanwhile, piglets scurried on to the verge and a lazy horse refused to move from its resting place in the middle of the road. I ducked down in the back when we passed through the town where we had previously been stopped by the police. Then we passed rows of ploughed soil and planted steppes, a satellite dish balanced on a rickety stone house, clay settlements and strings of rain-washed prayer flags, patchwork hillsides, cattle corrals and holy mountain upon holy mountain, with *ndashung* standing sentry on each peak. We crossed white picket bridges and glistening streams, passed nomads wandering on the long, open road, and lethargic Chinese road-workers feigning industriousness with cocked spades and copious tea-breaks.

We met the girls in a side-street cluttered with ramshackle guest-houses and ran towards each other with all the melo-drama of a Bollywood blockbuster. Then, after they had got over the shock of Tsedup's scarred face, we all settled into the cool of their hotel room. It had been a long time since I had talked in depth to anyone of the same sex and the joy of speaking my own language was indescribable. Also, I had been living in the tent for so long now that I had almost forgotten the pleasure of sitting in an armchair and reclined, sighing with pleasure, as they spilled out the goodies they had brought from England. Sadly for them I was immune to the wonders of anything, except the chair. Even the scrumptious biscuits lay unopened on the table. I had lived without such trappings for so long that they no longer tempted me. Among the items they had carted lovingly across China were boxes of packet soup, soap, a huge mountain of books, a bottle of champagne from our friend Tenzin – we would save that for a special day – and magazines, one sporting a semi-naked woman on the cover. I tore out the page inside that revealed a little more than was necessary – a small dose at a time of western anatomy for the tribal elders. Censorship was a must if I was to protect them from the wantonness of my culture. I pored over the pages of the magazines, discovering a world I had forgotten. I learnt that kitten heels were in, and that black was out. I enjoyed the glossy images, but had trouble finding a relevance to them now.

Then Ells inspected my neck, gave me her washbag and pointed to the door. 'Shower. Now!' she commanded. Her father was in the army. The layer of grime that I had been lovingly cultivating for the past few months would have to go, along with leg hair of unmentionable length. So far I had only escaped once to de-fuzz. Ells was here to instil some order.

The next day we drove back to the tribe listening to some

strange Moroccan music the girls had brought with them, which they proclaimed 'atmospheric'. I don't know what the driver thought of it, but he seemed happy to experiment. We stopped beneath some rocky mountains on the way and Ells, overcome with emotion, cried at the beauty of her surroundings. When we finally arrived home in the tribe, the family ran out of the tent to greet their guests. Everyone except Gorbo, of course, who had mysteriously disappeared, fearing that he would be devoured by his 'bride'. He didn't know how these weird English people would behave and he wasn't going to risk it. Ells and Chloë were ushered inside, where they took pride of place by the fire. Annay served them tea and they sat in embarrassed silence as everyone stared at them. It was difficult being scrutinised at such intimate quarters and I knew how they felt, for that had been me, not so long ago. On the journey, Tsedup had taught them how to say, 'Hello, how are you? I am very happy to be here,' at their instruction, but they had forgotten it in the rush of emotion. They both spoke a bit of the Lhasa dialect, but nobody understood that here.

'*Arro,*' they said instead, flushing crimson.

'Hello, dog!' replied Tsedo, grinning.

These were the only two English words I had so far managed to teach him, though I had not intended him to use them simultaneously. He was well aware of his clever joke, though, and the whole tent burst into laughter. As I had discovered, a nomad needed little excuse to tease and the girls were going to have to get used to it. Rhanjer asked for their passports and examined them in his usual, serious way. He asked about each country they had visited, what it had been like. He was fascinated by the world and everything in it. So was Ells. Tsedup's job as translator was thus secured. I hoped he wouldn't tire of it too quickly over the next couple of weeks as Ells and Rhanjer became more and more animated: he thirsty for new knowledge, she characteristically happy with her role as informant. Ells was a formidable talker.

We talked long into the night, then settled them into their white tent. It had been especially lent by Tsedup's uncle, Gombo Sonnam, who had also made a clay fire for them inside. It was a splendid home and we all tucked under the quilts and listened to Tsedup strumming the guitar and Ells's voice until the small hours. Then, after squatting together under the stars, which we would not have done in England, and concluding that, in Chloë's words, we were now 'closer than close', we retired for the night. I was glad to have them there.

Since they had come so far to see us, Tsedup thought it was only right that he plan some excursions for them. The next day he went off to make some arrangements in town, leaving us to amuse ourselves. They wanted to go for a walk, so I suggested we go down to the Yellow river for a dip. Nomads don't walk anywhere – why walk when you have a horse, yak or motorbike at your disposal? Still, they felt protective enough to accompany us through the minefield of mastiffs. Amnye was worried. 'Be careful,' he warned, as we tripped off through the grasses.

But by the time we got to the river, we were too shy to go in. About six or seven young men from the tribe had chaperoned us and were now sitting impassively on the bank, smoking. They stared at our white legs as we paddled pathetically. Since we were all dressed in our Tibetan *chubas* (Lhasa-style dresses), swimming would involve stripping to our underwear, which none of us felt comfortable about. I hadn't seen any Tibetan women swimming here. Instead we watched the men splashing self-consciously and flexing their muscles. They really were a vain bunch.

No women played volleyball either, but somehow that afternoon we found ourselves invited to join a game in the middle of the tribe. It seemed that different rules applied to us. We tried to convince Sirmo to accompany us, but she declined and for the first time I felt uncomfortable with my role. I was aware that I needed to maintain an air of respectability and behave like the other women as much as I could, but the presence of my English friends meant that I was having to compromise my position. It was dawning on me that we Englishwomen occupied some sort of middle ground between the sexes here. With the women, I had been comforted to discover that despite our cultural differences there were universal female characteristics that bound us. Yet as foreign women we were able to enjoy similar freedom to the men, which set us apart from the nomad women. We drank beer, enjoyed the occasional cigarette, sat on the wrong side of the fire. It was complex. In the end I sat and watched most of the ball game. I was rubbish anyway.

In the evening the girls played with the children, who adored them, and, determined to get to grips with nomad life, helped tie up the yaks. Shermo Donker and Sirmo giggled as Ells chased them through the mud. Needless to say, it was harder than they had thought.

'Do you miss England?' Chloë asked.

It didn't take me long to reply. 'No,' I said.

We stood staring at the blaze of golden cloud, dazzling the vermilion horizon, our breath clouding, watching Ells spinning the children round, laughing. I think they both knew exactly what I meant. That evening was as seductively beautiful as every evening in this strange land. They, too, were falling under its spell.

A few days later, we found ourselves honoured to be accompanying the men up to the summit of Amnye Kula. For a woman to climb a holy mountain is a sensitive issue and the brothers had agreed that we could go, provided we did not climb on to the offering site or participate in the ritual for fear of offending the mountain god. Tsedup, Tsedo, Gondo, Cumchok (their monk brother), Samlo (Rhanjer's son), Tsering Tashi (our neighbour) and Tsering Samdup (Tsedup's sister Dombie's husband) were all escorting us. Our convoy left the encampment early that bright morning armed with tent poles, bread, dung and a rifle: essentials for a night in the wilderness. We trailed through the dewy valley and through a deep gorge of fresh spring water, as the mountains closed in around us. These guys knew how to ride. They guided the horses with such adept ease and grace, and as we ascended the sheer slopes, they wove a lateral path through the dense scrub for us to follow. The girls were also experienced riders. I was undeniably the worst. My bravado went when I was unable to grasp the infinitely subtle complexities of using the reins. My horse got bored and confused by my ineptitude and began to stumble and descend. Below me the ground receded into a dizzy kaleidoscope of scrub, rocks and gushing water as the poor beast struggled to find a foothold. Tsedup attempted to save me, but his frisky horse refused to obey him and he fell down the slope, the horse tumbling after him. He wasn't crushed, just swung himself back into the saddle, swearing, but I was terrified. If he couldn't stay in the saddle, there was little chance for me. Thankfully, Gondo, with more sense than I and with the aura of an experienced mustang drover, took my reins and led me the rest of the way to our base camp, where I slipped gingerly from the saddle with aching knees. I was disappointed not to have impressed them with my equestrian skills, but told myself that for me, on my second ride, to try to compete with men who had been born in the saddle was ludicrous.

They erected the white tent and we continued up to the craggy heights of the mountain top, abandoning the horses when the route became inaccessible for them. The rest of the way we managed on foot, scrambling among the shale and rocks, pausing to gasp for oxygen, which was sparse at this altitude. The view from the summit took our breath away. Below us was the great grassy desert of our home. Beyond, the Machu river snaked between the flatland and the undulating mountains, which receded into an azure horizon. The tribe's tents formed a circle in the middle of the scene, smoke drifting from each tiny roof and the black and white dots of yaks and sheep formed pointillist brush marks on the canvas.

We were making history. No woman had ever before set foot on Amnye Kula. We sat in silence on a rock beneath the men, and as I watched the rain-stained prayer flags fluttering in the wind, I felt a deep sense of humility. Rhanjer and our neighbour, Namjher, had arrived on horseback at the summit, from the east. We sat and watched as the men heaped their offerings of *tsampa* and butter on to the platform of rocks and soil and lit a fire underneath using sheepskin bellows. Each one began to mutter rhythmically, calling on the mountain spirit to protect them. Some were more vocal than others, crying out then resuming a hypnotic chant, delivering their own personal messages to the mountain. All the while they tossed into the sky fistfuls of wind horses, which caught the breeze and danced down into the dark valley behind Kula. Namjher fired off a round from his pistol and they all fell silent as we sat among the paper snow, watching the black stormclouds roll in from the northern mountain range.

We returned to our camp and lit a fire, which proved difficult as it had begun to hail gently. We girls bundled up in blankets inside the tent, while the boys braved it, squatting in their *tsarers* around a bubbling cauldron of tea. Then the sky sealed over in a thick, grey shroud and the wind quenched the thin flame. Most of the men set off for home on horseback, leaving seven of us to brave the night. Tsedo sat for the remainder of the afternoon feeding the fire with the bellows, hunched in the snow in his *tsarer* and Stetson. He didn't seem ruffled, just puffed at his cigarette for hours, and I realised that this was no big deal for him. A bit of light snow and a sharp wind were nothing compared to a harsh Tibetan winter in the mountains with his flock, where temperatures can reach below zero.

That night was a veritable *tuckpa* of arms, legs and feet. The tent, which had been made to sleep two comfortably, now seemed inadequate. The competition for space under Ells's British army-issue survival blanket, which resembled a sheet of tinfoil, was tremendous. We had consumed the bottle of Veuve Clicquot that they had brought and were comfortable for about an hour, until its effects had worn off. I lay contorted in the dark, remembering the last time I had drunk champagne. It was at a celebrity-packed party for the magazine at the Mirabelle. I had worn my wedding *chuba* and the massive coral ring Annay had sent me. Lying on top of the holy mountain, I felt divorced from that previous world. I came round to the poke of a toe in my bottom. Reality was a cauldron of tea, more bread and a wet tent full of nomad cowboys.

Midway through our pretence at slumber, Chloë and I needed to relieve ourselves. We slunk out of the tent into a pea-souper of a fog and, as we squatted in the blackness, were alarmed to hear horses and men's voices. Then a gunshot. We tugged at our jeans as torchlight pierced the mist and swung in our direction. Petrified, we split for the tent only to meet Tsedo, rifle in hand, reassuring us that it was only some wandering nomads who had stolen some yaks and were transporting them under cover of night. A restful night's sleep was thus assured.

We woke again at daybreak, disentangled and washed in the mountain stream. After more tea we took down the tent and saddled up. The men led us down the sheer mountainside by the reins, as we lay horizontal in the saddle for balance. Back on flat valley ground, Tsedo shot a prairie dog for no particular reason. It seemed that despite his compassion for the sheep he killed, he also enjoyed the odd hunt. This was a man's world, and although we girls were appalled by his savagery, there was something about the masculinity of it that appealed.

A few days later we made a pilgrimage to a religious festival. But it was not an average pilgrimage, as we soon found out. The town of Tugsung Lhamo was two hours away by road, and on that chilly morning, about twenty bikers converged on the crossroads in the middle of Machu, revving their engines. Everyone was dressed in their *tsokwas* with their heads wrapped in balaclavas and scarves. Tsedo and Gondo took Chloë and Ells on the back of their bikes and I hopped

on behind our friend Wharden. We sped out of town in a
convoy, straight through a swollen river, lifting our feet in the
air to keep from getting soaked. Gondo, feeling particularly
chivalrous, commandeered a passing horse from a nomad
and ferried Chloë across. All the way, the boys overtook
each other, speeding forward then dropping back. I passed
Ells who grinned excitedly, cheeks flushed, clinging on for
dear life. She had developed a Tom Cruise fixation and
was singing the theme tune to *Top Gun* right into Tsedo's
ear. 'Take my breath away,' she wailed, before the wind
choked her.

Tugsung Lhamo was an old town that nestled in the
crook of a green valley, and spread on up a hill to where
its monastery stood. When we arrived it was packed with
pilgrims. They had come from far and wide for the annual
event, Rughda, and were all dressed in their finest costumes
and jewellery. We followed the train of chattering people up
through the town, over the bridge of a stream and past white
*chortens* until, breathless, we reached the top. The monastery
and its surrounding buildings resembled those I had seen in
Labrang. Their white walls sat close together in a jumble of
dwellings. Opposite the main monastery building was a steep
slope where everyone had congregated under the tall pine
trees. Men, women and children jostled for a patch of ground
so that they could see the performance. In the courtyard of
the monastery in front of us, rows of magenta-clad monks
were sitting on the steps under the huge black banners of
the overhead balconies.

In the cobbled square two monks, dressed in yellow, were
dancing. As they spun round, their skirts spread like twirling
umbrellas and they stared out at the crowd through the
white-painted eyeballs on their brown masks. They were

enacting the story of Milarepa and a monk bellowed a stream of dialogue through a loud-hailer, as the cymbals crashed wildly. It was the tale of a wandering yogi, who moved from cave to cave covered with rags, eating only nettle soup. He was a Tibetan peasant who, in the eleventh century, attained Buddhahood by practising tantric meditation while sitting in one cave for twelve years. The monk spoke of Milarepa's magical powers, of how he had walked through rock, flown in the sky, eaten stone. Then more monks came on, dressed as a deer, a dog and a hunter to perform the Deer Dance. The monk bellowed louder into the speaker, telling the story of the deer that dropped exhausted at Milarepa's feet one day while he was meditating in a cave in Nepal. It was pursued by a hunting dog that gave up its chase and lay down quietly. Then the hunter arrived and was converted by the holy man. The hunter spread Milarepa's fame throughout the land of Nepal.

Then they took us to see the holy cave. Long ago, it had been the lair of the last tiger in the area and a place of worship. It was how the town had acquired its name, for Tugsung means 'tiger's lair'. We walked up the other side of the hill past temples with rows of painted prayer wheels, turning each one and muttering, '*Om mani padme hum*', as they creaked and rattled on their axes. Small wooden hutches stood on stilts in the stream to our left and Tsedup explained that they were also prayer wheels, driven by the water. Soon we came to a tall cliff, surrounded by pines that sighed and rustled in the drizzly air. At the foot of the cliff, hundreds of *ndashung* speared the ground in a thick cluster and we realised that we had reached the tiger's lair. All around the bottom of the cliff were recesses containing *tsa tsa*, small triangular clay icons, a few inches high, depicting the Buddha, formed from a bronze mould and sun-dried. Around these were piles of *mani* stones, rocks that pilgrims had carved with sacred syllables. The white rock face was covered with the same brightly coloured mantras: huge '*om*' symbols scrawled like sacred graffiti. We squirmed into the cave mouth, only about a foot high, and ducked under the low crags, into the damp blackness. Someone lit a match and the flame cast eerie shadows around the walls of the deep, low cave. It felt strange to be inside the lair of a fierce beast and even though I knew it had been empty for a long time, I still felt the hairs on the back of my neck quiver.

On the journey home the wind drove like knives into our legs, and we were nearly attacked by mastiffs as we drove past a tribe whose encampment was close to the road. But safely back in Machu, we sat around the iron stove of a restaurant and ate huge, steaming bowls of *tuckpa*. It had been a good day, I said to Tsedup later. He looked at me earnestly, with a slight frown. 'You westerners are always measuring the days,' he said.

I hated being stereotyped. In fact, the girls' presence was making me realise a few things about myself. I was thrilled to have them here, but inside me there seemed to be some resistance to the little piece of England that they had brought with them. Things that had been part of my everyday vocabulary in London were now alien to my ear. As they talked, I was surprised by how my body bristled at the mention of Pizza Express, Camden Market, *lattes* in Ladbroke Grove and spritzers in Soho. It wasn't that I hated London, but I felt as if I was not in Amdo to reflect on the merits of McDonald's or the joy of a trip to Harvey Nicks. There was a clarity here that had been difficult to find in a throbbing metropolis. There was space, air and light. Time was only dictated by the circumference of the seasons and by the nomads' daily tasks of eating, milking the yaks in the morning, tying them up at night, preparing and collecting the dung. The most alien idea imaginable was of standing on the tube with my head in someone's armpit, crushed, breathless and late. Here, there was no late. It was only late when it was dark, but you were never late for anything. Vagueness pervaded. Maybe I will see you tomorrow, maybe not. No goodbyes when you left someone, you just went. This had been one of the most difficult things for me, as a western-bred person, to understand. But now, apart from mentioning that it had been a good day today, I felt as if I had slipped into that timelessness. I didn't want reminding of my hectic world. I was just content to be.

The next day the sun returned and we picnicked by the Machu river. We played tag like children, threw lizards at the boys and jumped into sand dunes. That night we went to a karaoke bar. The nomads sat uncomfortably under the neon bulbs as Chinese pop music boomed through the amplifier. Ells and Chloë were swept off their feet by many an obliging town boy. Gondo sat shaking, a cigarette butt in each ear, to block out the noise. Tsedup pleaded with me to make his brother dance with me. I had some trouble persuading him, but eventually he yielded and Tsedup laughed as I guided Gondo awkwardly round the floor. He had never danced before.

Later, they turned off the music and the nomads sang. Gondo might not have been a great dancer, but he was a formidable singer. He stood at the microphone, one hand cupping his cheek, his eyes closed. Everything stopped when he opened his mouth. No one talked, laughed, moved. The love song was plaintive; a deep yodel in his throat that echoed beyond that small room and out to the sleeping town. When I glanced at Ells and Chloë, their eyes were wet with tears.

Before they left there was another bike crash. We were all washing our hair in the stream's small waterfall. By this time, Ells had converted the men into glossy-haired, moisturiser-coated examples of maledom. Our neighbours were popping over for a shave. She had even located a shower in Machu town and insisted that, after she left, I went at least once a week. That day, she and I had been racing on the motorbikes in the grassland. We were going pretty fast and were impressed with each other, until it came to stopping. As we neared the bank of the stream, I remembered to brake, but forgot how heavy the bike was and fell off. Ells accelerated and flew over the handlebars on to the edge of the bank. She landed head first, knickers up, on the stones. We rushed into the stream and pulled the bike off her legs. Remarkably she was unhurt, thanks to a strong survival instinct – she had put out her hands to protect her head. This really wasn't the place for a major head injury. When we realised she was all right, we burst out laughing then made Sanjay promise not to tell anyone about it. Tsedup's father would be angry with him if he knew we had been allowed on the bikes. He was very protective of our guests. But back in the tent, Sanjay, a typical six-year-old, wasted no time in telling both Annay and Shermo Donker. 'You big mouth!' I said to him. He giggled and ran outside as we chased him. Tsedup was duly scolded.

When the girls left, in a trail of dust, I cried. Our 'holiday' was over. A piece of England had gone and a new phase would begin for me. The long autumn and winter lay ahead.

I would have to make the most of my female relationships here. Ells and Chloë had helped to reaffirm many of my good feelings for my new home, but now that they had left, I felt alone as I walked back into the town. They were part of my other life. They were the familiar, and even if that type of familiar had sometimes grated on me in this environment I knew that I would miss them.

I sat with the boys in a restaurant and we sipped tea quietly. 'Are you lonely?' they asked intuitively.

Tsedup, sensing my fragility, took me home on the bike. We made a detour on the way and, under the brilliant glare of the afternoon sun, we made love naked by a stream in the valley. Only the hawks watched us, spiralling lazily in the blue, as we lay together savouring the freedom, the breeze caressing our skin.

# ELEVEN

# *Blind Date*

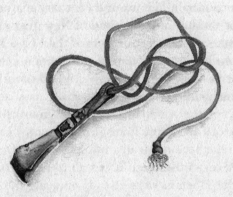

It was the end of September. Or perhaps October. I could never be sure. I had stopped measuring the days. To begin with I had kept my diary, but as one day drifted inconspicuously into the next, if I missed an entry I lost count. It was a strange feeling. Soon I felt the ridiculousness of monitoring each day as the family looked at my Filofax with bewilderment. It seemed out of place. When they saw all the phone numbers in the address section they were amazed. So many friends, they said. What they didn't grasp was that half of the numbers were required for the exhausting practicalities of urban living: the Gas Board, job contacts, pizza delivery. My only concession to time-keeping was my watch, which I could not abandon.

Of course they knew what date it was, but it wasn't the same: their time is laid down according to the sun, moon and the passage of the planet Jupiter around the sun, which marks a sixty-year cycle. Each sixty-year period is broken into five blocks of twelve solar years. Each year is named after an animal and an element, so that year, 1998, was the Earth Tiger year. Every year the most important festival, Losar, which usually falls around February, marks the annual passage of the sun and is a time of New Year celebrations. Around that time, the astrologers of the Lhasa Menzikhang are responsible for calculating next year's calendar. The solar year is divided into twelve lunar months and the Tibetans schedule all of their festival days according to the phase of the moon during these months. Many days are auspicious and some inauspicious. But my knowledge of their calendar system put an amusing perspective on the Millennium fever in the West. It was all rather inconsequential here, as the Tibetans were already enjoying the year 2125.

Without any real sense of time measurement I was learning to be more responsive to the changing seasons. One morning I woke, stepped out of the tent and turned to pass alongside the stream gushing freshly from a night of sky-falling. The sight of the snow-capped mountains sent my spirit soaring. I stood still for a moment and breathed in the moist air, watching the yaks grazing silently on the cloudy prairie. The land was changing. What had been a lush, emerald carpet flushed full with wild summer flowers of blue, violet and yellow, with skylarks whistling up out of their ground nests, was now a rough ochre expanse of autumnal shades. Welts of black earth and mahogany dung-spread patched the umber grass where the yaks were tied at night. Dotted about the encampment, like miniature mountains, were sculptured mounds of dung, taller than a man, some composed entirely of dense faeces, caked dry and smooth like an upturned mushroom head. Others were carefully constructed from dung pancakes, dried in the sun and arranged like intricate, vertical parquet flooring. Downwind the cliffs cleaved by the Yellow river stood like black scarps, shearing into the mud current that churned round the bend. The air was chilly these days and given to gusting under the lip of the *katsup*, threatening to carry off the tent on some blustery nights. We would huddle inside, drinking tea from soot-sprayed bowls, while outside the tethered yaks hugged the ground for comfort, those exposed at the end of a line catching the worst of it. For me, the component conspicuously missing from this autumn experience was the chorus of shivering leaves on creaking boughs, since as we were above the tree-line, there were no trees.

But winter had not yet taken a hold and we could still enjoy bright, hot days and sun-blistered cheeks. There was a change in the routine of the tribal workload. As we now had enough butter and cheese to last the winter, Amnye had given his permission for the yaks to be milked once a day only. Shermo Donker seemed happier. At this time the women were busy with textile chores and fuel preparations for the cold months ahead. Over the summer months they had collected yak wool in sacks and now they spun it into yarn for weaving. One morning, I helped Shermo Donker, Sirmo and our neighbour's daughter, Dolma. We emptied the raw fluff on to the tent floor and sorted and thinned it out by tufting it with our fingers, removing stubborn clumps and matted shanks. Then, inside the tent, I watched as they laid out yak skins to sit on, threw the good wool down and, with two long canes apiece, beat the hell out of it, until it rose and fell so lightly in the wake of each beat, it resembled spun sugar. Then they twisted it into stiff coils. All the while they joked and laughed until their cheeks flushed crimson and the sweat shone on their temples. What I could not gather of their conversation from my limited Tibetan, I could easily grasp from their blatant gesticulations and from their eyes, which sparkled with mischief. The topic, of course – what else when a gaggle of girls is out of earshot of their menfolk? – was sex. They were keen to draw me in and soon we were all hooting together. The black tent sucked in the heat of the noon sunshine and steep shafts of light cut through the roof, revealing the churning dust in the sweaty air. They became so hot that they took off their *tsarers* and sat on their knees in their leggings, teasing each other about the hottest parts of their anatomy, gesturing with their canes.

That day of the beating drums, of sweat and innuendo in the smouldering tent was revealing to me. Again I observed that although the women were quiet and obedient in front of the men, especially the older generation, at these times alone, they were bewitching, and their earthy humour was a welcome release. I was enraptured by them. They were clever, beautiful, spirited women, full of energy and life.

The next day they were up early spinning the yarn. They employed the children to sit in the hot sun and pull the strings of a small wooden instrument with raddles attached that turned on each tug, twisting the wool into a single-ply thin thread. The thread was gently eased away until the women stood at a distance of fifty metres, then trained straight over a pole and hook to keep it from the ground. When the yarn was plied they laid it on the grass to roll into a ball, then returned to repeat the process, until soon there were several tens of lines of black yarn stretched out on the ground.

Beyond the toil I could see our neighbour, Dolma, weaving a length of black fabric on a loom. It was triangular in shape, constructed of three vertical poles supporting a warp about a foot wide, which was spread flat on the ground. Bent double, she beat down the slack after each weft with enormous strength for such a slight girl, and as she worked she sang. Her voice carried to us on the westerly breeze. I joined her and she showed me how to do it.

I had studied weaving at university, but this was something else. With no treadle on the loom to pump with your foot, the fibrous yak yarn had a tendency to stick. To make a shed between the warp threads, I had to push a length of heavy wood between them and turn it upright, then slide the ball of weft through the space. Without a shuttle to feed the weft through, it was a laborious process. Still, I persisted and she laughed kindly at my efforts, sniggering and covering her impish face with her hand.

She was a cheeky girl of sixteen, with wide, almond-shaped eyes and red cheeks, which she diligently rubbed with white face cream. She wore a *rawa*, a length of red silk fabric embroidered with coloured stripes, which was sewn to the hair on the crown of her head and fell right down her back. Attached to the fabric were four huge, convex silver discs, covered in rich patterns. In the middle of each was a large coral stone. Above these were four smaller silver discs and three smooth amber stones set in silver. At the bottom of the fabric, five red tassels sprouted from thin silver tubes. Around her forehead she wore a *gorji*, a thick headband of huge lumps of old amber. This elaborate costume proclaimed her of pubescent and therefore, datable, age. She didn't wear it all the time, I presumed because it caused some discomfort, especially when it came to sleeping. Her mother, Annay Urgin, would sew it into her hair and she might wear it for a week or two, then take a break for a couple of weeks.

A few of the other girls in the tribe also wore *rawa*. The headpiece was handed down from mother to daughter throughout the generations. The girls would wear them for a year or two, then abandon them and begin to braid their hair in the style of the older women, with two plaits joined at the back. Until not so long ago the women wove their hair, in the traditional fashion, into 108 tiny plaits. That is a Tibetan's auspicious number, the length of their prayer beads. Tsedup remembered his mother having such elaborate hair, but today, although this hairstyle was still worn by some of the women I'd seen in Machu, it wasn't in our tribe, except for a special occasion, such as a marriage. It was considered too laborious a task.

Dolma and Sirmo were best friends. They were related too. Dolma's mother, Annay Urgin, was a real character. She had seven daughters by five different men and had never been married. This was not a problem in the tribe, although for Annay Urgin it was sometimes difficult because there were no men in the family to slaughter her animals. At these times she had to rely on Tsedo to help her. She lived next door to us with Dolma and her youngest daughter, Tselo, as all of her other daughters had married into other tribes and one daughter, Dado, was at school in Gannan. But despite the harshness of her existence, Annay Urgin never stopped laughing. She was the warmest and most earthy woman I had ever met. She was often in town visiting her sister, which left the tent empty for Dolma and Sirmo to have their sleepovers.

I had often heard them giggling long into the night, though exactly what they got up to was a mystery to me. If anyone knew about 'the beautiful one with the earring', it was Dolma. I asked her if she knew Sirmo's lover's name.

'Chuchong Tashi,' she said, tittering, as if she had betrayed a secret. 'He's very beautiful.' We laughed.

I was clearly becoming as fervent a gossip as the other tribeswomen. 'Does he have a good heart?' I asked. The nomads used this expression to mean 'kind'.

'A very good heart,' she confided.

I was satisfied. I had Dolma's testimony and was one step closer to uncovering the mystery, since Sirmo was not forthcoming.

That afternoon we made dung mountains. The children made round pancakes of dung and spread them out in rows to dry in the sun. Then we collected yesterday's, which were now biscuit crisp, and stacked them methodically, artistically too, on top of each other, like overlapping dominoes, twisting round and round until we had made a large cone. This ensured that the dung inside would stay dry and protected from rain during the winter months. When it was required the fuel would eventually be transported to the winter house in the valley, and also to Annay and Amnye's house in the town.

The rest of the day was devoted to felt-making. Amnye was spreading sheep's wool on to a plastic sheet beside the tent and sprinkling it with water. He rolled up the sheet as he went, until he had formed a long cylinder with all the wool wrapped inside. His job done, he retired to the tent to smoke and play cards with his friends. I joined Annay, Shermo Donker, Sirmo, Dolma and Dickir Che and we formed a line on our knees in front of the trunk of wrapped wool.

We rolled up our sleeves and began pummelling. Like all nomad tasks, it looked easy and, like all nomad tasks, it wasn't. The idea was to push the cylinder forward with the length of our forearms and let it roll back, rhythmically, with an even distribution of weight. Within a few minutes, I had developed a rash from the friction of the wool's coarse fibres on my work-shy, soft skin. But I laboured without complaint and accompanied the others as Annay led us in a counting song:

> Chick, ray
> Nyee, ray
> Sum, ray
> Jher, ray . . .

Little Dickir Che looked up at me and laughed as I started them all singing in English:

> One and
> Two and
> Three and
> Four and . . .

Even Annay was cackling and pummelling and struggling to form the words.

We continued in this fashion for an hour or so, until the welts on my arms had formed welts of their own. My face was stinging from the heat of the afternoon sun. Their familiarity with the outdoor life had given them naturally ruddy cheeks, but I resembled a lobster. They urged me to stop and go and rub on some butter to soothe my skin, while they saw the job through until nightfall.

The autumn heat had not only fired the women, as I had seen the day before, it seemed to have brought about a rise in activity among the teenage boys of the tribe. I was beginning to notice a pattern to each evening. On one particular night after dinner in the tent, a few boys turned up. They had come for Gorbo. They sat with us and ate as they waited. One was Wado, a tall lad with a permanent gormless grin. He was a bit of a clown and looked far more clueless than he was. His father, Athung, had been brought up with Amnye, and Gorbo and Wado were cousins. Tonight, under his *tsarer*, he sported a garish, silky, flower-patterned shirt that he had instructed his mother to make for him from a scarf he had bought in town. He felt rather special, but his new look caused an uproar in the tent. Tsedo and Tsedup teased him and slapped his back. '*Yucka!*' they cried, choking and spluttering on their noodle soup. He continued to grin gormlessly.

Accompanying him was Rinchen, Shermo Donker's youngest brother and a real Artful Dodger. He stood sniggering and hanging on to the tent pole by the fire. His head was covered in stiff stubble with bald patches where the razor had gone too far. He sniffed intermittently and wiped his nose with the back of his grubby hand. He had the same wide mouth as his sister and a huge silver hoop hung from his earlobe. He was fourteen but looked about eleven, such was his diminutive size, and this was his first night out with the older boys: his initiation. He was nervous. Tsedo and Tsedup gave him beer then spent the next hour teasing him as he reeled drunkenly, guffawed loudly and puffed on a cigarette, attempting to look grown-up. Meanwhile, Gorbo rummaged around quietly in the drawer under the altar and found what he had been looking for. He knew that Ells had given some perfume to Sirmo and, rising awkwardly from the corner of the tent, he moved among us in a pungent cloud of Chanel No. 5. This produced more laughter from the family. The boys were really going for it that night. They were on for a serious *hornig*.

*Hornig* was the nomads' dating game. I had laughed when I had first heard the word as it sounded strangely familiar. These boys were indeed horny as hell. Their task was to set off into the night on horseback or on a yak and seek out young girls in their tents at night. They often travelled miles under the stars if they had heard of a particularly beautiful young girl who lived in another tribe. Or they might have glanced at her in town or on the open road. The trick was to find one who was not 'locked in'. If a girl was locked in, it meant that her parents were in the tent with her. She could not be wooed. I had heard tales of boys being chased away by fathers wielding knives and throwing cooking pots. It was best to be careful. But the real art to entering a tent was to get past the mastiffs, a potentially life-threatening task. The boys each carried a *chukgor*, a steel weight on the end of a long leather thong, which they swung round threateningly in huge arcs as they approached the dogs on horseback, creating a path as the animals snapped crazily at their heels. When a dog got too close, its strangled cries rent the night sky.

A boy's second most prized possession was his torch. He was lost without it. Once inside the tent, he would seek out his loved one among the mass of her sleeping brothers and sisters, then silently lie down beside her. He would wake her and, if she liked the look of him, he would be permitted to stay. If not, he would be told to get lost and his quest would be over before it had even started. This was the young Romeo's first hurdle. It was easy to see how *hornig* might be a soul-destroying experience for less attractive wooers. But if a boy was considered desirable he would stay and talk with the girl, perhaps sing her an Amdo love song. Thus it was also imperative that he could sing. A girl would often judge him on the quality of his voice and those with a bad ear were at a major disadvantage. Despite the pitfalls, there were no hard and fast rules to *hornig*. A boy could roam freely until dawn from tent to tent, night after night, in the most promiscuous fashion, or he might find love and return again and again to the same girl. This was how the nomads eventually found a marriage partner.

For me, *hornig* seemed so mysterious and romantic. Here were all the ingredients of a first-rate drama: secrecy, danger, love and courage. I had visions of battling dogs, swaying torchlight and love songs whispered on young lips. Even these young boys, so unpractised in the art of seduction, were gallant in a way that had become old-fashioned in the West; this kind of custom did not translate into my culture. There, the most the average teenage girl could hope for was the promise of a slow dance and a grope in the dry ice at the local disco. As the boys swaggered out of the tent that night, I wished them luck and wondered what it was like for them to brave the night.

Perhaps I would never have found out if Tsedup hadn't stayed in town one night the next week, for then I shared my tent with Sirmo. As we lay down together, I noticed that she had on all of her jewellery, which I found curious. She usually placed the enormous coral beads and silver earrings by her pillow at night when she slept in the main tent. Still, I was green in these matters and didn't question her. We gossiped under the covers until I slipped into a deep slumber. Later, I woke in the darkness and heard her whispering to herself. Then I heard a young man's voice whispering back. At first I thought it must be her brother, Tsedo, but the voice was not sonorous or deep. It was the voice of a young man, not more than twenty perhaps, and they were talking to each other at great length. There was a man in our tent! Could it be Chuchong Tashi, the beautiful one with the earring? He was behind us, very close. I could feel the pressure of his head or his arm on the sheepskin pillow between us. I thought him most brave to have dared to enter the tent in the dark with me there and most stealthy to have reached his position of intimacy close to her by the tent wall. I lay motionless and listened curiously, trying to regulate my breathing so they would think that I was asleep.

'*Hja serro!* Yellow hair!' he exclaimed at one point, and I could feel the warmth of a torch bulb on my cheek as he amusedly examined the foreigner next to his love. I struggled to stop my eyelids flickering, listening to his horse outside, the chinking of the stirrups and bridle as it stood patiently in the moonlight. They talked for what seemed like hours, but I didn't understand a word. When I heard the zip opening on her sleeping-bag, I prayed they wouldn't be getting any more intimate – I was not that flagrant a voyeur. I must have drifted back to sleep for when I woke she was there in the candlelight and he had gone. She climbed into bed and leant over me to extinguish the flame but found no breath for a while and, unable to contain myself any longer, I laughed as she puffed, at last acknowledging that I was awake. She told me nervously that she had just been outside to the loo. I didn't say a thing.

I settled back into the folds of blanket, smiling silently. I had experienced a *hornig*, and even though it was not my own, I had still felt the thrill of it. Now, whenever I heard the baying of dogs and the dim thud of horses' hoofs around the tribe at night, I would know.

The next day I stayed silent. I had resolved not to divulge my secret to anyone, not even Tsedup. I felt I had trespassed on Sirmo's private moment and in the stark light of morning I felt cheap. But it soon transpired that Sirmo's business was to become a matter for the whole family.

One morning I walked into the main tent and Tsedup and his mother were arguing. Annay was crying as Tsedup berated her. He was frowning and worrying at a piece of bone with his knife as he addressed her sharply. I felt uncomfortable and sat down and ate my *tsampa* quietly as the two harangued each other.

'Namma, Tsedup is not good,' Annay said to me, through her tears. 'He's always telling me off.'

I had no idea what they had been talking about, but decided it was probably best to remain impartial. I was upset to see him treating his mother like that. She was an emotional woman at the best of times, but to have her son speaking to her so harshly was too much.

'Tsedup, have some respect,' I implored. He had sounded authoritarian, like a father talking to his child. But I realised that, despite the atmosphere of hostility, the family were getting closer. Now that they had returned to normal family squabbles Tsedup had truly settled in. The strange time of reunion and self-assessment was over. Tsedup had the confidence to act in this way. He was no longer racked with guilt for having run away and he had left behind the peculiar limbo state of his early days at home, when he had been struggling to find a foothold among the people he had left behind. I had watched him tentatively reasserting himself, reacquainting himself with his nomad ways and reconciling his modern mind with his past values. Today he seemed strong and very much at home, if a little petulant.

I asked him what they had been arguing about. It was Sirmo. Her lover had proposed to her. With a thrill of recognition I realised that I had probably witnessed it that night in the dark of the tent. This morning Tsedup had walked in on his mother worrying and fussing at Sirmo. 'If you can't make your mind up, make sure you don't get pregnant,' she had said, never one to mince her words.

Sirmo sat embarrassed, churning milk in the corner of the tent and blushing. As a private sort of girl she was visibly cringing. It reminded me of myself and my own mother. But Sirmo's family were concerned for her: she was the youngest girl in the family, maybe even a little spoilt, especially by her father, and they wanted the best for her. Was it the right thing to marry this boy?

Tsedup knew that his mother had been applying the pressure. He accused her of pushing Sirmo into marriage. The older nomad women were always telling Sirmo she was getting old and should find a husband, and Tsedup was sick of it. He urged Annay to leave Sirmo alone. She was only twenty-one and, as far as he was concerned, she was too young to get married. It was a grievance that, as a nomad man, he would not have expressed and I could see how much the West had influenced him. He turned to Sirmo: 'You're too young,' he pleaded. 'Why don't you wait and do some different things with your life? You'll find someone later on.' Then he continued to rail against his mother, who wept into the sleeve of her *tsarer*. Sirmo sat subdued in the corner, quietly churning the milk and staring at the hem of her skirt, listening as they discussed her future. She didn't say a word, and whatever she held inside, she did not share it.

For some light relief, when Sirmo had finished churning I suggested we go out and wash the clothes together. We carried the load in a tin basin down to the stream, crouched in a hollow of the bank and scrubbed as the hot sun shimmered on the wet pebbles. She didn't sing.

'You are still young. Don't rush into marriage,' I said.

'I am old, Shermo,' she stated matter-of-factly, and with what I felt was a glimmer of irony.

'No, you're not.'

'Yes, I am.'

It was useless to argue. What was young for me, was not for her. Here people married in their teens and to stray too far into your twenties without finding a mate was frowned upon. I just didn't want her to feel pressured into marrying Chuchong Tashi. If she chose him, I hoped he deserved her. Dolma had said he had a good heart and I hoped so. It was really none of my business what she chose to do. I was imposing my western values, as Tsedup had.

We didn't speak any more. She sighed and the corners of her mouth curled up into a curious smile. I wondered what she was thinking.

# TWELVE

## *End of an Era*

Snow, soft and white, through the crack in the tent flap. When I had slipped out of the tent for a pee at dawn, it had been unusually dark, the air thick round the yaks. A couple of hours later, I could see the glare of sharp white light through the doorway. I wrapped up in a double layer of tights and my *tsarer* and stepped out into the drifting flakes. The whole landscape had become invisible: no mountains, no sky. The sheep, usually wandering to the boundaries of our land, stood inert and silent in the middle of the encampment, heads bowed.

I knew there was a bowl of warm water for me to wash

in at the main tent, but in my maniacal drive for privacy, I obstinately made my way towards the stream. When I got there it had turned to ice; but I took a small rock and smashed a hole in the surface, cupped my hand into the water and splashed it on my face. It stung. Two young girls collecting water on the other side of the bank smiled and waved at me. They must have thought I was mad.

Inside the main tent it was miserable. The grass floor had turned to mud slush around the edges. We sat in front of the fire on damp Tibetan carpets in our *tsarers*, as the snow spiralled down through the roof-opening. When the flakes began drifting in earnest, Amnye closed the flap and we sat in darkness, listening to the drips that fell from the yak hair on to the plastic sheeting tied on for makeshift protection. The dogs, usually banished outside, were allowed to come close to the fire. They lay still and sighing as their thick fur prickled with melting snow. Amnye occasionally cursed them when they scrounged for scraps. Shermo Donker coughed consumptively in the smoky gloom.

Despite the conditions today, the offerings of *hdir* were to be made. The brick-shaped bundles of yellow cloth, containing sacred blessings that Tsedup had bought in Labrang, were to be buried at the foot of Amnye Kula, to propitiate the mountain god. Rhanjer ducked inside the tent blowing fiercely on his hands and settled down to smoke with his father and brothers in front of the fire. He and Tsedup were going to town to collect a monk from the monastery who was to help perform the ritual. After a bowl of hot tea, they set off. Tsedup, who had bandaged his head with a woollen scarf, started up the bike and skidded immediately on the slippery ground, falling into the snow. After a second successful attempt they disappeared. Within seconds the buzz of the engine was mute, swallowed in the silence of falling flakes.

Once they had gone Shermo Donker began flitting from corner to corner like an agitated sparrow, frantically fetching *tsampa*, butter, the *langwha*, basin, and *kadaks*, prayer scarves, all of which were packed into a saddle-bag. Annay brandished a smoking juniper branch around the bag then let it smoulder in the ashes; the tent was filled with the bitter-fresh fragrance of the aromatic sticks. Lhamochab and Donkerchab, two young men from the tribe, arrived on horseback and when the saddle-bag was loaded, set off in the direction of the mountain. I played with the children that day, as I did on most days. They could all count to five in English now and were usually clamouring for my attention, the girls sitting close and holding my hands and Sanjay leaping into my lap. Amnye or Tsedo would frequently scold them for getting so close and they would obediently skulk away. But I didn't mind. I loved them and, anyway, the closer we were, the warmer it was.

It was nearly time to move on. The days were closing in and the nip of frosted air bit deeper with each nightfall. A cold wind blew from the east and as the seasons shifted, the family and the rest of the tribe busied themselves with preparations. We were moving back into the valley soon from the open grassland. The family had their winter house close to where we had been living when we first arrived and every effort was being made to furnish and equip it for our arrival. Apart from Annay and Amnye, who had their house in town, the family had never lived under a roof before; this was to be the first year. The tribe had decided to try to live more comfortably this winter and everyone was busy building and fashioning their new dwellings. Most of them were to occupy the 'railway arch' constructions, built during the Cultural Revolution. There were two rows of them in that valley and they were to provide a convenient, if somewhat ugly, shelter. Our house was separate and stood at the base of a range of hills that ran the length of the stream valley up to the mountain peak of Kula. It was a simple home. The front was covered in a layer of clay and, above it, white plaster. It had a wooden door in the middle with odd windows on either side and a flat, corrugated-metal roof. Inside, there were two small rooms, one with a floor of brick and the other of earth. The walls were made from turf and were plastered over. Shermo Donker had built a clay stove on the earth side and the bricked side awaited an iron stove, which Tsedo would buy from town. It was only partially habitable and a couple of Chinese builders were still finishing off. Tsedo went to check on their progress each day on his motorbike.

Behind the house was a corral with a central dividing wall, one side for the sheep and one for the yaks. During the winter months the animals would be penned inside at night for safety – the mountains around us were full of wolves. Tsedup, Tsedo and Gorbo pegged the exterior walls with sharp spikes to prevent the predators from jumping in and savaging our flock. I helped clear the corral of long grass, which the family had grown there throughout the spring and summer. Tsedo cut it with a crude scythe and Shermo Donker and I gathered it up into bundles and bound each one into a sheaf with stalks. We stored the sheafs in a pit at the rear of the house. This was to be fodder for the animals when the weather was too harsh for them to forage for themselves. At the end of each day after our work, our hands were mapped with tiny cuts, scratches and weals from the sharp stems.

Despite the family's insistence that I should not work, I continued harvesting a few days later at Annay and Amnye's house near the town. The more they spoilt me, the more pale and feeble I felt, like some wan character from a Jane Austen novel, and I wanted to be involved with the preparations as much as possible to prove my worth. Ama-lo-lun sat on the step outside the tumbledown house spinning her prayer wheel and watching us toil. It tried to snow, but we ignored the flakes and I ignored Tsedo, who kept urging me to rest. '*Mar sho! Mar sho!*' he cried every five minutes, but I relished the work. When we did rest, we all lay in the piles of grass together and compared injuries to our hands and fingers. At night we slept in a row on the low platform of wood and straw, Shermo Donker cradling Sanjay inside her *tsarer*. I listened to their regular breathing in the dark and to Ama-lo-lun's small voice as she chanted prayers in the adjoining room, before she gradually ceased and fell asleep.

One morning when we were working at the winter house, I was given the responsibility of driving Rhanjer's enormous truck. I had to collect clay from a nearby hill, which was daunting, as I had never driven a heavy-goods vehicle before. Even more perturbing was that half of our family and most of the tribe's children were in the back. It was a challenge and I took it slowly. With much gear-grinding and screeching of brakes I managed to park precariously on a steep slope at the foot of a cliff. Everyone leapt off excitedly and began to dig then sling the earth on to the lorry with spades. Dolma and Wado were in charge of ensuring an even dispersal of clay, in case the truck toppled over, and they stood in the back, spreading fiercely with their hands. They laughed as the diggers lobbed their spades'-worth into the air and showered them with earth. Before we had use of the truck, we had laboriously loaded the clay on to two yaks and returned it to the house over the stream. This was going to make life easier. As usual it was also a chance for everyone to be boisterous and soon we were all covered in clay.

I drove the lorry through the stream and back to the house in first gear; my manipulation of the clutch had somehow failed. The noise of the engine was painful. Tsedo and Amnye laughed at me when I got back. To them, it was an amazing thing that a woman could drive a truck, as none of the women here drove, but it was amusing that she wasn't quite good enough. Women drivers. When their laughter had subsided, Shermo Donker, Sirmo, Amnye, Tsedo, Tsedup and I started making an extension to the house, the extra room were Tsedup and I would sleep. The men built the walls from turf and stone, and we girls spent the day slapping clay on top to create a smooth surface and block up the cracks. It was the hardest job I have ever done. The clay, which was mixed with water, had to be squelched in our hands to form a good strong mix, then slapped on the walls and spread with our palms.

Although the sun shone brilliantly from a perfectly blue sky, the earth was so cold our hands ached. It was even worse when we came to do the interior: it was freezing in the shade and there was no longer the psychological comfort of seeing the sun on our skin. I had to take a break as I had lost all feeling in my hands. To make myself useful I collected water from the stream for the workers, then rejoined them outside the house and enjoyed smearing in the sunshine, the feel of the sludge between my fingers. It was incredibly messy work and I couldn't help thinking that a manicure wouldn't go amiss; also a revision of the wardrobe situation, as I looked nothing less than eight months' pregnant in my multiple layers of mud-splattered clothing.

'You have a baby inside,' they teased.

When the walls were finished, the roof was put together from beams, bamboo and earth. Shermo Donker shinned up and set about spreading thick handfuls of twigs from the mountain bushes on top of the beams. She then spread plastic sheeting over it and completed the canopy with a layer of clay to seal it. Soon we had an extra room on the house. There was a hole for a small window in the front, which lacked glass, and a hole for a door to be put in. Although glad of a roof, I hoped they wouldn't forget these details. This was to be our bedroom for the next three months and it was below freezing at night now. Sometimes, by morning, my glass of water had turned to ice.

By sunset we had finished toiling and rode home. About fifteen of us made a caravan on horses and yaks back to the tribe over the hill from the winter houses. The evening light shone gold over the scorched grassland, and everyone was in jovial spirits. Soon they were whipping each other's yaks and racing one another. Shermo Donker, overtaking me on the inside, giggled devilishly and cracked a rope on the rear of my beast as she passed. It bolted and I shrieked into the wind, as I hung on for dear life. Ahead of me Sirmo fell off her yak and everyone teased her. My breath caught in my throat, not because of the wind but because I was overcome by an intense surge of emotion. I felt a strange sense of unreality, as if I was in a film. I think you would call it elation. If there had to be one defining moment that depicted Tibet in all its beauty and wildness, then surely that was it for me.

The next day I woke up to a seven-year-old piping Amdo

songs. Dickir Ziggy had shared my bed while Tsedup had stayed with his brother, Gondo, on the other side of Machu. We lay and chatted about my brother Phil and his naughty antics as a child while the frost gathered on our breath. She was especially interested to hear the story I told her about him lying in the road and pretending to be dead. When the cars had stopped to see what had happened and the drivers got out to check on him, he would jump up laughing and run away. Ziggy giggled.

I went and washed in the cold stream in the morning sunshine while the sheep collected curiously around me. In the tent I made *tsampa* and the milk boiled over in the pot on the fire, leaving a pungent smell from the burnt splashes on the clay. Outside, Gorbo led the white stallion across the open entrance. It was the most seductively beautiful creature I had ever seen; pure white and graceful, like a unicorn without the horn. The tents had all but disappeared now. The river valley looked bare, apart from we few stragglers, and the dung mountains that the early movers had left behind. Next door Annay Urgin's tent had gone and only a lonely clay stove was left on the ground where her home had been. The nomads never destroyed a fire. I had watched the tent being dismantled while everyone stood fussing round the yaks, packing huge sacks of belongings – cheese, butter, barley, clothes, the altar, tent poles and the tent itself – on to the animals' backs. Excitement and change had permeated our daily routine and I was looking forward to our move in a few days' time. We had been away in Labrang during the first migration and I was not going to miss this experience. But first we had to go visiting. Apparently this tribe was bigger than I had thought and we had been invited to the other half by the families on the opposite side of Amnye Kula. Tsedup promised we would be back in time.

I was collected by jeep from the town and driven to a northern valley on the other side of Machu by Namjher, a jovial, portly man. Tsedup followed behind on the bike. He had known Namjher since birth and had grown up with all of the people I was about to meet. It was a sad fact but today the tribe was split in half. During Tsedup's years away the introduction of new legislation from the government meant that there were now land-division policies, with which the nomads were forced to comply. Large tribes were discouraged from cohabiting in favour of small groups of families occupying their own sections of land within the wire-fenced boundaries. A way of life that had been practised for centuries had been changed irrevocably. The very nature of nomadic pastoralism was at threat.

Before the legislation, a meeting of the heads of the eighty tribes in the Lhardey Nyima area, north of the Yellow river, would have determined where and when they should move within their vast grasslands. Tsedup remembered the land available to his own tribe as covering an area of between ten and twenty miles. At that time, they also moved more frequently, every month in the summer, to allow the grass to regenerate more quickly. Today they were confined to moving only three times a year within their designated areas and the grass was of poorer quality.

When the nomads had been given the order to divide up, they had been left to sort it out for themselves since the authorities did not have the ability to organise vast areas of nomadic pasture and were concerned about tribal conflict. A group of officials inspected it annually to ensure that the nomads had conformed to the guidelines, and enforced restrictions if they thought there had been any cheating. The Tibetans also had local influence in the form of governors, such as Tsedup's father, so a method of democratic demarcation was employed, in the same way that they had always organised their choice of settlement. They divided it up with dice.

In Tsedup's tribe they had thrown three dice to see who had the choice of land, and the size of each tract was decided according to population numbers. Their land encompassed the stretch from the valley to the north of Kula down to the Yellow river. They decided to divide the tribe in half. A natural split emerged, with certain families wanting to stay together. From that day the two halves would live separately and see little of each other. The original tribe had consisted of fifty families, and today twenty lived on our land to the south of Kula and the remainder with Namjher in the north. I thought it a tragic rift.

Tsedo and some of the other men from our half of the tribe had wanted the northern land, as it was deemed more sheltered and had better grass at the time. Where we were, on the flat grassland, the wind could sweep mercilessly down the river valley whipping up the topsoil of the overgrazed land and further eroding it. However, when we arrived at Namjher's half of the tribe it was clear that they were not doing so well. The valley was steep and heavily grazed, covered in heather and sparse areas of grass, which had dried up in the winter sunshine. It was beautiful with the snow-capped Kula rising majestically above us, but because of its northern aspect, it was also shady beneath the mountain slopes and in these dark shadows the temperatures were at zero and below. Ironically, this place had turned out to be the worst of the two sites, although Namjher's half of the tribe had chosen it.

They had already all moved into their winter houses and their dwellings were at various stages of comfort. Most were clay-built, with wooden roofs and brick floors, sparsely decorated, with newspaper displacing wallpaper and the odd picture of a Chinese pop star. We were greeted with warmth and hospitality by our hosts, most of whom were relations. Tsedup explained patiently who was related to whom and by what connection, but it was so hard to keep up with that I was soon lost. We had come with Aka Choedak, a monk who was a relative and who had also been in India. He was a cheerful soul, always laughing and chatting. He accompanied us to each dwelling – where we must have been offered about five hundred *momos* in all, and at every house a plate of *djomdi*, small brown beans dug from the earth, with rice, sugar and melted butter. When we reached the last house that day, we were forced to decline any further sustenance and sat sipping bowls of tea.

I had the greatest pleasure in meeting one relative who was tirelessly inquisitive about life in the West, staring intently with the smallest, most close-set eyes I have ever seen, exclaiming, '*hschuck chair*! Scary, wow!' over and over as he listened to Tsedup's descriptions of routine things, such as trains that carried people under the ground. Tsedup spoke with authority about life in England. He sounded confident and settled and yet I knew that, deep down, he was neither back home. He still felt like a stranger. England hadn't matched up to his expectations and he had found it hard to forge a living there, but now we were in Amdo, I was glad that he sounded proud to be part of that life in the West, for it had rarely appeared so when we were there. I supposed that the grass was always greener on the other side of the fence.

That night I went to bed earlier than the rest of the throng, who carried on into the small hours. I was slightly overcome by the heat from the iron stove in Medo's tiny house and bewildered by the language barrier. I found it hard sometimes to appear attentive at these gatherings, as after a while of not understanding a conversation, my mind would wander. I retired to Namjher's house, and slept wrapped up in my *tsarer* next to Aka Choedak, who was snuggled up in his fuchsia robes. I had never slept in such close proximity to a monk before, and although we were separated by a low table in the middle of the platform, it felt sacrilegious.

In the morning Tsedup told me that I should have politely declined Namjher's offer of the platform to sleep on. All guests were treated as equals, but according to protocol, it had been wrong of me to sleep next to a monk. I felt embarrassed by my ignorance once again.

That day we had another seven houses to visit. At the first, there were so many children inside and they looked so alike that it was hard to tell whose they were. Tsedup and I talked about them with our host for some time, as they huddled together in the corner with wide eyes, eating their *djomdi* and whispering. It was amazing how much Tibetans talked about children. The word *shyee*, child, was mentioned frequently in conversation and it was clear that they loved their children deeply. They were also fiercely proud of their family heritage, and their children were important to them as they represented the immortality of the blood line. The children clustered eagerly outside as we photographed them, then an elderly relative called Gayko arrived to escort us.

Like Azjung, he was a man of distinguished features. We walked over the hill and through the heather with a view of Amnye Kula. It looked different from this side of the valley, inaccessible and monolithic. It towered above us and I couldn't envisage that we had actually climbed it. As we walked, Tsedup told me that his family had lived here during the Cultural Revolution. He pointed to a hillock. It seemed innocuous enough.

'When I was a boy, I watched my father being made to stand there and hold a wooden post above his shoulders for a day,' he said. 'His arms were shaking uncontrollably, but they wouldn't let him put it down.'

As I stared at the spot I had a mental image of the scene, a glimpse of more brutal times. For Tsedup, the land was mapped with memories and ghosts and at times he would draw back the veil for me, so that I understood that it was not just a manifestation of physical beauty. There was much more to it than that.

Gayko led us patiently from family to family as we ate and I listened to them talk. At his own house, his two sons took turns with Tsedup to shoot a gun at a bottle perched on the mud wall outside. They whooped with delight when they struck it. Then we set off to the last house up the valley, which was probably the most interesting of all.

It was the home of two brothers, Karko and Cumchockchab, who shared one wife. As we sat in the shafts of sunlight on yak skins I watched, intrigued, as the family entertained us. Karko was an amiable old man, naked except for his sheepskin *tsarer*, a real nomad. He sat on the dried mud floor smoking his pipe and laughing. Tsedup informed me that he was considered a man of integrity and intelligence among the nomads. His brother Cumchockchab was the joker of the two. It had been he who had exclaimed at the wonders of western culture the night before. Their wife sat between them and made *momos*, which she placed in front of me on a wooden dish. She smiled and urged me to eat. '*Sou! Sou!*' She was unremarkable in appearance and looked incongruous in their mud hut. Her eyes were quite round and she was almost western-looking. I felt as if I might have bumped into her in the supermarket back home. Yet she had the pleasure of two men's company on those cold winter nights. It set me wondering about their sleeping arrangements. Was there some kind of rota system? Did she tire at all? Apparently polyandry was quite acceptable in these parts, although it was not widely practised. My astonishment was greeted later with mirth by Tsedup, who found my ignorance amusing.

After an exhausting but enjoyable tribal tour we left, armed with presents of cloth, *kadaks* and money, for it was a Tibetan custom not only to fill guests' stomachs but to send them away with a gift. We skidded home through the heather, aided by Gayko on his antiquated motorbike; he showed us how to pick a path across the river and down the valley.

We drove straight to Annay and Amnye's house near the town. They were leaving for Lhasa the next morning. As part of Amnye's work, they were to accompany a lama from Ganden Monastery and would stay on for a month in the city. They were both excited and more animated than I had ever seen them. This was their pilgrimage and they were to visit the great monasteries of their Tibetan heritage to pay homage to their gods. Tsedo and Gondo arrived soon after and we all chatted as Annay and Amnye packed their travel bags and warm clothes for the seven-day journey on the truck. Amnye had his *bourgea*, a fine Tibetan hat, fur-lined and silk-trimmed, and his traditional Tibetan boots, *shangtee*, which they urged me to try on. Everyone including Amnye, who was usually so serious, then fell about laughing at me, as they are rather comical in appearance, although functional and warm. Annay was ill with swollen glands. She could hardly speak, but would not let that curb her excitement and her stubborn will to complete the journey.

We went to bed early, and awoke at five the next morning to accompany them to the truck. It was dark and bitterly cold. Annay and I held hands and followed behind the men, slipping on the frosted ground, but she had forgotten her hat, which I ran back to collect from the house. Their neighbour, Annay Gee Gee, called to us to come through her gate as it was a short-cut. We walked through and caught sight of the vehicle that would take them on the seven-day journey. In the light cast from the window of the house in front, I was appalled by what I saw. The truck was piled high with boxes of butter so heavy that it had sunk on its axles. On top of this mountain of produce were about ten people, all trying to negotiate a place to sit. So precarious was their situation, that it would only have taken a sharp bend on an icy mountain road to send them flying out into the valley below.

This was the potential destiny of my dear parents-in-law, and I was filled with dread as they clambered up on top of the pile. I handed Annay her prayer scarf, placing it over her head as she boarded, and gave Rhanjer's monk son, Tinlee, who was accompanying them, another scarf for good luck. It was his first trip to his capital and I hoped he would get there. Suddenly, as the truck began to grind towards the road, Tsedup jumped up on top and pleaded with his father to take the bus instead. '*Drucker, drucker.* It's no problem,' cried his father and Tsedup was forced to throw himself clear, as they disappeared into the dark. I whimpered quietly to myself as I watched the lights of the truck swing out of sight. Was this the last time I would see them? We walked back to the house and went to bed. Later we heard that the truck's wheel had broken on the Wild Yak range, not three miles from the house, and they had taken the bus after all. Relieved, we returned to the tents.

The next day the move was on. True nomadic spirit prevailed, but with no yaks this time. Technology had made life easier for the nomads and today a truck would do nicely instead. We got up early and began to take down the black tent. Sirmo unstitched the sides and we dismantled the enormous length of heavy fabric. Our hands were black, as it was covered in soot from the fire, and I was impressed to see how small a shape it could be folded into. Our home now sat on the grass, the size of a cardboard box. The day was chaotic: the truck got stuck in the mud and overturned when Tsedo was trying to tow Rhanjer's decrepit car so he had to fetch cable from the town to pull it out. We girls sat around among the sacks with the children and scrabbling puppies – the bitch had given birth to three – surrounded by mountains of ephemera, giggling and joking to pass the time. We waited till late afternoon around the lonely clay stove in the middle of the grassland, drinking tea and eating *tsampa*, the last of the tribe to go. There was no tent around us, just chilled autumn air and vast space. It had a surreal feel about it. Then Tsedo returned, cursing, in the truck and we heaved everything into the back. We were so overloaded that I was afraid the vehicle would keel over again, but we went on our way, a family on the move in the evening sunlight. We reached the house and unpacked, throwing the sacks on to the ground unceremoniously and, exhausted, piled into Annay Urgin's clay house next door for *momos*.

After that, life took on a singularly domestic air. As it was the first year that the tribe had lived in the winter houses, we still had plenty of jobs to do: painting window-frames, sewing curtains, building a house for the dung and another to store the meat, fixing gates on the cattle corrals and constructing a dung wall at the front of the house. It was less strenuous work for the women in comparison to their tasks in the grassland and, these days, I noted that they were more content to be indoors than the men. Soon the milking would stop altogether, and as they completed each household job, there would be less and less to do. Everything was slowing down to a few undemanding tasks. It was like hibernation. However, Tsedo, who had enjoyed a leisurely lifestyle in the grassland that summer, said that he would like to blow up the house and erect the tent again, since he was in charge of DIY. There was no pleasing some people.

One day Sirmo and I were sent to town to run errands for Shermo Donker. Young Dolma accompanied us, and when we had done the shopping we all retired to Annay and Amnye's house to roast barley. Since they were in Lhasa, we had the place to ourselves. *Tsampa*, which was made from barley, was an essential part of their diet and it was our responsibility to prepare it and bring back fresh stores to the winter house. We heaved out the old sacks from behind the cloth at the back of the house. It had been so long since they were opened that the fabric had rotted into a mesh. We had to force open the mouth of each bag with a wooden cosh. I watched as they tossed the raw barley grains on to some sand which had been heated in a pan over the fire. After a few seconds, the kernels popped open without burning, since the sand had diffused the heat. Then they sieved out the sand, poured the barley into another sack and the sand back into the pan. By the time they had finished, we were all smudged with smoke.

That night we drank some beer that Tsedup had dropped off for us and ate fried *momos* from a tin pot. They plaited my hair, Amdo style, in two braids. Then we lay in a row on the platform of hay and wood, singing songs before falling asleep.

The next day we took the roasted barley to town for grinding. Nowadays it was done in an electric machine, but in the old days they had used a hand mill of two flat round stones. The nomads were fond of labour-saving devices. In the late afternoon, Sirmo and I walked back to the house through the thick snow. When we arrived it was locked and our neighbour, Annay Pughlo, who kept the key, was out. Annay Gee Gee asked us in and we sat in her house to wait, watching the snow fall and darkness descend. When the blinding white of the window-pane had turned to black, we realised Annay Pughlo wasn't coming back. We would have to stay the night with our neighbour. Annay Gee Gee prepared us a meal, spread sheepskins on the dusty brick floor and wrapped us up in our *tsarers*. I lay next to the clay fire and listened to her tiny granddaughter, Tselo, chattering away. It was cosy. The walls of the house were covered in Chinese newspaper and a picture of Mao reclining in a wicker chair on a hilltop, smoking nonchalantly. As we fell asleep, Annay Gee Gee turned the prayer wheel and a small bell tinkled.

In the morning we washed and Annay took a tiny pot from the cupboard and put cream on her face. She lit a fire and we ate *tanthuk* from the night before. I watched as she brushed her long hair and wove it into two fine plaits, then hung her earrings over the top of her head. The snow was still falling steadily and silently outside. The blank air had erased our view of the town. Annay Gee Gee fed Tselo from a small wooden bowl, and she sipped the warm milk gently in the dusky, dim light cast through the fogged panes of glass in the window. An expressive child, Tselo seemed older than her years. She was dressed in home-made dungarees, patched and stained: big padded pink trousers with a slit cut in the bottom for her to go to the loo. She stood holding the door open by a string, smiling at me, and I could see the snow thick and deep in the yard outside beyond the stone step. Then she closed the door behind her to go and visit the poor kitten that was tied up outside, crying in the snow. Sirmo spoke to Annay Gee Gee for hours as we sewed and waited. I could hear Annay Gee Gee telling her she was getting old. She should find a husband. Time was running out.

I didn't realise then that soon things would never be the same again.

# THIRTEEN

## *A Family Affair*

The strangest night of all began with pancakes. It was a bit easier to manoeuvre now that we were in a house, so I had mixed up some batter and was busy making them for Dickir Ziggy, Sanjay, Gorbo and Shermo Donker. It was already dark. The yaks and sheep were safely in their corral, the evening's tasks were finished. Tsedup and Tsedo were away, Dickir Che was at her grandmother's and Sirmo was staying next door with Dolma in the Kambo household, as Annay Urgin was in town. We were a skeleton crew. I squirted mandarin juice and heaped sugar on top of the fried batter, as they smacked their lips in anticipation. Such was their new-found lust for this English treat that two hours later I was still ladling the thick mixture into the pan when Dolma appeared. I thought that she and Sirmo might have come over and joined in our feast, but concluded that they were probably too preoccupied with the evening's impending *hornig*. Two girls alone in a house was a perfect opportunity for young horsemen wandering the night and they knew it. Dolma hadn't come for pancakes, she had come to ask Shermo Donker something and, after some suspicious whispering, the two left the house.

The children and I finished eating then sat and played cards together. An hour passed and still Shermo Donker had not returned. I sensed that something odd was going on. Then, just as I was getting bored with playing patience for the twenty-fifth time, Dolma appeared again. She was alone and told me, giggling, that we should all go to bed, as Shermo Donker had gone to *hornig* with Sirmo. I was shocked and thought how strange it was that a woman could go off into the night on her horse looking for men, without even putting the children to bed. I laughed, but felt uncomfortable. As I was not really sure of the etiquette of the situation, I asked Gorbo if it would be a problem for Tsedo that she had gone to *hornig* and he replied that it would be. It was obvious that this was not a normal thing for women to do. But before I could grill him further, Gorbo decided to go off girl-hunting himself and disappeared on one of the yaks, leaving Ziggy, Sanjay and me to go to bed.

I tucked up both children next to the clay fire in their sheepskin and shut the door to the dark house, leaving them alone. But although they had assured me they were all right, when I came back in to clean my teeth they were afraid. Not knowing what time their mother would be coming home, I told them we could all sleep in my bed in the room outside. They jumped at the chance, although Ziggy was worried that her mother would tell them off.

'Where is Mother?' she asked me.

'Kambo,' I lied, meaning Annay Urgin's.

I assured them that Shermo Donker was not going to tell them off – she wouldn't get a chance, if I could help it. I was angry with her for leaving them. The three of us snuggled up together in the straw bed as the cold wind breathed through the glassless window and the doorless door. They soon fell asleep after some initial excited chatter and I lay quietly looking out at the stars. What a strange place this was. Their father had gone to the next valley and was supposed to be coming back later, although he had joked that he had a wife nearby and might visit her tonight, and their mother was herself off to *hornig*. I didn't know what to think.

Eventually I heard footsteps outside and someone opening the door to the house. Shermo Donker called to the children, but of course there was no one inside and she came straight to my room. 'Shermo,' she called nervously. She came and sat on the edge of the straw bed in the blackness and laughing, told me that she had been to *hornig*. To humour her, I asked if she had found a man. She said that she hadn't, then suddenly became serious and said that it had been a cover-up. She hadn't been at all. 'Sirmo has eloped!' she exclaimed.

So that was it. I was so shocked that I didn't know how to reply. Sirmo's lover had come on horseback for her and the two had made off in the moonlight to his tribe. Tomorrow she would be his bride. Immediately a string of thoughts filled my mind. That day she had led me to the Kambo house and had asked me for her *chadmay*, silver and coral belt, which she had always let me wear. I gave it to her. Earlier that day she had also complained that her feet hurt and had shown us her blistered heels in her dirty old shoes. Tsedup had told her to put on the new shoes she had bought for Losar, Tibetan new year. She had. This girl was clever. It had all been a plan to escape without suspicion. Annay and Amnye were in Lhasa, and her older brothers were away that night. Sirmo had planned it all. I was shocked and sad. I hoped she would be happy, but I knew I would miss her. Shermo Donker and I exchanged exclamations along these lines, then she went to bed and I lay thinking for a long time.

Sirmo had gone. I recalled all the things we had done together. I remembered talking to her by the stream when I had told her not to rush into marriage. Now I knew that she hadn't listened to a word. She loved this man, I supposed, and had made a brave decision to go with him. She had sensed her family's doubts for her future and had rebelled. Elopement was not common here: usually there was a marriage ceremony uniting both sides of the family. I knew that her mother and father would be sad when they returned from Lhasa, and that Tsedup would be angry and disappointed with her for not listening to him. But I felt an empathy with her. In a sense we were similar. I had run away to India to marry my husband and, like a hot-headed teenager, had not told my parents we were married. I was all too familiar with what love could make you do and I knew why Sirmo had gone.

The next morning when I came out of my room Tsedo was outside stretching and yawning. I asked him if he was angry that Sirmo had run away and, in his usual relaxed fashion, he said not at all. I knew that Tsedup would not share his indifference. They might have been brothers, but when it came down to it they were quite different. Tsedo could easily watch the world go by, while Tsedup would set it spinning on its axis. Sure enough, Tsedup pulled up on the motorbike in the morning sunshine, with a pot of paint I had asked him to buy for the window. He was looking pleased with himself for remembering it. Then I broke the news: his sister had gone. At first he didn't believe it and started laughing, but when I insisted it was true, he swore in a rage. Skidding the bike a full 180 degrees, he disappeared in a cloud of dust and shortly after returned with Rhanjer. It was time for a family conference.

The three brothers argued while Shermo Donker and I stitched the curtains. Once, Tsedup turned from his tirade to address my sister-in-law. He blamed her for being one of the women who had pressured Sirmo into marriage by always saying she needed a husband. Shermo Donker kept her head down, uttering stifled protestations through the pins in her mouth.

Tsedup was in full flood. He ignored family protocol and began condemning his older brothers. A younger sibling usually deferred. 'Why didn't you make Sirmo stay at school?' he demanded. 'This would never have happened if you had.' He was referring to the knife attack. As far as Tsedup was concerned, nobody had made enough effort to encourage her to go back after she had been assaulted, especially not his father. With Amnye away, Tsedup targeted his fury at his brothers. He felt responsible for Sirmo's education: nobody else in his family seemed to believe in the value of schooling. He had taken himself off to school in the town when he was twelve. It was not compulsory, and his father had told him that if he didn't like it he could come home at any time. But he had loved it, and when he was older he had taken both his brother Samba and sister Sirmo to school because he had recognised their academic potential. He told me later that subconsciously he had wanted them to be closer to him; none of his other brothers and sisters were in the town. But I suspect it wasn't just a question of geography: he wanted them to be like him. I thought it charismatic and resourceful for such a young boy to try to influence his family like that. There was something heroic and rebellious about it. But Tsedup had always been bossy. He was still full of the strength of his own conviction. He had had high hopes for them. Except that, in the end, he had left them both behind when he ran away to India. Samba had become a monk and Sirmo had left town to come back to the tribe. He felt guilty for having left them. Perhaps he couldn't have kept Samba from his religious devotion – it was good for every family to have one son who was a monk and his parents had desired it. But if he had stayed he would certainly have ensured that Sirmo went back to school.

Now he was back and he had implored Sirmo not to get married so young, believing that she could have an easier life in town. But she had rejected town life already, when she failed to return to school. It wasn't that the nomads were averse to education, but it was a complex debate. Both Rhanjer and Tsedo saw the value in Tsedup's beliefs – Rhanjer's son, Samlo, was at school – but compromises had to be made in order for the brothers to understand each other. Tsedup felt strongly that, with an education, a nomad could have a strong hold in both his own community and in the town. He felt that it was becoming increasingly important, now that the nomads were more a part of town life. Even a true nomad, such as his father, was a figure in town now, attending his regular meetings.

But the nomads valued their lifestyle, which they saw was under threat. Not only were restrictions being imposed on their land and herds, but they were having fewer children. According to the authorities, it was permissible for rural people to have two, but that was considerably less than they were accustomed to – Tsedup's generation came mostly from large families. With so few children the nomads also felt that in sending them to school, they would be initiating a departure from the tribe for future generations, weakening their infrastructure. Although there was a Tibetan School in Machu, which taught the Tibetan language as well as Chinese and the standard subjects such as maths, history, geography and the sciences, the tribes knew that their strength was in their unity and the preservation of traditions held for centuries. It was a timeless existence that was clearly being threatened by the inevitable pressure of development and encroaching 'civilisation'. School would take their children away from them, both physically and mentally, and they also believed that there would be a Chinese influence on their characters. A man like Tsedo thought that if he sent his son, Sanjay, to school, then Sanjay would surely not return to a nomadic life after graduation. What would be the future of his family with no one to inherit? In our tribe alone there were thirty-two children who were not at school. I considered this sufficient evidence of their parents' anxiety. But who could say what was right? It was true that these children had a right to education and were being deprived of it, but it was also true that without the children, the tribe could not survive. It seemed that Tsedup hoped these two points could be reconciled.

But there was to be no reconciliation between the brothers now.

'Go and bring her back!' Tsedup ordered Tsedo.

'No way, big-head!' said Tsedo indignantly. '*You* can go if you want to.'

Tsedo had had enough of his younger brother's hysteria. Tsedup was way out of line. But Tsedup didn't go to fetch Sirmo. Instead, rather childishly, he said he wasn't coming back to the house until his mother and father returned from Lhasa. Then, I imagined, he planned a real showdown. Outside the house, he asked me if I would come away with him for a few days. I quickly prepared a small bag and we left on the bike.

We went to stay with his sister Dombie for his cooling-off period. She lived with her husband, Tsering Samdup, and their vast herd on the other side of Machu. They were safely ensconced in their winter house, which stood in a collection of three dwellings in a deep, remote valley. Their two young children, a girl, Dawa, and a boy, Yeshe, were at school in the town. Dombie was younger than Tsedup and the eldest of the two sisters in the family. She was beautiful, like Sirmo, but shy. She spoke softly and laughed huskily as she served us tea. We were most welcome. I hadn't spent any time with her since my arrival and she was keen to befriend me. We sat inside the clay house, on green vinyl flooring and rugs, while Tsedup related Sirmo's saga. Dombie made cooing, soothing noises as Tsedup repeated the tale. Tsering Samdup sat polishing his knife, his short bursts of laughter interspersed with the swear-words: '*Hartsay viron!*' and '*Garo geywa!*' Most men's speech was liberally punctuated with a dose of swearing on the good deeds of their ancestors, for this was what it meant. He looked like a Roman centurion with his close-cropped wavy hair and aquiline nose and he wore the most enormous coral necklace I had ever seen. It was a sign of his status, as his family were quite wealthy. Dombie had married well, but she had an enormous workload. The family's seventy female yaks, *dro*, needed milking each day, twice a day in the summer, and it was Dombie's responsibility to do it.

The next day I attempted to help her with some of her tasks, as Tsedup had accompanied Tsering Samdup on his daily trip to town. I sensed that she was probably lonely sometimes. The other two houses in the valley were occupied by Tsering Samdup's sisters and their spouses, but she missed her children whom she saw only at weekends. As it was Friday Tsering Samdup was to bring them back tonight, she told me animatedly. She was one nomad who certainly knew what day of the week it was. We spent the afternoon collecting fresh dung pats from the floor of her corral and slinging them into a pit from our wicker baskets. She had the biggest mountain of excrement I had ever seen outside the fence to her house. She was a good *namma*. That evening the men did not return and she tried to hide her disappointment at not seeing her children. 'Tomorrow,' I assured her, feeling silently cheated that we had been abandoned.

In the morning we walked down the valley of dried grass, the swishing stems higher than our knees. She lassoed two yaks, and we rode back up towards the mountains to collect water from a fresh stream. Her niece, Norgentso, accompanied us, a bold young girl with bluntly chopped hair, who had an amazing voice and entertained us all the way with folk songs. Later, we sat against a mud wall in the sun-trap of Dombie's yard for a rare work-break and she told me about herself, as she brushed her hair, thick as a yak's tail. She had eloped, just like Sirmo. She was seventeen and her father had thought her too young to marry, but she had run away with Tsering Samdup anyway. Dombie was not worried about her sister. She had seen it all before.

That night it snowed. The men arrived without the children, but Dombie didn't complain. She was an obedient wife and I felt her restraint. If it had been me, it would have been a different matter. Tsering Samdup, ignorant of his failure to deliver, sat in his leopardskin *tsokwa* and tipped out his winnings on the floor. He had spent a hard day and night gambling and was pleased with himself. He was a seasoned professional. Tsedup looked at me and, smiling nervously, told me he had tried his hand, but with only a few yuan. I was not amused. We had little money to last us to the end of our six-month stay and I hoped the peer pressure wouldn't get to him. A lot of men were gamblers here, and Tsedup's brother Gondo even made offerings to the mountain spirit to ensure that the cards worked in his favour. Of course, Rhanjer and Tsedo, the sensible brothers, didn't indulge, and there would be trouble from them if Tsedup got involved in it. There would be trouble from me too.

The morning we left them, I watched Tsering Samdup propitiating the gods outside his house. He poured hot ashes on to the offering site, a metre-high cube standing outside the yard, which Dombie had constructed from clay. Then he sprinkled *tsampa* and milk on top and yelled aloud to the spirits as he tossed handfuls of wind horses into the bright sky. I had never seen such a vocal display as a daily practice. Amnye's morning ritual, which I had observed outside our tent door, had been far more restrained. After breakfast we left for town and I waved from the back of the bike at the receding figure of my sister-in-law standing sentry at the gate. She looked small and isolated. I hoped her children would come home soon.

I had never really thought of myself as a feminist, but sometimes, even though I was loath to impose my western values here, I found it hard to be objective when I observed the way men and women interacted. For me, the most alien aspect of nomad society was the structure of gender relationships. Tsedup had told me that there was an equilibrium; that, in metaphorical terms, the nomads saw the man as the tent pole and the woman as the tent. They existed interdependently. One was useless without the other. But, as far as I could see, this egalitarian outlook required something of a compromise on the part of the woman. This was a man's world, and Machu man was indeed macho. This was a place where men were men and women were women; each had their clearly defined role and it was virtually impossible for members of the indigenous tribes to cross the barrier. Not that they wanted to.

It was largely a question of the public and private domain. Men occupied the public quarter and women the private. Apart from a trip to town to do the shopping, or to visit relatives, women stayed in the tribe and busied themselves tirelessly from dawn to dusk. An idle wife was a bad wife and this view was upheld by the men but enforced by the senior women in each family. I had witnessed Shermo Donker toiling in foul weather with flu but no one urged her to rest, neither Annay nor Tsedo. She always complained and sighed with pain or discomfort, however, just to remind everyone that she was suffering. Nomad women were good at that. Many were workaholics, and if there was no work to be done, they invented it for themselves. It was not permitted for a woman to go to bed before the rest of the family either, and if the men chose to sit and talk for hours, then she was required to stay to pour the tea and stoke the fire, even though she had risen at dawn when the men were at liberty to lie in. It was all accepted behaviour.

Apart from deep in midwinter, when they lived up in the mountains with the herds for a couple of months, the young men had it easy. They rose at a respectable hour, ate a leisurely breakfast, then sometimes they mounted their horses and checked the herd, but usually they took a trip to town on the motorbike and hung out playing pool, gambling in hotel rooms, eating in the restaurants, then returned home before dark. But Tsedup told me that it had not always been like this. Before the land division, men were occupied with shepherding over a huge area of grassland. They were dedicated to their task and rarely slept. Such was the fear of theft that they guarded the cattle with guns all night, hardly ever sleeping in the tent. Armed bandits would stake out tribes and hide for days, waiting for an opportunity. Then they would swoop, sometimes taking a hundred horses at once. They had been a formidable threat. Tsedup remembered his father remaining outside in storms and snow. It was a hard life in those days, but everyone was equal. The nomads were a tough and diligent people, but now, the men had been rendered impotent. Because of the fences there was no reason to herd the animals and it was more difficult for bandits to attack an enclosed encampment. Their role in the family had been all but erased. The new laws had tragically accomplished their goal of nomad domestication.

Nowadays, sometimes the men chose to stay in town overnight and their wives waited, anxiously, for their return, as I had seen with Dombie. I knew the women had excellent hearing. I was used to them jumping at the faint purr of an engine on the distant track. When the men came back the whole family would run out to greet them. Sometimes they brought treats of sweets or noodles for the children, who rarely went to town and these were received with hasty enthusiasm and devoured instantly. In fact, the men were exceptionally good at shopping, and since it was they who frequented the town, it was their responsibility to buy all the necessities for the family. I had been impressed to witness Tsedo quite shamelessly purchasing face cream, shampoo and other unmanly items. Thanks to Chinese entrepreneurialism, the nomads were now avid consumers and cosmetics had become more of a feature in their lives, although the older generation still used butter to moisten their skin.

As Tsedup and I made our way to town I prepared myself for the change. It was difficult to be together there, and although I sometimes looked forward to a break from the remoteness of the grassland, I always approached the town with a mixture of excitement and trepidation. We pulled up at our usual restaurant and warmed ourselves by the iron stove as the waiter fetched tea and Tsedup chatted with some friends. I sat watching men and women going about their business through the window to the street. I was secretly looking for Sirmo, but she was nowhere to be seen. Men cruised around on bikes or sat on the pavement looking around. Women huddled together in groups, parading themselves up and down like peacocks, shopping and giggling. Rarely did you see a husband and wife together, although they might sit together in a restaurant to eat with their children. For a Machu man, it was simply not cool to be seen in public with his wife. Indeed, to be cool was a much practised and refined art here. I had never seen anything like it.

The nomad men's use of language was fundamental to their character. Tsedup could never suffer chit-chat in western society: in England, I had watched him struggle to comprehend what was going on as someone attempted to engage him in some spurious discussion. He simply could not and would not join in. Sometimes people thought him unsociable, but he wasn't. He was genuine. Here, people spoke from the heart and practised an economy of language unmatched in my experience.

In Machu, this restraint was evident. For instance, a nomad would be in a restaurant with friends and, having barely eaten the last morsel, he would stand, mutter casually '*Jo ray*, I'm off,' and leave without a glance. His friends might offer a 'Yeah,' which is the same in English, in reply, but that was it. It had taken me some time to get used to such casual greetings. When I had first arrived I had tried to kiss friends goodbye, but this was unheard-of so I refrained. Likewise, when a man greeted someone in the street he would usually just look at them, maybe smile, usually not, and instead of saying the equivalent of 'Hi, how are you?' he would ask them where they were going: '*Cho gung an jowjer?*' Since this was a small town, there weren't many places that a man could be going, so the reply was usually something along the lines of 'Oh, I'm just hanging around.' The conversation just about wrapped up there, and both parties would mutter, 'Yeah,' and walk on. The essence of it was not to be over-enthusiastic. Otherwise you risked seriously losing your cool. This place might have had a stress-factor of nil compared to London, but it had a cool-factor far exceeding anything I had ever seen on the streets of Soho.

As far as I could see, if you were a nomad bloke, to be really cool the following ten prerequisites had to be observed. You should:

1. Ride around town on your horse or Honda really slowly. Since town consisted of two T-junctions you would frequently be seen. This was good.

2. Wear your *tsarer* (or leopardskin *tsokwa* in winter) in all weathers, even when it was 90 degrees, your left sleeve almost touching the ground. (Since there appeared to be no conceivable reason why one sleeve should be so long except that it made a good pillow to sleep on, the design, at some point in history, must have incorporated the cool-factor.)

3. Wear your five-metre-long red sash, *kirok*, wound as low and as tight as possible round your hips. This made it difficult to walk with anything approaching ease, but it was cool. It was important to walk slowly with a bowling gait at all times.

4. Carry a knife, preferably in a sheath with coral or turquoise embellishment. This hung from your hip and gave you the appearance of being ready for action, even if you had only used it for cutting sheep's intestines.

5. Carry a pistol. This should be tucked into the bulk of your *kirok*, leaving the butt visible. People had to see it was there.

6. Carry a pipe, *ratcho*, the bigger the better. Silver was best; horn not bad. Preferably, again, encrusted with coral and turquoise. It should be tucked inside your *tsarer* in its embroidered pouch and puffed on regularly.

7. Wear dark glasses. Some people thought big and

square was best, but those in the know rejected the seventies look in favour of the small John Lennon variety.

8. Not wash your hair. Unkempt was cool, but not too long. Shoulder-length and straggly was good, for that just-got-out-of-the-sack look.

9. Wear an earring. One thick silver hoop hanging heavily from the lobe.

10. Try not to look busy.

Of course, this behaviour was not just about getting respect from a young nomad's peer group. It was also about trying to look sexy. For although men and women occupied different spaces in the town and remained quite apart, they were very much aware of each other, observing from a distance. Town was a hotbed of gossip: here, men and women from distant surrounding tribes came into contact with each other and provided the basis for a future *hornig*. A glance from a gamine to a young man might signify an invitation for a nocturnal visit.

Affairs were common. Tsedup had told me that there was often a curiously liberal attitude to sex outside marriage here. A man could take a lover and have a casual liaison for a while without hindrance. He might even discuss it with his wife, she might tease him, and they might laugh about it together. However, if the relationship developed into something more serious, this represented a threat to the stability of the family unit and would be actively discouraged by elder family members. Of course, these liaisons resulted in random offspring, but it was not acceptable for the man who had sired the child to visit it or take any part in its fathering, even if he wanted to. Also, if a woman's husband was away she would be within her rights to an extramarital affair. If he heard about it the husband would stay away. Tsedup explained that it was shameful for a man to demonstrate jealousy.

This was all very strange to me. I could not imagine Tsedup surviving in this environment. If he had stayed and married a nomad woman he would never have coped. He demanded loyalty. And, similarly, if he had any ideas himself about skipping off in the night as I smiled on, he was mistaken. But it was clearly not uniform behaviour, as I had discovered from my conversations with Shermo Donker. I had also noted Gorbo's reaction when we had thought she had run away with Sirmo to *hornig*: Tsedo would not have been pleased. The social codes were more complex than they appeared. It seemed to me that, in reality, men were capable of having extramarital relations without fear of guilt. It was part of the macho charisma and was something to be proud of, while women, who carried the burden of domestic chores and who looked after the children, had less opportunity or had more responsibility for the cohesion of the family unit. Nomadic society, like western society, was full of contradiction.

With all this in mind, it was difficult to see how a western woman who was also an Amdo bride fitted into this environment. I was still hugely conspicuous and felt self-conscious in town, even though I wore traditional Tibetan costume. This consisted of my cumbersome leopardskin *tsarer*, and a *kirchi*, a knitted tube of fabric that could be worn as a hat or pulled down over the face for warmth. All the women wore them. I had two, one luminous pink and the other lime green, since these were the fashionable colours, but although I felt as if I looked just like a nomad woman, I obviously didn't. I concluded that it must be my marble eyes and protruding nose that gave me away. Despite my attire, or perhaps because of it, I was still a constant source of curiosity for the nomads and Chinese alike.

Yet harder than this feeling of alienation, was the difficulty I was experiencing in spending time with my husband. After nearly nine years away, he was in his element hanging out with the boys in town. I understood why, he had missed them so much when he was in England. But somehow I had imagined he would enjoy the grassland more. Back home I had envisaged him as a nomad, riding, hunting and herding; it was these images that Tsedup had nurtured back then, when he had endlessly recounted stories of his homeland, but it was different now that we were here. I knew that he was a nomad at heart, but I could see that he had already made a departure from that life when he had left the tribe and gone to school. Yet this taming and 'civilising' had been a necessary part of his history if we were ever to have met and made a successful marriage. Without it, even if we had had the chance to meet, which would have been highly unlikely, I guessed that we would not have been able to relate to one another so well and our expectations of each other would have been irreconcilable. Certainly we would not have achieved the level of intimacy that we had. Somehow we had reached middle ground.

But now – despite his concern for my welfare – to have a wife at his side in this macho land was a slight embarrassment. And, as we sat in the restaurant, once again I felt extraneous. As usual there were no women present in our group and, after listening to the men's conversation for a while, I had to admit that gambling successes and recent fights had never been my hot topics of conversation. They had never been Tsedup's either. I was forced to accept that, in town, the new gender definitions I was encountering were certainly changing the dynamics of my marriage. What had been a symbiotic synthesis of shared time and experience in England had been transformed into a necessary parting of the ways. Sometimes he made me angry. I made my excuses and left the table; it was time to visit my female friends.

I walked to Dolma's house past the ditches of rubbish and snuffling pigs at the far end of town. Tsedup's cousin ran out to meet me with her small son, Gonbochab, who cried, 'Ajay Kate! Ajay Kate! Aunty.' The mongrel in the kennel by the gate strained on its leash and gnashed furiously in the direction of my ankles. At least I was welcomed by the family. Dolma showed me into the parlour and poured me black tea. She set down the *gamtuk*, the box containing *tsampa*, cheese and butter, in front of me and took up her knitting on the bench at the other side of the iron stove. Gonbochab played with a puppy on the brick floor and grinned at me. Then Dolma spoke to me in her high-pitched voice at great speed. She made no allowances for the fact that I could not understand her, and laughed at me when I made mistakes with my Tibetan. If I asked her to repeat something she looked at me with a glazed expression and repeated exactly what she had said before, but with different emphasis on the words, as if it would help. It did not. Then she would smile and mumble something to herself. Unlike Annay, Sirmo and Shermo Donker she did not gesticulate and simplify her language for me, but I enjoyed her company nevertheless. She was warm and kind, with the cheeky grin of a teenager and twinkling eyes. I'm sure she felt sorry for me as she was always asking if I missed home. In fact, everyone asked that. I supposed they could not imagine being so far away from their own home and thought I was suffering. I was not . . . but they could sense that sometimes it was hard for me.

That night Sando, her husband, tempted me to stay the

night with the promise of an English-language wildlife VCD. I felt obliged to watch it as I suspected he had bought it specifically to entertain me. About thirteen of us squeezed into their tiny parlour. He had recently purchased a brand-new VCD machine, silver and shiny with a winking, spiralling electronic light display. He was most proud of it. However, there was insufficient electricity from the mains to power it, until after 10 p.m. We sat in anticipation, he rather frustrated, twiddling knobs furiously. Then when he had cracked it he played not one but five wildlife films all about the plains of Africa. I was touched, because I was the only one there who understood them. Typically Rhanjer, who was also there, wanted me to explain about every single animal that appeared on the screen. After the third film, I began to wilt and at one o'clock in the morning, after Dolma had collapsed with boredom and fatigue beside me, I insisted on going to bed despite his attempts to play me the latest Kenny G VCD of saxophone songs, which he told me was a big hit.

The next day Tsedup stopped by and I asked him to drive me to Tashintso's. As I stepped into her back kitchen our policewoman friend flashed a couple of tickets in front of me. 'We're going to a show!' she said. That night, along with half of the town, we made our way to the big local theatre. Nomads and townspeople collected around the entrance and filtered through the turnstiles. When we walked in I was amazed at the size and grandeur of the building. It was just like an auditorium at home, with a sloping floor and wooden flip-seats. But there were striking differences to the proceedings. There was no hushed anticipation as the lights went down and the curtain came up. Instead it was a riot. Nomads shouted and smoked, laughed and joked with each other. The women called from row to row. About thirty small children, who had rushed to the front, now fought each other, writhing around on the floor in a grubby rumpus. Meanwhile the dancers danced on and the singers turned up their microphones. When it was time for a comedy act the whole place was in uproar. I had never seen such an unabashed display of audience participation. All around me people were fighting to control their laughter, tears dripping down their faces. I laughed too, but since I didn't understand a word of the performance, I was really laughing at them. After each act the nomads burst into applause and whistles ricocheted around the walls.

It was a rare thing, to be out on the town, sharing time with men and women. Usually the only women I saw out at night were the platform-heeled barmaids in the karaoke houses. I missed going out with my friends in England and the ease of the male-female mixed social scene at home. This town was a difficult place for me to be and I was pleased to leave the next day. The haven of the grassland was calling me. It was where I preferred to be. I wasn't sure if Tsedup would be joining me, due to his self-imposed exile from his family, but I knew I had to go back. Before I returned, we made one more stop at Gondo's home nearby.

His tribe were still in their tents and that night the two brothers insisted that we sleep under the stars. It was sub-zero outside, but that wasn't a problem for them: it was something they had always done together when they were boys. Gondo's wife, Tseten, propped up the flap of yak fabric on one side of the tent with a stick and made a bed for us from sheepskins and thick quilts. Gondo, Tsedup and I lay three in a row with our balaclava-clad heads protruding outside and our feet facing the glow of the fire. Tseten, perhaps, had had more sense – she stayed inside.

It was a clear night and the ground was covered in a thick frost. I looked straight up into the deep blue-black sky, and puffed out my breath, watching it cloud away on the freezing air. The yaks stood grunting resignedly behind our heads. The air was fresh and clean on my face, and although I had thought they were mad for wanting to sleep out like this, I was grateful for the beauty of the experience. Once again, I was coming close to nature in a way I hadn't known before. At home in England, Tsedup could only sleep with the window wide open, even in midwinter. He craved the Tibetan night air. I now knew why. But it wasn't the same. In London he hadn't had the spectacular dome of the galaxy to ponder. Nor had his tears turned to ice.

# FOURTEEN

## *Winter Chronicles*

He didn't come home for a while. But it was no longer childish obstinacy that kept him away. Tsedup's friend, Nawang, had been shot a few weeks ago. A man from a distant tribe had tried to swindle his brother, Tsering Samdup, during one of their gambling sessions. The man had ripped off Tsering Samdup's enormous coral necklace. Nawang had got involved, and in the skirmish, the man had pulled a gun from inside his leopardskin *tsokwa* and shot him in the back. The bullet had passed right through him and out. There had been a lot of blood, but he had recovered well and I discovered that Tsedup had accompanied him to

Labrang to the hospital there for a check-up. It worried me. At times like this I was all too aware of the lawless nature of this place.

In the week that followed I remained in the safety of the family home. Since Tsedup had left, I had become accustomed to sharing my sleeping quarters with a whole new collection of life. As usual, I awoke to a small bird scrabbling in the eaves above my head. I watched the outline of its body as it shuffled between the fabric pinned to the wooden beams. It had somehow found a home between the wood and flower-print material and I listened to the rustling of the straw against its feathers. Next to me, the old flea-ridden bitch lay snoring quietly, content to be free of her yapping brood, though on most nights the pups joined us and scrabbled and whined in the straw next to my head. Their mother had recently taken refuge with me in the clay hut, since the nights were freezing and she was no longer as hardy as the other dogs. Behind the woven sacks, saddles and plastic drums of frozen curd, a small rodent called an *abra* had set up residence. It was much prized by the nomads as a creature of gentle nature, which had been known to exhibit domestic tendencies, accepting tempting treats from outstretched hands, sometimes sitting beside the fire with a generous child. At night it scurried across my bed, furtively seeking out scraps to nibble, and left a pile of droppings at my feet.

That morning, however, I woke to someone walking on the roof and the shrill tones of Shermo Donker, ordering everyone in the house out of bed. If I had had glass in my window, surely her dulcet tones would have broken it. As usual, there was no response from the slumbering Tsedo and I lay drowsily, tasting the wet snow on the sheepskin around my face from the night's light fall, feeling a faint rumble in my stomach. Her persistent shrieks eventually roused him and the rest of the family, and a small commotion ensued outside in the yard. I could hear a ripping sound and was curious to see what I was missing. I disentangled myself from the considerable mountain of quilts and peered through the window. In the yard, not five feet from me, I saw the enormous carcass of a yak, half skinned, legs akimbo, the taut flesh of its stomach stripped pink and naked, steam flushing from the deep gash carved in its chest. Tsedo and Annay Urgin were butchering it. Both were panting from the effort of cleaving this vast beast and their breath clouded white in the hazy morning sunshine. Shermo Donker was running around fetching huge cauldrons in which to spill the fresh blood and her brother, Rinchin, had his arm inside the yak's strained neck, rummaging around for something. I decided to lie down again for a while and let them get on with it. The sounds of cracking bones and swilling blood, flaccid organs flung on to plastic and snapping tendons entertained me for a while, then I got up. I went to the house to watch the proceedings from the window, respectfully muttering, '*Om mani padme hum*,' as I passed them.

From inside, I could hear their chaotic chatter and inter-mittent bursts of laughter. The children were all helping to pare the yak and one of the puppies was tearing excitedly at an enormous pile of offal, until it was dragged away by Sanjay. Tsedo came to the window to sharpen his knife on a stone and I saw the skin of his forearms stained crimson. An enormous liver sat on the gatepost and various organs were trailed along the wall like washing on a line. Soon the job was done. Tsedo came in and sat with me while I prepared him a bowl of water to wash in. 'Our Amdo home is not good,' he said. I thought that maybe he was unsure how I felt about the killing. I knew how much he regretted his task, but we all realised that we couldn't carry on eating just *tsampa* every day. The kill was long overdue. Until the next death we would have good food.

As they prepared the offal, I played with the children. They were a wild bunch, fascinated by everything and constantly asking me questions. Sometimes I would find one of them alone in the hut, rooting around in my rucksack for a new oddity from the West. As with every day, I took out my book of blank paper and a pen to write, and within moments it was wheedled from my grasp by small, furtive fingers. They wanted to draw. I don't know if they had ever drawn before I came, but I suspected not. It had become a new delight for them, and a fascination for me. It had started with me drawing for them, then I had encouraged them to try for themselves. At first they had touched the paper hesitantly with the end of the nib, intimidated by the white space, then gently and slowly they made tiny shaky marks, maybe a few squiggly circles, not really trusting themselves. As they gained confidence they began to draw yaks, horses, sheep, and eventually people. By now they had each developed a style. Dickir Che drew large, deliberate figures with huge round heads and stick arms, Dickir Ziggy's people were covered in intricate checked clothes and had tiny facial features, while Sanjay's people sometimes had no bodies at all, just heads, arms and exaggeratedly long stick-legs. It reminded me of English children's early drawings, known as 'tadpole men', a primitive body image. Sanjay's drawings were less developed than the other two children's.

I offered him my pad and asked him to draw his mother and father. Instead, he drew his grandmother, Annay Labko, large on the page, then his grandfather, Amnye Karko, smaller, and then Gorbo, with no body. All had enormously long legs. Gorbo was a tadpole man. These three were Sanjay's most treasured relations. As the smallest child in the family, he was unashamedly spoilt by his grandparents, and Gorbo was his hero; I wasn't surprised that he had preferred to draw them. In nomad society it was usually the grandparents who had most physical contact with the children, hugging and kissing them frequently, while their parents seemed more inclined to discipline them. Sometimes, Shermo Donker was particularly hard with the children. She barked her orders at them as they scurried around performing tasks for her. When they fell asleep at night on the floor, she sometimes wrenched them up by the arms to put them to bed, bellowing their names at the top of her voice. I saw their tiny faces contorted with discomfort and heavy with sleep.

The children were always looking nervously at their parents to see if they could get away with doing something and were often seen as a nuisance. If they leant on me affectionately they were reprimanded for getting in my way, and if they scribbled on my drawing book, they were told to stop because they didn't know how to draw. I knew that Tsedo and Shermo Donker were trying to make life easier for me, but I didn't mind the children. I tried to encourage them as much as possible, whenever possible. But I was not naïve enough to spoil them. I was aware that without discipline a nomad child possesses the innate qualities of a feral beast and will run wild through the vast grassland unhindered: I knew that Shermo Donker loved them. She was always telling me how good it was to have children and how Tsedup and I should have one soon. I had been thinking about it a lot. I had never spent so much time with children before and I had discovered they made me happy. I thought how good it would be to have my own family.

Sanjay giggled and chewed his dirt-encrusted finger as he surveyed his creation. The snot dribbled from his nose.

'*Marger!* I can't do it,' he said.

'*Warger!* You can do it,' I replied.

He was a tiny boy for a six-year-old. Tibetan children were generally much smaller than their western counterparts, but even among his nomad peers Sanjay was small. He was an excellent mimic, copying Tsedup when he sang English songs and making the whole family laugh. Now, bored with drawing, he went outside and ran around pushing a small wheel fixed to a metal rod. He reminded me of a Victorian child with his simple toy.

I gave Dickir Che the pen and asked her to draw something, but she hesitated. Although bossy, she was the least confident of the three. I could feel her desperation for affection in the way she clung to me. Unfortunately, at eleven she was too old to be sweet, and her attempts to attract attention meant that she still spoke in a baby voice and recounted any random piece of information to the family, no matter how mundane, to entertain them. Consequently, she was largely ignored. But she was my great companion, and I loved her.

Dickir Ziggy snatched the pen from her elder sister and went to sit in a corner, where she aimed, no doubt, to draw better pictures than any of them. As she drew, she talked incessantly to herself in a hyperactive babble. I felt that if any of the children should go to school, Ziggy should. She was amazingly quick with numbers and had so much energy and enthusiasm that she didn't know what to do with. She was also very affectionate and would often spontaneously take my hand or hug me.

Afterwards we sat outside in the sunshine and made clay animals, which we painted with water-colours. The children were pleased with the results and lined them up on the window-sill of the hut to dry in the sun. Then Shermo Donker shouted something to them and they scurried off. I watched them from the house as they ran across the far hill in the morning sunshine chasing a stray yak. They called to me, 'Ajay Shermo, Ajay Shermo! Aunty, Aunty!' and I called back across the flat plain, my voice carrying to the depths of the deep shadow at the foot of the hill where they now stood, like matchsticks in a row, waiting for my reply.

That afternoon I saw two distant figures hunched over a hole in the ice of the frozen stream. Dickir Che was helping her father, Tsedo, to wash his clothes. They were scrubbing furiously and occasionally rubbing their hands together for comfort. Shermo Donker had refused to wash them. She had found them filthy in a rice sack and had quickly folded them up and put them away again, giggling with me. Was this nomad feminism, or just common sense? Obviously Tsedo was proud enough of his appearance to risk losing his fingers from frostbite, and Dickir Che would do anything to help.

That evening, when the children had gone to sleep, Tsedo, Shermo Donker and I washed our hair together. The iron stove was well stoked and we sat around in our T-shirts in the stifling heat and took turns to pour warm water over each other's heads from the kettle. They were very impressed by my shampoo. 'Our hair is so soft,' they said, after using it – sounding, ironically, like an advertisement. I laughed. Tsedo and Shermo Donker insisted on regular beauty sessions, and I loved the intimacy of these evenings. With Amnye and Annay away, the atmosphere in the house was far more relaxed, and we laughed and joked outrageously sometimes. Dado, a young man from the tribe, dropped by on his way to *hornig* and we teased him about not having a wife. He was only twenty-three, poor fellow. Luckily he could take a joke. He asked for a hairwash too, then rode off to impress some girl.

The skin on my hands had become ingrained with dirt and had cracked open in places. I realised that I now had the hands of a nomad woman. At least part of me was like them. I guessed it was because of their exposure to such extremes of temperature and that it was impossible to keep them clean; no matter how often I washed them, they were dirty again within minutes. The winter dust was everywhere.

Going to the loo was now something of an endeavour since, on bad days, the wind gusted through the valley, bringing small cyclones of spiralling dust and billowing clouds of grit. We often went in twos for comfort, and that night I pulled up my *kirchi* as far as I could when Shermo Donker and I braved the night. We crouched next to each other in the darkness on a slope of dried grass and rocks at the side of the house. The wind was howling eerily and a shape was moving in the blackness. I began to feel uneasy. The nomads were firm believers in ghosts and I was becoming influenced by their fear. I had always been afraid of the dark and this land had been the site of much bloodshed. And Tsedup had told me that people had been abducted by ghosts. I had been sceptical, but as I felt the cold fingers of the frosty night air on me, I wasn't so sure. 'Did you see it?' I whispered to Shermo Donker. She shuffled over and gripped my arm. We peered anxiously into the ebony night as the sound of panting got louder. Then, in desperation, I turned on the flashlight and two eyes shone back at us. It was the dog. Cherger began to jump all over me in greeting and to lick my face, threatening to push me over. I laughed and stroked him. He was warm and his thick fur crackled with static and lit up in magical, neon-green flashes under my hand.

There was no threat of me being mauled any more as, under Annay's supervision, I had spent many days in the summer offering him scraps of dried meat to befriend him. Now he was my good friend. I was part of the pack. He even preferred me to Tsedup. When we pulled up on the bike outside the house and the dogs raced out to attack, Tsedup asked me to call to them, to pacify them. Because he was often away they weren't sure how to treat him. The dogs were fiercely territorial: even Rhanjer, who visited the family every day from his own home, was attacked regularly by the bitch, who seemed to have a personal vendetta against him. There were always fights outside between them, as she lunged at him and he beat her off with a stick. He didn't live in the family so he was not part of the pack. The rules were simple. I felt honoured that I had been accepted.

The next day, I climbed up the foothill of the mountain behind the house with Sanjay and Tselo, Annay Urgin's little daughter. They ran ahead of me, like goats over the rocks, as I puffed my way to the top, feeling the full weight of my *tsarer*. We sat in the tall grass on top and surveyed the land. Below, the house looked minuscule and isolated within the enormity of the arid landscape. The valley floor stretched away from us down to the glistening river and the blue mountain ranges. Beyond, the tips of the powder-white snow mountains flecked the horizon. Above our heads, hawks spiralled on the warm thermals in the sunlight. We played for a while, then the children scrambled back down the hillside, as I paused to watch the last light sinking behind the silhouette of the Ngoo Ra, Mount Silver Horn.

A shock of grey cloud drifted like a deep canopy above the orange and blue dusk. Pockets of phosphorescence illuminated the distant glaciers on the other side of the Yellow river, and a chill breeze rustled the dry grass at my feet. I could hear the children singing and their voices echoed in the valley among the bleating sheep and lambs as they called them to their corral for the night. Sanjay was now trundling around on his bike and crashing every so often. He had wanted a bike so much that he had said he would sell one of the puppies to buy it. Tsedup and I had saved him the trouble and now it was his prized possession, his only possession. He had tied a yellow prayer scarf around the handlebars as if it was his favourite horse and I watched him mounting it, as his father did his dapple-grey, swinging one leg up and jumping into the seat. His excited squeals carried to me on the breeze.

Gorbo was on the other side of the rocky stream, herding the yaks home for the night. I could just make out his orange hat as he came towards the house between the mountains on his horse, accompanied by a ewe and her lamb that had strayed. The mass of yak hoofs tripped across the valley like showering pebbles and crunched across the ice of the frozen stream. I could hear the whir and crack of his sling, as he chucked a well-aimed stone at a wandering yak. He was singing. His voice rang out clearly and soulfully, alternating between high and low pitch with a gentle vibrato, in the style of a traditional Tibetan song. The words were swallowed at the end of each phrase in a blunt staccato and the rhythm wove a steady pattern, almost hypnotic in the twilight, rebounding and reverberating up the valley.

It might have been a song of love or a song about his land: the mountains, the air, the light, the flowers, the life of the animals and their intrinsic value. Gorbo had said he wanted to be a bird. When he herded in the valleys, he would look up and wish he could be there, soaring over the mountains. In song the theme of nature was always used as an image of man's profound emotions. A song would be riddled with metaphor and had a unique relevance to the people of this land; Machu was renowned all over Amdo for its talented singers and many of the best Tibetan songs came from here. The Amdo people were imbued with the spirit of the land and their lyricism was a direct reflection of the profound love they felt for their culture. They sang with a raw energy unmatched in western society. This was a place where young lovers still sang across the valleys to each other; the two would spontaneously construct a song using metaphor and innuendo. These love songs, called *kabshat* or *lazjhee*, literally 'mountain song', were the most beautiful. They were flexible in their subject matter and might contain messages of love or teasing and sarcasm. It depended on the singers' mood. Sometimes they would deliver a verse alternately, which resulted in witty retorts, as each tried to come up with a better reply than the other. It was a formidable challenge and required a creative mind – but, then, they thought in that way. In Amdo, everyone was a poet. It was no exaggeration.

The music was often sorrowful. Amdowas had a strong sense of identity, an unfaltering concept of home, and an acute sense of the visual. Their vocabulary directly reflected this and they had a startlingly subtle variety of adjectives at their disposal. They had specific words for each minute colour variation of their horses and that colour could not be used to describe anything other than a horse. I was often reminded of the inadequacies of my own language in this respect, as some things were impossible to translate without sounding clumsy.

Tsedup's cousin, Lugerjar, was a singer-songwriter famed throughout Amdo. He made his living producing audio cassettes, which were sold across Tibet, and running the local School for the Performing Arts. I was privileged to have heard him sing for us one night in a restaurant. It was a melancholy sound, a lingering, crystal vibrato. He delivered it with passionate force from the pit of his solar plexus. Everyone stopped eating when they heard it:

*My guru has winged into the blue space,*
*Tears well up in my eyes as I long for him.*
*Lend me your wings, white condor,*
*And I will go to the guru in the azure sky.*

*My brotherhood has been scattered to the four corners*
    *of the world,*
*Sorrow floods my heart as I long for my little brother.*
*Lend me your speed, wild horse,*
*And I will go in search of him.*

*My beloved parents have departed to the darkness of death,*
*I am lost in timeless nights and days as I long for them.*
*Bestow me with your beams, O great sun,*
*And I will search for them in the world of the dead.*

Another relative, Choegetar, had just produced his first

cassette. He was the one who had sung the reunion song for us in the tent when we had first arrived home with Tsedup. His music was haunting, revealing the drama and strife of this land, and now that I knew more about him I understood why. A few years ago, his father had been killed over a land dispute. All of his sons displayed creative tendencies – Choegetar's younger brother, Sherab, had published a book of poetry, and the youngest, Jachwar, was a dancer and singer at the local School for the Performing Arts – and their work was imbued with a sensitivity and an acute sense of empathy that perhaps is only felt by those who have truly suffered.

But not all nomad lyrics were sorrowful. At our marriage blessing in England our Amdo friend Lamakyab had stood at the altar and read Tsedup and me the words to a *lazjhee*.

> *Let you be the yonder snow mountain,*
> *Let me be the pure virgin snow.*
> *Even though the blazing sun rises*
> *I will never melt.*
>
> *Let you be the sandalwood tree*
> *And I will be the scented leaves.*
> *As long as you are not harmed by the wind*
> *Leaves will never fall.*
>
> *Let you be the glistening lake*
> *And I will be the golden fish.*
> *For where would I exist*
> *If not for your rippling waters?*
>
> *Let you be the statue of Dolma, the female saviour,*
> *And I will be your dazzling, brocade robe.*
> *Who would don me*
> *If you were not there in all your sculpted splendour?*

> *The cedar in the forest*
> *Neither perishes in the bleak winter,*
> *Nor is changed by the sweltering summer,*
> *Such are our thoughts.*
>
> *The snow-white Waller flower*
> *Is neither withered by the bitter wind,*
> *Nor suffocated by the weight of snow,*
> *Such is our love.*

I had also heard Tsedo and Rhanjer chanting aloud a traditional rhyme that chronicled the transition of the various stages of winter, which were split into units of nine days:

> *The first ninth, the chilled ground cracks,*
> *The second ninth, the cold stone splits,*
> *The third ninth, the icy iron cleaves,*
> *The fourth ninth, the shuddering bull groans in the barn,*
> *The fifth ninth, a spark of fire warms the sea bed,*
> *The sixth ninth, ice reveals its entombed treasures,*
> *The seventh ninth, water brings seeds of life,*
> *The eighth ninth, the horseman takes off his hat,*
> *The ninth ninth, the wayfarer takes off his shoes,*
> *The tenth ninth, the fertile land heralds the spring.*

We were deep into the winter and still had a long way to go before spring. I regretted that Tsedup and I would not be here then: we would be leaving, and as the daylight hours shortened I knew that our time here was running out. We were somewhere in November and my awareness of the date was gradually becoming all too keen. We were dreading going back to England and the closer it came to the end of December, the more sad and reflective we both became. I missed my family and it would be good to see them and our friends, but we also had responsibilities I would rather have forgotten about. Our days of living in the wilderness were drawing to a close. London and a mortgage beckoned. I had also missed Tsedup's parents while they had been in Lhasa. They were due to return soon and it would be good to spend some time with them before we left.

A few days later the children came running breathlessly down from the mountains, their sacks bulging. They had been collecting grass worms. Previously I had denied the existence of a worm that could turn into a piece of grass, dismissing it as a Tibetan myth. I had heard many things, but this topped the bill. In England I remembered Tsedup telling me that in Tibet there was a tiny dog that was known to hatch from an egg. I had trouble swallowing this one too. But in the case of the grass worm, I was disproved. Indeed there did exist a worm that grew fungus on its head in autumn, which looked like grass, then died. It was called *yarsa gunba*. The Chinese used it as an expensive medicine, and at this time of year the nomad children were despatched by their parents to collect as many as they could from the mountains to sell in town. They were pleased with their haul today, but were even more ecstatic to be able to inform us that they had seen the *tolla* bringing Annay and Amnye up the track to the tribe.

Sure enough, the rickety vehicle was chugging towards us in a dustcloud. We hadn't had snow for a month now. It was bad news for the road, which, through lack of moisture had achieved the consistency of powdered turmeric. It was like driving on a beach. That day the wind was up and the powder enveloped the *tolla* in whipping clouds as the hunched figures of Tsedup's parents clung on tightly and lurched through the landscape, their faces covered with scarves. They pulled up at a distance, as the Chinese driver was nervous of the dogs, and the children ran whooping and squealing from the house to greet their grandparents. Annay Urgin, Shermo Donker and I followed and helped to unload the sacks and boxes that Annay and Amnye had brought back from Lhasa. Everyone was talking at once, grinning and laughing, happy to be reunited. The dogs were barking and jumping around Annay excitedly. Sanjay was pulling at the skirt of her *tsarer* and Dickir Che clung, chattering, to her grandfather's arm.

Then, in the commotion of voices and fervour of chuckling faces, Annay asked, 'Where is Sirmo?'

There was silence. It was the moment we had all been dreading. Annay and Amnye would have to be told that their daughter had eloped. But who was to do it? Shermo Donker busied herself silently with the luggage. I stared at the ground.

'She's gone,' said Annay Urgin. 'We thought you might have heard on the way.' This sort of news travelled fast.

'No,' said Annay, her voice quavering. She began to fuss with the dogs while Amnye spat the dust from his mouth. An uncomfortable lull descended on the welcoming party.

Inside, Annay cried. Amnye sat quietly in the other room with the children. I could hear him asking them where his daughter had gone. He asked Sanjay, Dickir Che and Ziggy, but none had the courage to answer him. They shied away, sensing that something wasn't right but not fully understanding what.

That evening, Tsedup returned. As promised, it was only the presence of his parents that had brought him home. Despite the circumstances, I was excited to see him as his bike screeched to a throbbing halt in the yard and his dust-clogged hair flapped around his face. He was followed by his brothers, Tsedo, Gondo and Rhanjer, who pulled up behind. When the whole family had assembled in the small house, there began a heated discussion. Tsedup challenged his father over the schooling issue, but with less force than I had anticipated. He had cooled down now, and was capable of discussing it man to man. Indeed, his relationship with his father had changed from when he was there last. He had told me that he didn't really talk to him much, apart from the obvious 'Can I borrow your rifle?' requests, to which his father usually replied no. But Amnye was jubilant to see Tsedup again and must have realised how much his son had grown up since he left. Just as Tsedup had noticed how old his parents had become. But I also realised how nervous of Tsedup his family were sometimes. Apparently he had always held strong opinions, but now that he was a man he could be quite intimidating. The iron stove pumped out heat and the air was thick with smoke. Shermo Donker and I sat on the floor and I slipped her a sip of my beer every now and again. She giggled quietly as Amnye railed in the corner and Annay sat rocking on her haunches, cuddling the puppies for comfort.

'One day he will leave her,' repeated Amnye, over and over again, as he coughed on his cigarette. He was angry with Sirmo and Chuchong. The match was clearly not approved. He seemed suspicious of her suitor and I supposed he thought it a weakness in Chuchong's character that he had stolen his daughter. Didn't all fathers deserve respect? But he didn't just blame Sirmo's unexpected new husband. As he debated with his sons, I discovered that he had anticipated the possibility of his hot-headed girl's flight before he went to Lhasa. He had implored her not to run away while he and Annay were gone and she had agreed. Now he knew she had ignored him and he was furious. He knew that Sirmo had gone to a huge family and would be living communally with them all and he insisted that, over time, she would not get on with so many in-laws. Only if they were given their own home would Amnye agree to give Sirmo her share of the family wealth that was due to her. As a new bride, traditionally, Sirmo should be lavished with silver, coral, turquoise, new leopardskin *tsarers* and her own quota of yaks.

Amnye slept outside that night beside the clay house where we stored the meat. He had missed Amdo when he was in the city and had had enough of sleeping on beds, he said. As for the food, he told us he preferred plain Amdo fare. He had dreamt of a bowl of *tanthuk*. Lhasa had changed beyond recognition. Now it was another Chinese city: too many people, too many buildings. Tsedup and Tsedo tried to dissuade him from sleeping outside, as he clearly had flu, but he grunted obstinately and they tucked him up on the frost-bitten ground. The sand blustered around his head, but he didn't care. He needed to feel the earth again.

Two days later the mediator arrived, a goblin-like man. His name was Garsay and he had been selected by Sirmo's new family to act as go-between in this most sensitive of issues as it was not appropriate for the two families to meet. He arrived from Sirmo's tribe in the morning and Amnye entertained him, despite the severity of his illness. The diminutive man had brought cloth from the groom's family as an offering. The exchange was heated, Amnye speaking most. The mediator was there merely to listen and relate Amnye's words to the unfortunate new bride and her in-laws, but he was in for an earful.

We sat in the adjacent room, sewing quietly and listening to Amnye's passionate protestations. '*Zuncha ma*, liar,' he said, over and over. Sirmo had lied to him by leaving. Annay interrupted his stream of invective with her own hysterical tirade, until Tsedo told her to shut up. She came out to sit with us by the clay stove, muttering to herself. Shermo Donker and Annay Urgin tutted along. From the huge mound of matted sheepskin piled between them came a faint odour of damp and cheese. They were making a *tsokwa* for Dado, who needed a wife. I asked them if Amnye had been as angry when Tsedup had run away all those years ago. They said no. No doubt, it was different for boys. Then Annay Urgin stopped sewing, as if recalling a moment from that time. She told me that Amnye had cried when, after five years of no communication because the mail hadn't got through from India, he had received Tsedup's first letter. I realised how devastating the waiting must have been for him. Although I was ignorant of the subtle complexities of matrimonial negotiation, I thought it strange that such a sensitive man wished to punish his daughter. For I had heard his ultimatum.

'She is not welcome back here,' he bellowed. 'Not until this problem is settled and they are given their own home.'

The goblin shuffled out of the door, somewhat abashed, followed by Amnye and Tsedo. I knew that when he returned to Sirmo and related her father's words, she would be unhappy. This dispute had signalled a real rift from her own family. She had been banished until the negotiations were complete, and how long that would take nobody knew.

She would be missed. Tsedup and I would probably not see her until we returned to Amdo, and we had no idea how long that would be. As Garsay mounted his horse to ride back to the other tribe, Annay waved the cloth he had brought. 'Look, we have swapped our girl for this!' she cried, as he disappeared down the dusty track.

# FIFTEEN

# *Where the Heart Is*

The social pressures of life in Amdo were considerable. Since it was now common knowledge that we would be leaving soon, we received daily invitations to visit people. Even Tsedup was exhausted with the spirit of Tibetan hospitality. That morning we were woken early by Rinchen. The Artful Dodger danced around our hut excitedly and told us to get up. Our neighbour, Gabo, had arrived to escort us to his brother Sangta's home in the next westerly valley. We dressed quickly, then jumped on the back of the bike and followed him on his horse. In their valley we passed a small temple, painted white and orange in traditional Tibetan style. Two elderly nomad women were circumambulating in the morning sunshine.

We arrived at Sangta's home, to find that the family had slaughtered a yak and several people were huddled around it, busily dissecting it. Sangta's wife hurried us inside their small clay house, steering me away from the sight of the dead animal. She didn't realise I was used to it. Inside, it was stifling. The heat from the iron stove-pipe and the sun on the plastic-sheeted windows, combined to offer little in the name of oxygen but we settled ourselves for the day. I watched Sangta talking. In contrast to his brother, who was the stout, cheerful wrestler, he had long, sleek hair, a generous moustache and the largest Roman nose I had seen on a Tibetan. He sat pondering his guests like a stalking polecat with his sly eyes. Sangta was a real nomad, a wanderer. Rarely at home, he preferred to spend his time travelling from place to place on horseback. Tsedup told me that there was not one area of Amdo that he hadn't seen. His children eyed me suspiciously from the corner of the room; the elder attempted a smile while the younger stared unblinking from beneath a shock of dreadlocks dangling from the crown of her head.

We ate *momos* as the crows squawked and flapped on the tin roof above our heads, and I listened as the men talked for hours. Then just before the sun tipped down below the mountain ridges, we left. Gabo asked me if I'd like to ride his horse home and, seized by the challenge, I said yes. I mounted the black steed, rather self-consciously, since everyone in the valley was watching. It was important to appear professional at such times, but as I gripped the sides of the enormous beast with my knees and it began to move off I felt nervous. This was it: my first ride alone. I deceived the crowd of onlookers with a huge smile and willed the horse to respond as I tugged cautiously on the reins. He was obedient and I began to feel confident. Ahead, Tsedup and Gabo revved the bike and roared away down the track. They would watch me from the road beneath the mountains, they said.

I set off across the low hills bordering the grassland. From the saddle I could see the receding blues and greys of the undulating Silver Horn range on the other side of the Yellow river and the barren dustbowl of the abandoned grassland. A train of golden sand billowed from the bike on the track far beneath me. It was silent apart from the swish of the horse's hoofs through the parched grass and a skylark's song. I rode through a herd of grazing yaks, who parted ranks grudgingly, and I felt an overwhelming sense of exhilaration and freedom, that I was alone, that I was on this horse, that I was in Tibet. I knew that this image would be preserved for ever in my imagination, like a camera shutter closing.

For the next few days there was to be an interesting break from the social rounds. It was Nyon Nyi, the twenty-fourth day of the tenth month in the Tibetan calendar: an auspicious time and an occasion for fasting and prayer. It consisted of two days dedicated to contemplation, prayer and self-purification. Tsedup told me that during the fast one was supposed to think of all those who were less fortunate than oneself, who were starving, or whose lives were difficult and miserable. This applied to both people and animals. He explained that on the first day, Gonsuch, we would be allowed to eat lunch, but thereafter we could not touch food for the rest of the day apart from a drink of tea in the evening. On the second day, Nachchet, it would be forbidden to eat, drink or talk, as one assumed the embodiment of an animal. Also, during Nyon Nyi there were rules to be obeyed. There could be no sex, chastising of children or animals, motorbike riding, or anything other than was practically necessary in terms of work around the home and with the animals. I had decided to stay and fast with Shermo Donker, Dickir Che, Gorbo, Annay Urgin and little Tselo. Although they had participated when they were children, Tsedup and his brother Tsedo did not feel up to the challenge and went to town, leaving us to it.

That morning I rose before dawn to pee. Outside, the scene reminded me of a biblical setting. The small clay houses nestled at the foot of the mountain under the stars, winking in the ethereal sky. I felt as if I had arrived at Bethlehem. It was probably the fact that I knew Christmas was approaching back home, combined with the knowledge that I was about to have a religious experience of a different kind over here. I was sleeping in the house as the men were in town and I snuggled down again next to Shermo Donker, feeling pleasantly confused. At seven thirty she woke us and we washed our faces. We did three prostrations on the sleeping platform and then she told us to go back to sleep as she had some jobs to do. I lay down and dozed, in and out of sleep.

When we woke, I prepared breakfast for the two Chinese carpenters who were staying with us. They had come to make a cupboard for the house and scoffed their rice broth through rotting, gold-capped teeth. I guessed that we would all have to tolerate each other. It was a bit of bad timing that they were here for Nyon Nyi, but on the other hand, they didn't understand us anyway, so conversation was limited even before we had started the mute part of our fast. They smiled at us nervously and we grinned back. Those of us who were fasting were only allowed to drink tea for breakfast. I didn't realise that you couldn't get up from where you were sitting while drinking it. You were supposed to finish by purifying yourself with a drink of water, then spitting it out. Only then were you permitted to move. I would remember that for the next meal. Also I didn't realise you couldn't brush your hair, which I already had. In the future, I thought it prudent to ask if it was permitted to do something before I did it. Could I brush my teeth? Could I wash clothes? Could I put on lip balm? I could. But then, seizing the opportunity to exploit my ignorance, the children started humouring themselves by telling me it wasn't permitted to go to the loo and other naughty fibs.

By midday I was feeling quite hungry. I wasn't alone and, since I was the only one with a watch, everyone who had missed breakfast was asking me the time. At last we were given the signal by Shermo Donker and we all went next door to Annay Urgin's house for a feast. Her clay home was dark and damp. In contrast to our house everything was made from earth: the walls, the roof, the floor, the sleeping platform. It was indeed basic, yet she had constructed an incredibly vibrant altar in the darkest corner, housing golden cups – *thib* – candles and pictures of the lamas. It was the only colourful thing inside the plain dwelling and proudly declared her religious devotion. We prostrated three times before the altar and Annay Urgin placed a small golden bowl of *djoma* and bread in front of the lamas' pictures as an offering. We then stuffed ourselves. Meat was omitted from this meal as an act of compassion, so instead we ate *djoma*, *tsampa*, bread and satsumas, and drank tea. Dickir Ziggy, who was not fasting, had become our slave during the meal as we weren't allowed to move. She scurried around pouring tea and filling the iron stove with dung. Aware of the encroaching fast, we ate so much we felt sick. Then fully satiated and nursing swollen stomachs, we each made a little *lanchuch*, which looked like a small boat with a bowl on top made from *tsampa*, filled with a piece of everything we had eaten. We spat water into it to purify ourselves again before we were allowed to get up. Sanjay ran and put our boats on the wall outside and we watched through the window, as the dog ate our handiwork.

There would be no more food until the day after tomorrow. I hoped I could make it. I was enjoying myself so far. Contrary to my expectations, for a religious experience the mood was far from sombre; everyone chatted and laughed and the children shrieked so much that Annay Urgin developed a headache. I hadn't had much time for the contemplation of sentient beings today, but perhaps that would come tomorrow with the silence.

The next morning, I woke to see Shermo Donker pulling on her *tsarer* in the dark. I turned on the light and she smiled at me in recognition. Today it was forbidden to talk. Only prayers could be uttered, but since I didn't know any apart from '*Om mani padme hum*', I would have to be silent. We prostrated three times and I lay down, listening to Dickir Che mumbling incoherently through closed lips in the next room. She was being teased by Sanjay and Dickir Ziggy, who were not part of the ritual and were trying to make her talk. Then she and Gorbo came into my room to prostrate and we smiled at each other and giggled. It was funny not being able to talk. I nestled down into my thick *tsarer* and watched the ice crystals melt very slowly on the frosted window-pane. They looked like intricate flowers, flashing white as the sun

Photograph by Eleanor Thorp

*Clockwise from top,* milking my yak, Karee Ma; women from our tribe; me,
Chloë and Ells on top of the holy mountain, Amnye Kula; Annay Urgin shows
me Tibetan weaving techniques.

Dickir Che and Ziggy.

Photograph by Eleanor Thorp   Photograph by Eleanor Thorp

*Top,* friend Tseqwar, Tsedup's brother, Tsedo, friend Wharden, Tsedup's eldest brother, Rhanjer and younger brother, Gondo. *Bottom from left,* Gondo's son, Dorlo; Tsering Samdup outside the tiger's lair at Lhamo; Rhanjer's son, Samlo.

Photograph by Katrina Edwards

*Top,* Tsedup in winter *tsokwa*; *bottom,* Gondo's wife, Tseten, Gondo, Tamba and friend.

Tsedup's sister, Dombie.

Photograph by Cloë Lederman

Opposite page, *clockwise from top left*,
Dombie's son Yeshe; her daughter
Dawa with Dickir Che; girls in *tsokwas
– in front*, Rhanjer's girls, Lhamo
Tsering and Rinchenchet with eldest
daughter, Gurra *centre back*; Tselo in
the grassland.
This page *top*, Dickir Che and
Rinchenchet knitting; *above*, Sirmo's
son, Tsering Dhondup; *right*, me
wearing the rings that Annay gave me.

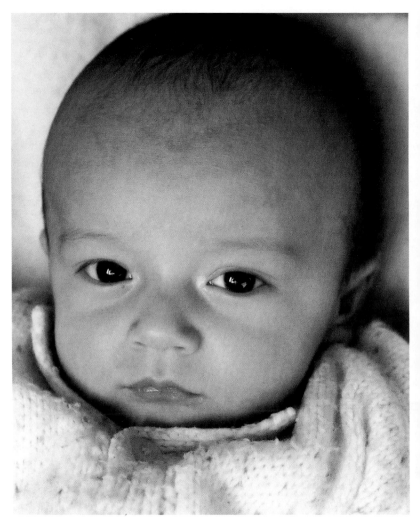

Our son, Gonbochab.

rose behind them. But too soon they were gone, dribbling in rivulets and racing each other down the warm glass.

By mid-morning I was deep in thought and hungry. I began to think about the fact that I was the embodiment of an animal. What did that mean? Which animal did I represent? I thought about the *abra*, the small rodent – which the bitch had killed yesterday. It had still been alive when I picked it up and its tiny body had shaken as I held it in my *tsarer* for comfort. I had guessed it was a mess inside, although it had looked all right. The children and I had made it a home out of an old shoebox and straw, but its damaged intestines had given up an hour afterwards. In all its pain it hadn't made a sound, not a squeak. I was silent. I was the *abra*. Or maybe I was a bird? I tried to internalise the feeling of being able to fly, then decided that maybe I was trying too hard. Perhaps I wasn't supposed to represent one single beast, but the whole spectrum of creeping, crawling, flying, skulking, living things.

At lunch-time the bitch bit the Chinese carpenter and Shermo Donker hit her with a stick. The bitch was a sentient being worthy of respect, but my sister-in-law had forgotten that rule. Then Rhanjer came round from his house, specifically to tease us. He encouraged us to be less pious by beating us with wet towels and, of course, we were forced to defend ourselves. He giggled like a naughty child and hit Shermo Donker with his silver pipe, which unfortunately hurt her hand. She was struggling so hard not to laugh that the tears poured down her cheeks. It seemed that nobody was prepared to take Nyon Nyi seriously.

That afternoon the hunger set in. It was twenty-four hours since I had eaten anything and a full nineteen since my last drink. I felt tired and my eyelids were heavy, but it was forbidden to sleep during the day, so I fought the fatigue. Although talking was banned, it seemed quite permissible to hum phonetically through pursed lips and it was now becoming something of a game, guessing what people were saying. Of course, my job was much harder. As Dickir Che tried for the fourth time to convey some piece of information to me, I had to give up. Trying to talk in a foreign language with your mouth closed is impossible. The others were quite good at interpreting each other, but Dickir Ziggy had decided to feign ignorance and was taking full advantage of the situation today. If the rules meant that her mother couldn't reprimand her, then she could be as bad as she liked and get away with it. Or so she thought. After a concentrated period of chanting prayers and quietly suffering Ziggy's antics, Shermo Donker thrashed her. Ziggy fled wailing and her mother began swearing under her breath; a weird, dull muttering sound. A new mantra.

I decided to give prayer a try. But I did it in the only way I knew how: in my head and to my God. I had always resorted to prayer in times of need. Whoever I prayed for, I asked God to hold them in His hand, as if He was some benevolent giant. Right now, something in the back of my mind was preventing me from relaxing fully into this experience and I knew what it was. Guilt. I was reminded of the words from Exodus: 'You may worship no other god than me. You shall not make yourselves any idols: any images resembling animals, birds, or fish. You must never bow to an image or worship it in any way; for I, the Lord your God, am very possessive. I will not share your affection with any other god!'

According to the Bible, I was committing sacrilege. But I preferred to think of it as showing respect for Tsedup's culture. I had always despised the zeal with which Christian missionaries had sought to convert indigenous peoples throughout the world. Although I wasn't a disciple of Buddhism, I afforded it the greatest respect. I wanted to learn about the nomads' rituals and, through participating, would be able to understand this place and, consequently, know more about my husband. I also wanted to share this special time with Tsedup's family. I would just have to avoid any mighty thunderbolts that the possessive giant threw at me.

Neither Tsedup nor I were exceptionally religious in terms of either Buddhism or Christianity. I had been confirmed when I was eleven with my best friend, yet I was suspicious of my motivation. In retrospect I had probably just wanted to copy her. My mother had been my main source of encouragement in matters of faith. When I was a child our house had been littered with religious paraphernalia. There were palm crosses tacked to the walls and postcards of Jesus on the dresser. On the wall in the toilet was a rhyme I had pondered throughout my youth. It began, 'Go placidly amid the noise and the haste and remember what peace there may be in silence . . .'

Today I felt peaceful and silent. I prayed to God for all the sentient beings and was satisfied with that compromise. Whatever else I felt about my religion, I knew that God was love and Buddha was compassion. When you stripped the religions down to their bare essentials, that was it for me.

I went outside to see the world covered in dust. The washing on the line had frozen solid and was creaking in the wind. Then Tsedo pulled up on his motorbike. He had been to the other side of Machu to feed the fish. Apparently there were masses of them at a convergence of two rivers and it was customary for people to go there and feed them on this day.

That evening Tsedo and Shermo Donker lit a candle in a bucket and placed it before the altar cupboard. It glowed from within the red plastic. Then he took a small book wrapped in a cotton wallet from behind the glass door and began to read. It was a prayer and his voice wove a familiar, hypnotic chant as he read, deeply and resonantly, like the monks in the monastery, passing his prayer beads through his fingers. Around him the children shrieked with the squealing puppies, the Chinese carpenters played cards and chatted, the kettle hummed, steam whistled from the spout and Shermo Donker bustled around making rice broth for the workers. I appeared to be the only one listening. Then the children began to join in and there was a resonant chorus in the room. I took the prayer wheel and softly chanted, '*Om mani padme hum.*' It was soothing, along with the voices rising and falling in cadence.

That night we fell asleep early to escape the pain in our empty stomachs. I woke before daybreak, feeling weak and dizzy, my mouth parched. Shermo Donker felt the same. She pointed to her throat and rasped. We dressed in our *tsarers* and went to Annay Urgin's house. It was still dark, but the sky was ablaze with stars and a crescent moon shone like a smile in the deep, purple sky. Inside, we prostrated three times in front of her altar and then drank *samker*, a broth of *tsampa*, water and salt. It was hearty but not very tasty. I was past caring by that stage and would probably have eaten grass if they had given it to me. We then spat the soup three times into a bowl of earth to end the ritual. Nyon Nyi was over. Now we could talk freely. The candle in the oil lamp flickered in the dim clay room. Gorbo giggled, Dickir Che reclined in my lap, Annay Urgin and Shermo Donker chattered animatedly and loudly, relieved to have the freedom of speech, while Dolma ladled out the thick, brown soup. I lay down and felt the warm, dark atmosphere of the room, as the butter lamps burned softly in front of the altar and the effigies of lamas. The tears welled in my eyes. Once again I realised how difficult it would be to leave them all.

A couple of weeks later it was Christmas. I had decided to show them what it was like. I knew there was no church here, no carol singers, no turkey or mince-pies. *Momos* and some games would have to do. Mostly, I wanted the children to feel as excited as the children in the West did at this time of year. That meant presents; lots of them. They had never had presents on such a scale before; probably because their parents were not such shameless consumers as their western counterparts. Still, it would be fun for once. Tsedup and I announced our intentions and asked Rhanjer if we could hold the celebrations at his house. We wanted the whole family to be united there on Christmas Eve, including Gondo and Dombie and their families from the other side of Machu. The invitations despatched, we set off for town, Rhanjer following the bike in his truck. We had some serious shopping to do.

We bought enough food and drink for a real feast and loaded up the lorry. Then Tsedup and I went browsing round the bazaars and sifting through the jumble of plastic in the shops. We bought toy guns, cars, a football, a model dinosaur, dolls, colouring pens, books, hats, a fluffy dog that barked when you touched it; we even found glass paper-weights with snow-scenes. I was delighted to find wrapping paper, ribbon and spangly decorations in one particular shop. At the end of the day we had a sackful. It sat between

Tsedup and me on the back of the bike as we trundled to his parents' house at the foot of the monastery. Annay had asked me to stay with her that night and Tsedup was my taxi ride.

That evening we talked. I relished my conversations with Annay. This was the only time that we had been alone since the men had gone to worship the holy mountain. By now my language skills had improved to the stage where I could understand most of what she said; she knew my limitations and was patient and kind. It was a freezing night outside and the stove burned furiously in the sweltering room. She made me some broth and we wrapped ourselves in blankets and sat on the sleeping platform. I asked her what Tsedup had been like as a boy and she told me he had been naughty. His idea of fun was not hers, she said. She told me about the time when he had kicked down the sacred clay fire in the tent. In desperation she had tied him up by his ankles and suspended him from the beam above the fire. I laughed. I asked her what it had been like to give birth to her children and she recounted the details of each one. Dombie's birth was the worst. Annay had nearly died and had to be taken to hospital, where she received sixteen injections (of what drug, I had no idea, but I assumed it was painkillers). Also, Sirmo was born when Annay was alone in the tent. Tsedup and Gondo, who were about seven and six then, had been sleeping in the corner as she struggled, unaided and crying. As I listened, I had trouble understanding why no one had come to help her. Men were always banished at such times, as it was deemed inappropriate for them to witness childbirth; it was the women's domain. There was usually a woman present who acted as midwife. I guessed that it had been a spontaneous delivery and no one had heard her cries.

I tried to imagine the awful spectre of childbirth without drugs or anyone for company, in a tent in the middle of the grassland. For me, nothing could be more horrific. Annay was an amazingly strong woman.

She had been forty years old when she had carried her last child, Gorbo; an old woman, she said. Tsedup had told me that he remembered his father scolding her for getting pregnant. 'At your age, Labko,' he'd scoffed. 'Do you have no shame?' He had spoken as if the event had had nothing to do with him. Annay had laughed. But as she became heavier, she had found it increasingly difficult. Seven previous births had taken their toll on her body and she grew weaker. Tsedup had been afraid she would die. He nursed her and helped her with her daily tasks. A teenage boy milking yaks was a sight to be seen among the nomads, but he hadn't cared. The tribe had teased him and called him Namma. I found it moving that he had behaved so instinctively and with such compassion at an age when boys are usually self-conscious. He was a good son.

As she stirred the embers with a stick, Annay told me how happy she and Amnye would be if Tsedup and I had a child. She smiled at me. She wasn't interfering, she was simply stating a fact. I told her I wanted a child. I meant it too. I just had to tell Tsedup about it, that was all. The feeling had been growing in me. The hardships we had suffered in England had faded to a distant memory, and here I had been nourished and imbued with the sense of well-being, of kinship. The fecundity of nature that surrounded me had, no doubt, also played its part. I felt bound to Tsedup as never before. A child would make us a family. A child who belonged to two worlds.

\*     \*     \*

The next day we had a surprise. Annay had been in discreet negotiation with her spies and despite Amnye's ultimatum, she had arranged for us to meet Sirmo for the last time before we left. Her daughter had been ostracised at home, but there was nothing in the rulebook to say that we couldn't meet her at Annay's brother's house. Annay had worked it all out. I began to see where her daughter had learnt her guile.

We arrived at Perko's house in the morning sunshine. His winter home was on a low hill overlooking the grassland, just above where the tribe had been in the summer. He had amazing views east and west up the valley, and I could see the clay cliffs of the Yellow river and the water's surface, shining as it twisted round the bend. Tsedup's cousin, Sonnam Sebay, had gone to collect Sirmo from her in-laws that morning: they had given their permission for her to leave them for a few days. After more than a month without her, I was dying to see how she was and nearly fell off the bike in my haste to dismount. She emerged from Perko's house, resplendent. Chuchong's family had obviously spoilt her and she wore a brand-new, elaborately embroidered *tsarer*, new shoes and a big silver and coral ring I hadn't seen before. As I looked at her I was filled with pride. She was a beautiful woman now, a wife, and she had truly blossomed. Her cheeks shone with new-found radiance and her hair was sleekly plaited. But she didn't meet my gaze. Instead, she stood with her head bowed in shame. I wanted to run and hug her, but that would have been a very English thing to do and I restrained myself. Tsedup turned off the bike engine irritably and we all went inside.

Perko and his wife, Annay Dobe, had done their best to make things easy for everyone, but the atmosphere was tense. We ate *momos* politely and Tsedup directed all conversation to his uncle, with whom he fell into a discussion about the tribe. Not once did he address Sirmo. I sat by the window with her and we held hands.

'Are you happy?' I whispered.

'Yes, I am,' she said, with a tiny smile.

And I felt that she was. Inside she radiated warmth and I realised that this was the hardest ordeal for her: dealing with the aftermath of her actions and the hurt that she had inflicted on her family. She was obviously in love and did not regret running away.

'Do you miss your husband?' I asked her, grinning.

She giggled quietly and blushed. 'I missed you, Shermo,' she murmured. 'Did you miss me?'

'I missed you very much,' I replied.

She kept her eyes firmly on her sewing for the next few hours. It was strange to see her so restrained and filled with propriety. She had always been so natural and spontaneous before. Later, she left the room and retired to the back parlour with Annay. They sat studiously picking the nits from each other's hair and talking at great length. I decided not to interrupt. There was a lot to cover and they didn't need any distraction from me. Annay was clearly thrilled to see her daughter and I imagined that she was grilling Sirmo for information about her new life. She would need to know that she was content and that her mother-in-law was good to her. All too often, a new bride was treated like a slave. But Annay seemed content with Sirmo's answers and cooed her approval.

Before we left, I went outside with Sirmo and her cousin, Malo. We squatted downwind from the dogs and I teased her. 'You're a *namma* now,' I said, chuckling. For a moment the mask slipped: as we girls were alone, Sirmo threw back her head and laughed. It was a joyful sound. I felt happy for her. We walked back to the house arm in arm and stood for photographs. Then I took a picture of her and Tsedup as he stood stiffly beside her, frowning. He mounted the bike and spoke to his sister for the first time. '*Shimo*, girl,' he bellowed, 'you have upset your father.' She stared at her feet and he seemed to give his blessing, for he modified his tone. 'I won't see you for a long time. You've made your choice, so try your best.' She began to cry softly and I put my arm around her. Tsedup's mode of address had shocked me. He had sounded patronising and stern. I had never heard him speak like this before. I knew he loved his sister and I didn't understand why he had to behave like this now, when he was leaving. Then, I saw him in context and with enormous clarity: he was an Amdo man. According to his culture, his behaviour was appropriate, but I didn't understand it. It seemed cruel.

I sighed in disapproval and turned to Sirmo. 'Goodbye,' I said. 'When I see you again, you'll have a child.' She was a newly-wed; what could have been more likely in this fertile land? She tried to smile, but couldn't look up. I wiped her eyes and kissed her head. For once I didn't care about nomad etiquette. She squeezed my hand as I mounted the bike. Then I left her, speeding down the hill to the track. I waved for a long time, clinging to Tsedup with one hand, staring until she was nothing more than a dot.

# SIXTEEN

## *The Parting*

On Christmas Eve, in the late afternoon, the streets of the town were bathed in a pale violet light. The mountains to the north had lost their brilliance. Black crows flocked across the sun as it added crimson and tangerine ripples to the feathered cloud. We had come to collect the children from school. Dawa and Yeshe, Dombie's children, had left their lessons early so that we could arrive at the winter house by dusk. Gondo's son, Dorlo, had been truanting again. Tsedup had found him in a video hall watching Kung Fu films and had threatened to leave him behind if he didn't behave. Dorlo swore he would.

Before hitting the road, we took the children to a restaurant. They were delirious with excitement, having been told they were getting presents, and nearly choked on the noodles in their haste to depart. Dorlo was having particular problems controlling himself. Unable to avoid the question threatening to implode his brain, he was forced to blurt out through spluttering lips, 'Is mine a gun? Is mine a gun?'

Tsedup laughed at him. 'No, it's a doll,' he teased.

'I *know* it's a big gun,' beamed Dorlo.

'You'll find out tomorrow,' I said. Thank God we had bought him a gun.

Yeshe, his junior, remained polite and restrained, kicking his legs under the table and blowing bubbles from his nose. For such a small boy he had a peculiar sense of propriety. He drove the food leisurely round his plate with one chopstick, as he surveyed us all curiously. His sister, Dawa, chattered and giggled and sniffed; snapping open and shut the pink, plastic purse that hung round her neck. The children were all dressed in their *tsarers* for the journey to the grassland. We would all have to go by *tolla*, as their parents weren't coming on the bikes until tomorrow.

Tsedup hailed one of the three-wheeled tractors on the street, as I waited with the children in Annay Latuck's *momo* shop. We warmed our hands on her stove. Dusk was falling and it was freezing outside. Annay Latuck ran the shop like an eccentric brigadier, shouting orders to the girls behind the curtain in the back kitchen. She was a no-nonsense woman, but her beady eyes twinkled and her wry smile betrayed a kindly nature. She was the mother of our friend Tamding Gyalpo, who now lived in Switzerland. She hadn't seen him for eight years and missed him terribly. We would often sit and talk as she held my hand and I assured her he would come home soon. He was waiting for his Swiss passport to enable him to travel. The scenario was all too familiar and I felt for her as I had for Tsedup's mother. Now, she placed a pile of *shabala*, meat fritters, in front of us and commanded me to eat. '*Sou*, Namma Kate! *Sou!*' I wasn't hungry, but I knew that there would be no escape if I didn't attempt her offer of sustenance. She always looked after me. Yet, half-way through our greasy snack, we were summoned to the road.

The *tolla* ride was predictably uncomfortable. The track resembled an ice-rink in places and we skidded precariously for most of the way, juddering in the back as the engine thundered in our ears. At one point we stalled after crossing a frozen stream and Dorlo decided to jump off. He ran away from us wielding a gun-shaped stick and mock-firing at us, crying, 'Dddddrrrr, dddddrrrrr!' like a machine-gun. Then the Chinese driver pumped the gas and the engine burst into its own rapid fire. Without waiting, he continued driving up the hill, as Dorlo, shocked at being abandoned, shouted obscenities in his high-pitched voice and chased behind until he got a grip on the tailgate and we pulled him in. That boy was a liability.

In the evening we congregated at our house. Annay held the fort as the children shrieked and fought together in the limited space. It was rare for all the cousins to be united and tonight it was mayhem. Two of Rhanjer's children, Samlo and Rinchenchet, had also turned up to stay the night. Although their own house was only a hundred yards away, there was no way they were going to miss out.

At bedtime the boys went to our hut outside. Gorbo was in charge. He supervised as Rinchen, Samlo, Dorlo and Sanjay squabbled together under the quilts. Yeshe did not want to join them. He had specifically asked Tsedup if he could sleep with him on top of the dung mountain outside. Tsedup was delighted. We wrapped them up in sheepskins as they lay together in sub-zero temperatures on the small summit, with only their noses poking out. Tsedup told me later that they spent a long time watching the shooting stars and then, thinking his uncle well travelled, Yeshe had asked him if he had ever been to the moon. It hadn't been such an unreasonable suggestion, since England seemed just as far away to Yeshe.

'When you went up in a plane, you must have been really close to the stars,' he had said. 'Did you see people and houses on them?' Tsedup had told him yes, and Yeshe had decided to go there when he grew up.

I put the girls to bed next to the clay stove. Dickir Che, Ziggy, Dawa and Rinchenchet were all inside one huge sheepskin that had been sewn together like an enormous sleeping-bag. I threatened to tickle them all and they retreated to the bottom of the bag, screeching and writhing to escape me. I left them breathless and giggling together. Then their mumblings became silence as they fell asleep. But just as Tsedo, Shermo Donker, Annay and I were about to bed down for the night, Dorlo burst into the room, tears pouring down his cheeks. He flung his arms round his grandmother.

'What's wrong?' Annay asked.

'There's a ghost out there,' he sobbed. 'Cousin Gorbo told me.'

We laughed as she hushed and rocked him, then let him settle in her bed on the floor. His gunslinging bravado had disappeared, and Dorlo was not the big man he professed to be, just a child. In fact now, a more lovable one.

I woke on Christmas morning to Dorlo climbing inside

my *tsarer*. 'It *is* a big gun, isn't it?' he said. I had to give him top marks for persistence, but I wasn't going to give in. It reminded me of my own Christmases as a child. The anguish I had suffered, waiting for my parents to wake up and make the tea, then drink it, before my brother and I were allowed to open our presents. Now Dorlo would have to learn the same patience. I went outside to check on Tsedup and Yeshe. They were still sound asleep on top of the dung heap. The early-morning frost sparkled on the mound of sheepskins. Not even a nose was visible. I hoped they had been warm enough in the night. We prodded them awake and Annay and I laughed at them as they emerged, blinking, from the pile. It was the most bizarre location for a bed.

When we were all assembled we went down to Rhanjer's home for the party. He lived with his wife and three girls in a smart brick house at the side of the railway-arch dwellings. Although he had five children, his two boys stayed in town. The eldest, Tinlee, was a monk and lived in the monastery, and the younger, Samlo, was at school in the week and lived with his uncle, a teacher. As we arrived at the house, Gurra, Rhanjer's eldest daughter, ran out to escort us past the dogs. Her father stood on the porch, grinning festively. He was proud of his home. It was much larger than ours, with steps up to the front door and brick floors throughout. He guided us in to where his wife, Shermo Domatso, was busy preparing for the festivities. She was a diminutive woman with a wide smile of perfectly white teeth and laughter lines fanning out from soft eyes. She spoke gently and melodiously. '*Losar zung!*' she said in greeting, as I walked in. It was the closest thing to 'Happy Christmas' in the nomad vocabulary, but really meant 'Happy New Year'. Losar was their biggest annual festival, and Tsedup had told them that Christmas in

England was like Losar in Tibet. In terms of seasonal status, this was true, but I was to discover that the nomads' idea of celebrating was quite different from our own.

The house had been festooned with silver decorations and the table was piled high with sweets, fruit, boiled meat and drinks. In the back room, several hundred *momos* awaited. We all went to sit down on the platform. Azjung sat in front of the table, the sunlight from the window mapping out the lines on his old skin with shadow. He thumbed his prayer beads. As we entered he smiled and motioned for Tsedup and me to come and sit with him.

'Why do the westerners celebrate Christmas?' he asked Tsedup curiously.

Not wishing to instigate a full-blown theological discussion, Tsedup found an analogy to make himself understood. 'It is their Buddha's birthday,' he explained.

Azjung nodded carefully. Tibetans didn't celebrate anybody's birthday, so no doubt he found this answer strange. I had always found it strange that they did not count birthdays. Here, everyone automatically advanced in age at the same time every New Year, which was around February. Sometimes this led to confusion for me: it meant that a baby born in January would be called a year old a month later. This was probably why nomad children always looked much younger than their western counterparts.

Many years before, when Tsedup had applied for his Indian passport to leave for England with me, he was supposed to have produced a birth certificate. He had had no idea what they were talking about. When I had explained, he had said, 'I exist. I don't need a piece of paper to prove it.' Nevertheless, the authorities seemed to think it was important. He had remembered his mother telling him he was born in winter, so he had picked a date at random: 2 December. From then on, to the outside world, he had existed. It had been Tsedup's first taste of the infuriating bureaucracy of modern society and it hadn't stopped there, for they had also asked his surname. Tibetans don't use their family names as we do in our everyday life in the West. In Tibet everyone is known by their first name. Although his family name was Kambo-Wasser, Tsedup had never used any other name but Tsedup. In his culture it simply wasn't necessary.

'What is your father's name?' the official had persisted.

Tsedup had stood confused. 'Karko,' he had said.

From that day, it had been Tsedup's surname and then mine.

The western Buddha's birthday was in full swing by mid-morning. Dombie and her husband Tsering Samdup, Gondo and Tseten had now arrived, having finished their morning chores at home. It was a rare thing for the women to come away for a whole day and night, and was only possible thanks to their neighbours, who had agreed to round up the animals at the end of the day. I was glad that they had made it. With all the family and half of the tribe competing for space in the parlour, it was time to distribute the presents. They had been stacked up on the family altar since we had arrived and the children had sat patiently, staring with saucer eyes at the bulky yellow-paper packages. It felt almost ceremonial as we began to give them out. Tsedup and I had chosen a different gift for each child and we felt around the shape of each parcel to determine what was inside, then gave it to them. Each time, nine other pairs of eager eyes followed the parcel to its destination. The children shrieked with delight when the contents were revealed. When Dorlo received his long-expected rifle, he jumped around hysterically on the platform. He loaded the plastic bullets into the cartridge with professional ease and cocked his weapon, ready to fire. He took aim at Yeshe and before anyone could stop him, he pulled the trigger. Annay screamed. But nothing happened. He squeezed the trigger again. Still nothing. Unbelievably, the gun was faulty and, feeling cheated and frustrated, Dorlo collapsed in tears as everyone tried to calm him. The excitement of Christmas was just too much for him. It was too much for little Sanjay too. Among other things, we had given him the plastic dinosaur and when he peeled back the paper and saw the hideous creature inside, he dropped it and ran away in shock.

The children's mothers collected up all the presents for safekeeping as soon as they were opened. I thought it strange that they didn't let the children play with them now, since that was what Christmas Day was all about. But they were shrewder than I. They knew that if today was to be anything like the Losar they were used to, those presents would shortly be garbage.

I soon saw what they meant. The nomads really knew how to party and, sure enough, I watched the day progress from the initial chatting and sipping of drinks into a full-scale riot. Most of the tribe had arrived to join in by now and since there was a severe overcrowding problem in the house, everyone spilled outside. It was a warm day, the wind had settled and the sun shone favourably from the sapphire sky. There was nothing to prevent a game or two out in the yard, I thought. Perhaps a football match with Samlo's new ball. But they had something less sedate in mind. The nomads like to wrestle. The women were the real hell-raisers and left most of the men inside with their beer. I watched as they chased the teenage boys, performing perfect rugby tackles and bringing them down in the dust. Grandmothers grappled grandchildren and nephews attacked aunts. Dombie, who was normally so quiet, had transformed into a raging Amazon and had her cousin Donkerchab in an armlock, as he cried for mercy. I saw Shermo Donker writhing and screeching on the ground, as Dado rubbed her head in the grit of the paddock floor. Dolma had been pinned to the floor by two young tribesmen and screamed and kicked as they tried to tether her to the yak ropes. The ensuing tumult whipped up a dust-storm in the yard and, one by one, the fighters retreated to rest by the porch, panting and covered in filth. They were crazy, and although a part of me wanted to join in, I found it hard to come to terms with the fact that at the end of the frenzy there would be no shower. I watched and laughed, absorbing their boisterous energy, and wished I had their freedom of spirit and blatant disregard of muck all over my body.

As they played, I thought of Christmas in England. Right now, my family would be dozing on the couch with a bellyful of bird, while the TV flickered and the fairy-lights winked on the tree. I couldn't have been further from them. I missed them, but not the familiar trappings of our festive season. These days, the excitement was mostly for children while we adults just sat around achieving various stages of inebriation. Here, the adults were content to behave like children sometimes. They knew how to have a good time.

I had heard other stories of their wildness. Last New Year the men from our tribe had driven a truck to the next valley. The men of that tribe were away and our men had kidnapped all of their women and brought them back to our valley for a joke. In retaliation, the abandoned husbands had then ridden over the ridge to claim back their stolen wives, along with our women. A mock battle had ensued with much wrestling and frivolity as Atung's wife, Annay Tseko, had ended up running around naked. She was certainly one grandmother with a sense of fun. Some day I would stay for New Year in Machu.

That night as the revellers straggled home, Rhanjer invited Tsedup and me to sleep over. With so many relatives staying, there was no room at home or inside his house, so we settled for the railway arches. Shermo Domatso made us a fire and brought enough dung for the night's fuel. She put down fresh straw on the earth floor and gave us sheepskins as bedding. Then she left through the curtain covering the doorway. The freezing air blustered in from outside and we wrapped ourselves in the skins and drew closer to the iron stove. The shadow cast by the flames danced mysteriously around the mud walls and between the clefts and ridges of the concave stone ceiling. It was a weird place, a cave full of memories. We shared a cigarette and Tsedup told me that these buildings had been part of a labour camp when he was a boy. His parents had worked here. All day he had been left in a tent, unsupervised, with the other children. He explained that no fire had been allowed in the tent. There had also been no food; that was supplied in the main mess, where strict rules governed eating times. I wondered how it had felt to be abandoned in such a way. His elder brother Tsedo, aged about nine, had looked after all the younger ones in their family until ten o'clock at night when his mother and father came back. Exhausted, his parents then sat reading from *The Little Red Book*. They might be asked to quote random passages from it in the morning and there would be trouble if they couldn't remember. Of course, like many nomads, Annay was illiterate. Those like her had had to learn the book by heart – or by head: their hearts had had nothing to do with it. Amnye had read it aloud to her.

As I listened, I felt the family's sadness. The gloomy interior of the hovel we now lay in served only to enhance the sense of misery for the strange time that they had suffered. I was glad that things were different now. They were all together and such fear had gone. The riot and elation of our Christmas Day had revealed their resilience. The past was past.

We lay quietly for a while. The straw and skins were warm and the fire crackled as stray sticks popped and split. I looked at Tsedup as he stared at the shadows, drawing pensively on his cigarette. I was full of love. His experience of life was hard to imagine because it was so far away from mine. He shared a sense of drama with all the people of this land, which I could only guess at, but I was grateful to be a part of him. He had enriched my life. I touched his face and turned his eyes to mine. Then I gently asked him the question I had wanted to ask for some time. 'Shall we have a child?' I said.

Even in the dim light of the room I could see the colour drain from his face. He choked on the smoke and laughed nervously. 'A child?' he spluttered. 'But we have no money, darling. How will we survive in England? If we lived here it would be easy. I would be happy to have as many children as you like. Here, you have people to help you look after the baby. In England it is so much harder. We live on our own.'

I knew he was worried about the idea of supporting a family. Although he had been in England for four years, he still didn't feel confident in his capabilities. He was the stranger without the right education and he didn't fit into a box. A regular, fulfilling job seemed impossible to find. The acting work had been too sporadic and he had taken up shop work in the hope of increasing his income. I had often seen him stripped of his dignity by a lacklustre people who did not appreciate him for who he was. Only our closest friends and my family cared about his unique cultural heritage. I had always known that he was an extraordinary person, like no one else. But he knew I could not live here for ever. I had grown to love it and knew I would always pine for it, but the cultural leap was too great for me to stay. The segregation of genders would always pose a problem for me, as I enjoyed the equality of modern society. Also, I would miss my family. And, for all its faults, neither of us could quite relinquish our grip on the western world. We would have to compromise and live between the two worlds. Our base would be England. That was our plan. But I knew it was merely a sensible compromise for a homesick man. I carried the guilt.

'We can do it together. We will help each other,' I said, ever the optimist. Tsedup and I had been through more difficulties than the average couple – in fact, the odds had been probably stacked heavily against a relationship like ours surviving. But over the years we had grown in strength and understanding. Whatever obstacles we encountered, things had always worked out in the end. He was the worrier, and I was the soother.

He smiled at me and said, 'Well, you're not getting any younger, are you?' It was just plain old nomad-speak (with, perhaps, a tinge of irony: I knew that he was well aware of the sensitivity of the subject of age in the West). I would be thirty-one tomorrow; a pretty average age for having a baby in my culture, but ancient in his. I could almost hear the cogs of his mind turning as he pondered the idea of fatherhood. 'Maybe we should have a child,' he resolved, accepting his challenge. He embraced me and we lay still, listening to each other's breathing.

The western Buddha's birthday was over, but the next day it was mine. I had always thought that Boxing Day was a bad time to be born, but this year was different. Tsedup took me to town in the afternoon and suggested we go to a karaoke bar in the evening. I felt like having a hot date with my husband and agreed. Then he left me waiting in a hotel room. I sat watching a wailing Chinese opera on the battered TV and took solace in a packet of biscuits. But after two hours I decided I was getting tired of his disappearing act. There would be some serious confrontation when he returned. I was just warming up for a showdown when he finally appeared and simply said, 'Come with me.'

He drove me to the bar and I rustled my way in through the plastic fringe curtain hanging over the door. There, in the tinsel, neon glare of the karaoke's interior, stood a huge crowd of people in leopardskin costume. I was shocked. This was not the nomads' usual hang-out. I looked around and realised I recognised every single face. Then it clicked. Tsedup had arranged a surprise party for me. Everyone cheered and smiled at me, ushering me towards an enormous iced cake, complete with candles. All of our friends were there, even my girlfriends from town who never went out. For a people who weren't used to birthdays, these days they were sure having a glut of them. I laughed as the town boys among them, who were familiar with such customs, sang 'Happy Birthday to you' in Chinese. Then

Tsering Samdup gave me his jewel-encrusted hunting knife to cut my cake. I made a wish.

It was overwhelming. I had never had a surprise party before. The nomads stood around grinning at me and trying to remain as macho as possible. This was not really their scene and the discomfort they felt at these unfamiliar surroundings only touched me deeper. Then our friend Dontuk approached me, carrying a small box in his hand. He held it out to me. 'For you, Shermo,' he said, and kissed my cheek. Inside was a huge gold ring. I took it out and placed it on my finger. It was heavy; an accessory of medallion proportions. On its flat surface, in relief, was the word 'Tashidelek', which the Tibetans use as a special greeting or a congratulation. Above the word was a crescent moon and below was the sun rising over a mountain top. On either side of the band, a peacock and a dragon had been engraved in intricate detail. Tsedup explained that it had been their idea and they had all contributed to have it made especially for me. I was speechless and just stood smiling at them all. They never ceased to amaze me and I felt the tears welling in my eyes. When I had finished struggling for composure, I asked Tsedup to translate for me as I thanked them all. I knew that they weren't used to outward displays of emotion, so I kept it short.

'When I came here, I never dreamt I would find so much love,' I said. 'You have given me a home and I will miss you. Every time I look at this ring I will think of you.'

Cheering, they raised their glasses, and through the blur of faces, I saw Tsedup smiling at me. Then one by one the nomads took the microphone and sang the songs of their homeland. We never did use the karaoke machine: its flashy Chinese pop songs were irrelevant to us. It was better to feel

282

the hairs on the back of your neck quivering and to share silence in the face of true beauty.

The evening before we left the grassland I went walking by myself. I wanted to absorb the last deep breaths of Amdo air, to savour the wilderness in which I had been living. It helped me to think. For I knew that sometimes, in the day-to-day routine of life, I had forgotten to register that I was *actually here.* I had forgotten the pain that we had gone through in waiting to be able to come. I had forgotten that six months ago I had not known these people or this land. I had heard so much about it, but I hadn't really *known* it. It had been a distant and inaccessible dreamscape somewhere in the deeper recesses of my mind.

That evening, I paused and stood very still. I looked up at the mountains. I listened to the children calling each other. I heard the icy stream rushing over the rocks. I watched flocks of tiny birds rushing up into the dying blue, the buzzards lazily arcing through the waning dusk. I heard the coarse grass rustling at my feet and smelt the dung smoke drifting from the tin chimney. I felt the vastness and irrepressible beauty of this place and I knew that I was home.

The morning we left the grassland, I followed the children to the river and watched them ice-skating in the sunshine. They took it in turns to sit cross-legged on a small wooden toboggan and pushed themselves along with a metal spike in each hand. Each time, they crashed and spun across the thick rutted surface of the ice, laughing. I stood sadly watching them from the bank. I was leaving them today. Tonight we would be staying in Annay and Amnye's town-house, as the car was coming to take us to Lanzhou at dawn the next day. Most of the family were coming to stay in the house with us, but the children would remain here. Perhaps they sensed my sadness, for they called out to me excitedly as they played, 'Come on, Ajay Shermo! You have a go.'

'I'll just watch you,' I replied, too morose to join in.

But Dickir Che was having none of it. 'Come on! Come on!' she cajoled. 'You'll be *so* happy if you try.' She was mothering me, as she always had from the day I arrived. I smiled at her and squatted down on the tiny sled. She put the picks into my hand and showed me how to dig them into the ice for speed. Then I scooted off and she ran along beside me laughing wildly and skidding in her broken boots. She was right. I was happy.

When it was time to go we loaded our bags on to Rhanjer's truck. Gorbo had disappeared so we couldn't say goodbye. I guessed he wasn't up to an emotional farewell. That wasn't a teenage boy's style. Then Rhanjer crunched the gears and we lurched off down the pitted track, stopping at the railway arches to pick up a sheep. Namjher was taking it to town to sell. As they hauled it into the back of the truck and we pulled away, everyone in the tribe ran out shouting goodbye. We waved and smiled, hanging on for dear life, as we bounced violently through the landscape, the poor sheep scuttling and skidding over our rucksacks. Way down the valley, my dear Dickir Che was still running alongside the truck, grinning and waving, her cheeks flushed from the sting of the wind. I stretched out my arms to her, but she couldn't keep up any more. Her joyful laughter was the last thing I heard of the grassland, before the truck's engine drowned it and we disappeared over the brow of the first hill.

That night we had our last supper. The small house was tight for space as twelve of us were staying. We talked and drank and laughed together in the hot room as Annay stoked up the fire. Shermo Donker made *tanthuk*, and Tsedup and I savoured the last bowl of real Amdo fare. Then we went up to the monastery to say goodbye to Ama-lo-lun and Azjung. Tsedup's grandmother lay on the floor of their house covered in yak skins. She was ill. She seemed to have shrunk and her tiny body was swamped by the mound of musty, animal hides. We sat and talked with her and Azjung for a while, and I held her hand. She looked so weak that I was worried we would never see her again. It was so hard to leave her, but she was too frail to talk and we decided to let her rest. As we said goodbye and stepped out of the room, she cried after us feebly, 'I will see you when the flowers blossom.'

Tsedup covered his face and walked away quickly, guided by Azjung, who saw us to the outer door. As I mounted the bike, the Sky Man gently took my face in his hands and pressed his forehead to mine. Then his cheek to mine. It was the closest thing to a kiss I could imagine. A gesture so spontaneous and pure, with no regard for nomad etiquette, that I would never forget it. 'It is so sad that you have to leave,' he said, over and over.

Tsedup and I said nothing to each other all the way back to the house.

The next morning we woke at dawn and moved quietly about our business. The car would be arriving soon to take us away. Although the house was crowded, everyone moved silently around each other in their long costumes, like a slow, sad dance of swishing skirts. Tsedup and I were dressed for the journey. His family had made him a wine-coloured, woollen *tsarer* with gold brocade. Amnye had bought the cloth in Lhasa. A huge knife dangled from his waistband in an elaborate silver holster. I had been given a green silk *tsarer*, with red and gold trim and a soft lambswool collar. The women tucked and tied the folds of fabric until they were satisfied and smiled at their work. Then I was presented with amber jewellery, which had been handed down through the generations. Annay Urgin strung them on to my necklace, then stood back to look at her finished work. 'Amdo Namma.' She smiled. It was like a ceremony and we were as resplendent as a bride and groom. I felt proud to be returning to my culture in traditional Tibetan costume. It felt normal. It was who I had become. I was going back to a grey place, but thanks to Tsedup, I had been blessed with a new knowledge. This was my beginning in a coloured world.

As I stepped out of the house Annay took my arm. We embraced and wept gently. 'Look after each other,' she said to me. Then she went to find her son. I stood alone on the step and took one last look at my new home. The sun had left a delicate thumbprint in the pink morning mist. The milky cloud drifted low over the river basin and the blue mountains smudged the horizon. The first silver slivers of light winked from the town. Out in our field, I heard the clink of the white stallion's bridle and the muffled voices of the farewell party, their leopardskin collars pulled tight against the frost. I breathed in the fresh fragrance of the yarsa weeds, tumbling over the stone wall. It reminded me of the autumn harvest when we had lain laughing in the bales of crisp straw. I picked some and put it in my bag.

Then I walked to the waiting car. All of the family crowded round and many of our friends had come from the town to say goodbye. I moved among the earnest faces; the same faces that had seemed so strange to me when they had greeted us so long ago. Today I knew them all. I was their *namma.* They were my heart. 'Come back soon,' they cried, as we climbed into the car. As we pulled away, I watched them waving and receding in the back window.

Don't cry, I told myself. You will see them when the flowers blossom.

# *Epilogue*

Everyone stared at us on the plane. We must have looked ridiculous to the other passengers, as we sat in our lavish costumes, but I didn't care. They were from the grey world. I looked out of the window at the land beneath the cloud and remembered the family running out of the tent to watch a passing plane. Planes hardly ever flew over the Tibetan plateau, so it was always an exciting event. 'One day you'll be inside and you'll look down at us and wave,' they had said. But, needless to say, they were not on our flight path.

Back in London I wore my *tsarer* for a week. Then I felt too bizarre and conscious of the strange looks in the street, so I put it away in favour of that season's fashions. It hung in the wardrobe, waiting, the leopardskin trim a reminder each morning when I selected my office clothes. The soft aroma of dung smoke still clung to the fibres when I nuzzled into them. It took a week to wash the dirt of the grassland from under my fingernails and even longer for the cracked skin on my hands to return to normal. For a while I sleepwalked around the city in a state of shock. It was strange to be surrounded by so many white faces. I went to a party and watched dancers flailing their limbs to a deafening rhythm. I was calm inside, the slow beat of my heart like a slip of the hawk's wing trembling on a thermal in the Valley of the Rocks.

But it was good to see my family and our friends again. To gossip and drink and be understood. We confined ourselves only to those who understood. For there were plenty of people who couldn't comprehend the kind of life we had led. The trip had brought Tsedup and me closer together than we had ever been. Now when he talked of the land and his people, I understood his passion and was able to share it with him. It had always been hard to live with him, knowing he would rather be somewhere else. Now I wanted to be somewhere else as well. But I hadn't forgotten that, not so long ago, he had extolled the virtues of western society to his friends in Tibet. It was true that the grass was always greener elsewhere.

In the spring I became pregnant. I will never forget the day I found out. I was sitting in the kitchen enjoying the warm breeze that trailed in from the back door. I had unloaded the shopping: fresh prawns, soft mangoes. I had been walking my brother's dog in the park, watching children playing in the sandpit. Then I had decided to do a test. I had a strange feeling inside. When the line went blue, I went pink. I looked at myself in the mirror, clutching my cheeks. Did I look any different? I had a life inside me. I paced up and down, talking to myself, laughing. I went to the back door, to the sunlit garden, where the voices of next-door's children trilled over the fence. I cried. Then, when Tsedup came home from work, I followed him along the hallway asking him how his day had been. He was half-way through a short soliloquy about infuriating customers in his shop, when I began giggling. I tried to cover my mouth, but was out of control with irrepressible excitement. He knew. His eyes twinkled in anticipation of my next few words. He went white then he smiled.

Both our families were overjoyed. When we phoned to tell Tsedup's parents, we learnt that Sirmo was pregnant too. I was thrilled to know that our child would have a cousin the same age and I couldn't wait to see Sirmo. A hospital scan revealed that I carried a son, and in the summer we took him for his first trip to Tibet. He was five months old in the womb. When we arrived the whole family ran out of the tent to greet us. I was euphoric as I went inside. Everything was just as it always had been, but the tent seemed bigger somehow. Shermo Donker smiled warmly at me. She was more beautiful than I had remembered. Tsedo looked wilder, with long, tangled hair and a beard. I hardly recognised him. After the first few tentative moments, everyone fell back into the old familiar humour, joking and laughing together. The children jumped all over me again, although they were told to be more careful this time. Dickir Ziggy was at school now and came back to see us one weekend, boasting to her brother and sister of her accomplishments. Dickir Che and Sanjay examined the contents of her satchel methodically and fought over the coloured pencils. It felt good to be home. Somehow the grassland looked different, strangely autumnal for this time of year. There were fewer flowers and it was not as lush as I remembered it last summer. The stream had cleaved a new path in the bank and a small waterfall gushed close to the tent. We lay and listened to it each night, inside the new tent that Amnye had made for us.

Being pregnant in the grassland was a revelation. I was treated differently this time. There were new rules. Annay explained carefully to me that I was not allowed to visit any other tents in the tribe apart from Rhanjer's and Annay Urgin's. Even in their homes I was not allowed to eat anything. I was baffled as to the reasons for my confinement, but Tsedup told me that it was a custom here: the nomads believed that the unborn child might be harmed by malevolent spirits associated with other families. He told me to be especially careful in Annay Urgin's tent, as the Kambo household had powerful deities. I bore it in mind. Also, on a practical level, Annay wanted to protect the baby and me from contamination by food. Only she would cook for me, she said. Sometimes I felt like an invalid, but at least it saved me from the hectic Tibetan social whirl.

I had to wear my costume differently too. Shermo Donker showed me how to tie it below my swollen stomach, which made me seem even more voluminous, but despite the discomfort, I was happy to be pregnant here. The women were always gently touching my bump and asking if I was all right. The scan picture, which I had brought especially to show them, provoked amazement. They had never seen anything like it. 'The western doctors are incredible,' they said. Annay asked if she could keep the image of her grandson.

'When will you bring him to Amdo?' she asked.

'Next year, when he's a bit bigger,' I replied. 'Maybe a year and a half old.' I wanted him to know them all, to learn the language, to ride yaks and run naked in the grass as his father had when he was a child. And to be proud of his nomad heritage. That summer was the first time I felt our son move. On hot days I lay in our tent watching the sheep shimmering in the midday heat. The children sat around me staring at my stomach, as the baby kicked inside. They put a stick on my belly to see if he could knock it off. 'He moved! He moved!' cried Sanjay, each time the stick quivered. Our boy was already part of the family.

I wanted him to be named in the traditional Tibetan way. A lama usually performs a divination to determine every Tibetan child's name, so Tsedup asked our monk friend Aka Tenzin for help. We waited anxiously for a few weeks as the monk went to consult the boy lama, Jarsung, in Labrang Monastery. You might think it reckless to leave the naming of our son to a thirteen-year-old child, but we felt it was the right thing to do and spent the time fantasising as to what the name would be. It was a bit of a lottery. When he returned Aka Tenzin sat us down and smiled broadly, as was his fashion. He looked at me as I grinned with anticipation and then he simply said, 'Gonbochab.' I turned the name over. It would be a mouthful for his relatives in England, that was for sure, but I loved it. 'It means "Blessed by the Saviour",' said Tsedup.

That summer, Sirmo was allowed home at last. The joy of our arrival seemed to have prompted Amnye to relent and he gave his permission for her to visit. It had been ten months since her elopement and her father hadn't seen her since she had left. The residue of those angry days still remained.

Everyone was nervous as to how he would react to her and her husband. We all ran out at the sight of three horses in the distance, straining to see them, and as they rode closer, the children flocked around them laughing and shrieking. Sirmo smiled weakly and her husband, Chuchong, was silent as they dismounted with the mediator. The goblin man had come again to offer his diplomatic assistance, but after his last encounter with Amnye he looked a little nervous. They were ushered into the tent, where Chuchong took his place of honour on the carpets by the fire. I was shocked at how young and vulnerable he looked as he listened politely to the elders' talk. He cast furtive glances at Sirmo as she stood on the women's side of the fire in her old place. She looked splendid in her finest clothes and jewellery, but also tired. She was heavily pregnant and her skin was discoloured with the dark patches women sometimes have, but she was ecstatic to be home.

It was clear that Amnye was moved to see her again. He remained calm and even smiled once or twice. Goblin was visibly relieved. Once the formalities of the reunion were over, Tsedo took Chuchong off to play volleyball and Sirmo busied herself with serving tea and bustling around the tent. Amnye spoke softly to her, calling her 'Babko', her child's name, and fussing over her. We were relieved that everything was back to normal. In his own quiet way, he had mellowed and forgiven her. Time was a great healer.

Over those few days of Sirmo's visit, the tribe were in the middle of a summer picnic. A huge white tent had been erected in the middle of the encampment and all day they played and ate and danced. There were water fights and everyone was thrown into the stream. Everyone except Sirmo and me, of course: we were forced to be more restrained.

Although we were permitted to enter the communal tent, since it had no harmful spirits, we were instructed by Annay not to eat anything. We sat quietly together holding hands, as the rest of the tribe rioted in traditional fashion. We compared stomachs and appetites and moaned about our tiredness. It was touching to be able to share the intimacies of our changing bodies. Even Ama-lo-lun, who had fully recovered from her illness, joined the party and teased the young men, waving her stick at them and challenging them to throw her in the water. The crazy atmosphere reminded me of our last Christmas.

Before we left Annay took me walking in the grassland. Tsedup had told me it was something to do with the baby and we would be going as far as the boundary fence, so I was curious as I set off with her. She led me through the grass carrying a bucket containing *tsampa*. At first she didn't seem to know where she was going and changed direction several times. I followed her, still oblivious to our task. We left the gush of the waterfall behind us, moving silently through the rough grasses and the last few blue flowers of late summer. All I could hear was the rustle of the grass around our shins and the breath of the wind. Annay began sprinkling *tsampa* about her on the ground and muttering, '*Om mani padme hum*,' as we headed for the railway arches, far away from the tribe. I still had no idea what we were supposed to be doing, until I stumbled over a mound on the ground. 'Well done. You've found one!' cried Annay. It was a small raised tuft of earth that looked like the offering site outside the tent. I thought perhaps Annay might start to burn offerings on it as I had seen Amnye do, but instead, she stamped the ground and sprinkled some *tsampa* on top of the mound. Suddenly hundreds of ants appeared and I realised that we had come to feed them. We were giving back to the earth and the tiniest of sentient beings for the sake of my son. 'It will be good for him,' said Annay.

We wandered deeper into fresh purple- and rose-tinted grasses. The yaks had not grazed this far and the flowers there were still blossoming yellow and blue. At each ants' nest we stopped to feed them, prayed and moved on. Then we reached the fence. But Annay was not deterred by the barbed-wire confines of her homeland. She urged me to lift it, then crawled underneath. I couldn't follow her because of my stomach, but I handed her the pail and watched her wander further into the wilderness, sprinkling around in the fuchsia flora. She seemed so beautiful at that moment. It was not in the awkwardness of her laboured gait, her loose grey hair or her soiled clothes; I was deeply humbled by the beauty of her spirit. Breathing in the fragrant air and blinded by the dazzling sun, I scanned the vast panorama of my Tibetan home: the mountains, the river, the grassland, the tribe. 'All this is for you, our son,' I said. 'All this is for you.'

It was still hard to leave after the six weeks, but somehow Tibet did not seem as inaccessible as it had. It was now part of our lives. We planned to build a house and come back each year. Tsedup and I would witness great changes in the lives of the nomads in our visits to come: those of Tsedup's generation had fewer children, less land, fewer livestock than their ancestors. Now some of the children were going to school and a few of their parents even had mobile phones. Only their unfaltering spirituality would stem the tide of modernisation. It was at the heart of the nomads and would be passed from father to son for ever. Tsedup and I would watch the children grow. They were the future.

\*     \*     \*

A few weeks after we had gone, Sirmo gave birth to a son. He was named Tsering Dhondup. Then, in the winter, our own son was born. Tsedup stayed for the birth along with my mother. It was not the custom for a nomad man, but somehow he defied one of the greatest taboos of his culture to be by my side. I hadn't demanded it. I soon forgot the pain, but I would never forget his tears falling on me.

Our boy, Gonbochab, is the bridge between our two worlds. We hope he will inherit the best of both, for he is loved in the East and in the West. Sometimes I stand with him at the kitchen window and we look out beyond the small yard and the fence and the backs of other people's houses. We look up at the sky and the planes flying east. I rock him gently and tell him that one day we'll take him to his other home.

One day soon.

# GLOSSARY

*ajay*          aunty

*arro*          Hello

*Bardo*         the intermediate state between death and rebirth

*bodhisattva*   a spiritual incarnate or emanation of Buddha, who cares for all sentient beings

*Bon, Bonpo*    indigenous shamanic tradition of Tibet and its practitioners

*bourgea*       traditional Tibetan hat made from silk and lined with fur

*chadmay*       leather belt worn by nomad women, decorated with coral or turquoise and silver discs

*Chenrezik*     the bodhisattva of compassion

*Cho demo*      How are you?

*chorten*       religious monument of brick or stone, consisting of a dome, a box, a spire and a plinth

*chuba*         traditional Lhasa-style pinafore dress

*chukgor*    steel weight attached to a long leather thong which is used by the nomads to defend them-selves against dogs

*dalin*    saddle-bag

*darchok*    prayer flags

*djoma*    small brown beans dug from the earth

*djomdi*    a dish of boiled brown beans, rice, sugar and melted butter

*dobshair*    woven hanging used to cover up the items stored at the back of the tent – sometimes embellished with coloured ribbon and bells

*dro*    female yak

*gamtuk*    wooden box containing *tsampa*, butter and cheese

*garchot*    non-blood offering

*gorji*    headband of amber stones worn by pubescent girls

*hdir*    'treasure' – offerings to the earth, contained in colourful cloth bags

*hornig*    the nomads' dating game: young men travel

|  |  |
|---|---|
|  | miles at night on horseback or yak to seek out young girls in their tents |
| *jib* | fireplace, the heart of the nomad tent, made from turf and clay |
| *jo* | wheat husks |
| *kabshat* or *lazjhee* | mountain love songs traditionally sung across the valleys by young boys and girls |
| *kacher* | long sheep's hair |
| *kadak* | white silk stole representing the purity of the Tibetan heart (sometimes referred to as 'prayer scarf') |
| *katsup* | the gap between the fabric in the middle of the tent roof, which allows the smoke from the fire to escape |
| *kirchi* | tube of brightly coloured, knitted fabric used as a hat or a face-covering in winter |
| *kirok* | sash worn around the *tsarer* |
| *korlo* | prayer wheel |
| *langwha* | washing basin |
| *laptse* | holy mountain |

| | |
|---|---|
| *long hda* | 'wind horses', small paper squares with pictures of horses printed on them which carry blessings when thrown to the wind |
| *lu/luma* | male and female demi-gods of the subterranean world; serpent spirits of earth and water |
| *mandala* | the 'Wheel of Life' – a symmetrical picture made from coloured sand. The simplest mandala is an empty circle and the centre represents 'emptiness', the pure awareness and limitless space of the Buddha mind. |
| *marcho* | blood offering |
| *merdach* | spun sheep's wool |
| *momos* | traditional dish of steamed parcels of meat |
| *Nam Nyeur* | 'Sky Man' or ancient man |
| *namma* | bride or daughter-in-law |
| *ndashung* | wooden spear, about six metres high, with a brightly painted flight for pegging the earth at spiritual offering sites |
| *nyen* | sky gods, of a warrior-like nature, who live on the mountain peaks |
| *Nyon Nyi* | a religious ritual dedicated to fasting, contemplation, prayer and self-purification |

| | |
|---|---|
| *phurba* | ritual dagger |
| *piju* | Chinese word for beer |
| *ratcho* | pipe |
| *rawa* | head ornament sewn into pubescent girls' hair, made of heavily embroidered silk fabric, silver and precious stones |
| *rungpizz* | ribbon rice noodles, served cold with garlic, vinegar, chilli and tofu – favourite dish of the nomad women |
| *samker* | broth of *tsampa*, salt, and milk with ginger or aniseed |
| *seeto* | wicker basket |
| *shabala* | meat fritters |
| *shangtee* | traditional Tibetan boots with pointed upturned toes, made from felt or leather and usually only worn by old people |
| *shermo* | sister-in-law |
| *shimo* | girl |
| *shinlab* | literally 'wave of grace': the feeling experienced after receiving the Buddha's blessing |

| | |
|---|---|
| *shogshung* | 'Staff of Life' – the main spear which marks the site of mountain worship |
| *shugndot* | knotted protection cord given by a lama, which is worn around the neck |
| *shyee* | child |
| *sockwa* | shoulder blade |
| *sonnam* | religious merit |
| *tanthuk* | soup of meat and small squares of cooked dough |
| *thanka* | religious painting, usually on a silk scroll and depicting the Buddha |
| *thib* | small brass cups for filling with water as an altar offering |
| *tolla* | three-wheeled tractor-like vehicle, which is sometimes hired along with a Chinese driver, to transport the nomads to the grassland |
| *tranger* | prayer beads |
| *tsa tsa* | small triangular clay icons, a few inches high, formed from a bronze mould and sun-dried, depicting the Buddha |
| *tsampa* | ground barley flour |

| | |
|---|---|
| *tsarer* | traditional Tibetan dress resembling a large wrap-around cloth coat with woven or leopard-skin trim and embroidered detailing |
| *tsokwa* | thick sheepskin *tsarer* with leopardskin collar, worn especially in winter |
| *tuckpa* | soup or rice noodles and meat |
| *tugh* | colourful woven hem of *tsarer* |
| *turnkor* | churn |
| *tzorgin* | yak/cow half-breed |
| *yarsa gunba* | grass worm – this particular phenomenon is a worm which grows fungus on its head and dies in autumn. The nomads say the worm turns into grass. It is highly prized by the Chinese for its medicinal properties and the nomads collect them in the grassland to sell. |
| *yucka* | beautiful |